NYSTCE
001 LAST

Liberal Arts and Sciences Test
Teacher Certification Exam

By: Sharon Wynne, M.S.
Southern Connecticut State University

"And, while there's no reason yet to panic, I think it's only prudent that we make preparations to panic."

XAMonline, INC.
Boston

XAMonline, Inc.
21 Orient Ave.
Melrose, MA 02176
Toll Free 1-800-509-4128
Email: info@xamonline.com
Web www.xamonline.com
Fax: 1-781-662-9268

Library of Congress Cataloging-in-Publication Data

Wynne, Sharon A.
    LAST Liberal Arts and Sciences Test 001: Teacher Certification / Sharon A. Wynne. -2nd ed.
    ISBN 978-1-58197-344-0
    1. LAST Assessment of Teaching Assistant Skills 001.   2. Study Guides.
    3. LAST   4. Teachers' Certification & Licensure.   5. Careers

Disclaimer:
The opinions expressed in this publication are the sole works of XAMonline and were created independently from the National Education Association, Educational Testing Service, or any State Department of Education, National Evaluation Systems or other testing affiliates.

Between the time of publication and printing, state specific standards as well as testing formats and website information may change. Such changes are not addressed in part or in whole within this product. Sample test questions are developed by XAMonline and reflect content similar to that found on real tests; however, they are not former tests. XAMonline assembles content that aligns with state standards but makes no claims nor guarantees that teacher candidates will achieve a passing score. Numerical scores are determined by testing companies such as NES or ETS and then are compared with individual state standards. A passing score varies from state to state.

Printed in the United States of America

NYSTCE: LAST Assessment of Teaching Assistant Skills 001
ISBN: 978-1-58197-344-0

Table of Contents

Great Study and Testing Tips!

What to study in order to prepare for the subject assessments is the focus of this study guide, but equally important is *how* you study.

You can increase your chances of truly mastering the information by taking some simple, but effective, steps.

Study Tips:

1. <u>Some foods aid the learning process</u>. Foods such as milk, nuts, seeds, rice, and oats help your study efforts by releasing natural memory enhancers called CCKs (*cholecystokinin*) composed of *tryptophan*, *choline*, and *phenylalanine*. All of these chemicals enhance the neurotransmitters associated with memory. Before studying, try a light, protein-rich meal of eggs, turkey, and fish. All of these foods release the memory-enhancing chemicals. The better the connections, the more you comprehend.

Likewise, before you take a test, stick to a light snack of energy-boosting and relaxing foods. A glass of milk, a piece of fruit, or some peanuts all release various memory-boosting chemicals and help you to relax and focus on the subject at hand.

2. <u>Learn to take great notes</u>. A by-product of our modern culture is that we have grown accustomed to getting our information in short doses (i.e. TV news sound bites or USA Today style newspaper articles.)

Consequently, we've subconsciously trained ourselves to assimilate information better in <u>neat little packages</u>. If your notes are scrawled all over the paper, it fragments the flow of the information. Strive for clarity. Newspapers use a standard format to achieve clarity. Your notes can be much clearer through use of proper formatting. A very effective format is called the <u>*"Cornell Method."*</u>

> Take a sheet of loose-leaf lined notebook paper, and draw a line all the way down the paper about 1-2" from the left-hand edge.

> Draw another line across the width of the paper about 1-2" up from the bottom. Repeat this process on the reverse side of the page.

Look at the highly effective result. You have ample room for notes, a left hand margin for special emphasis items or inserting supplementary data from the textbook, a large area at the bottom for a brief summary, and a little rectangular space for just about anything you want.

3. Get the concept, then the details. Too often we focus on the details and don't gather an understanding of the concept. However, if you simply memorize only dates, places, or names; you may well miss the whole point of the subject.

A key way to understand things is to put them in your own words. If you are working from a textbook, automatically summarize each paragraph in your mind. If you are outlining text, don't simply copy the author's words.

Rephrase them in your own words (paraphrase). You remember your own thoughts and words much better than someone else's and subconsciously tend to associate the important details to the core concepts.

4. Ask Why? Pull apart written material paragraph-by-paragraph, and don't forget the captions under the illustrations.

Example: If the heading is "Stream Erosion", flip it around to read "Why do streams erode?" Then answer the questions.

If you train your mind to think in a series of questions and answers, then not only will you learn more, but you will also experience less test anxiety because you are used to answering questions.

5. Read for reinforcement and future needs. Even if you only have ten minutes, put your notes or a book in your hand. Your mind is similar to a computer; you have to input data in order to have it processed. *By reading, you are creating the neural connections for future retrieval.* The more times you read something, the more you reinforce the learning of ideas.

Even if you don't fully understand something on the first pass, *your mind stores much of the material for later recall.*

6. Relax to learn, so go into exile. Our bodies respond to an inner clock comprised of various biorhythms. Burning the midnight oil works well for some people, but not for everyone.

If possible, set aside a particular place to study that is free of distractions. Shut off the television, cell phone, and pager; and exile your friends and family during your study period.

If you really are bothered by silence, try background music. Light classical music at a low volume has been shown to aid in concentration over other types of music. Music that evokes pleasant emotions without lyrics is highly suggested. Try just about anything by Mozart. It relaxes you.

7. <u>Use arrows, not highlighters</u>. At best, it's difficult to read a page full of yellow, pink, blue, and green streaks. Try staring at a neon sign for a while, and you'll soon see that the horde of colors obscures the message.

A quick note, a brief dash of color, an underline, and an arrow pointing to a particular passage are much clearer than a horde of highlighted words.

8. <u>Budget your study time</u>. Although you shouldn't ignore any of the material, *allocate your available study time in the same ratio that topics are likely to appear on the test.*

Testing Tips:

1. Get smart, play dumb. Don't read anything into the question. Don't make an assumption that the test writer is looking for something else than what is asked. Stick to the question as written, and don't read extra things into it.

2. Read the question and all the choices *twice* before answering the question. You may miss something by not carefully reading, and then re-reading, both the question and the answers.

If you really don't have a clue as to the right answer, leave it blank on the first time through. Go on to the other questions because they may provide a clue as to how to answer the skipped questions.

If, later on, you still can't answer the skipped ones, then **guess.** The only penalty for guessing is that you *might* get it wrong. Only one thing is certain; if you don't put anything down, you will get it wrong!

3. Turn the question into a statement. Look at the way the questions are worded. The syntax of the question usually provides a clue. Does it seem more familiar as a statement rather than as a question? Does it sound strange?

By turning a question into a statement, you may be able to spot if an answer sounds right, and it may also trigger memories of material you have read.

4. Look for hidden clues. It's actually very difficult to compose multiple-foil (choice) questions without giving away part of the answer in the options presented.

In most multiple-choice questions, you can often readily eliminate one or two of the potential answers. This leaves you with only two real possibilities, and automatically your odds go to fifty-fifty.

5. Trust your instincts. For every fact that you have read, you subconsciously retain something of that knowledge. On questions that you aren't really certain about, go with your basic instincts. **Your first impression on how to answer a question is usually correct.**

6. Mark your answers directly on the test booklet. Don't bother trying to fill in the optical scan sheet on the first pass through the test.

Just be very careful not to miss-mark your answers when you eventually transcribe them to the scan sheet.

7. Watch the clock! You have a set amount of time to answer the questions. Don't get bogged down trying to answer a single question at the expense of ten questions you can more readily answer.

SUBAREA I. **SCIENTIFIC, MATHEMATICAL AND TECHNOLOGICAL PROCESSES**

COMPETENCY 1.0 **USE MATHEMATICAL REASONING IN PROBLEM-SOLVING SITUATIONS TO ARRIVE AT LOGICAL CONCLUSIONS AND TO ANALYZE THE PROBLEM-SOLVING PROCESS**

Skill 1.1 Analyze problem solutions for logical flaws

Deductive reasoning is the process of arriving at a conclusion based on other statements that are all known to be true.

A symbolic argument consists of a set of premises and a conclusion in the format of if [Premise 1 and premise 2] then [conclusion].

An argument is **valid** when the conclusion follows necessarily from the premises. An argument is **invalid** or a fallacy when the conclusion does not follow from the premises.

There are 4 standard forms of valid arguments which must be remembered.

1. Law of Detachment   If p, then q   (premise 1)
                              p,   (premise 2)
                              Therefore, q

2. Law of Contraposition   If p, then q
                              not q,
                              Therefore not p

3. Law of Syllogism   If p, then q
                              If q, then r
                              Therefore if p, then r

4. Disjunctive Syllogism   p or q
                              not p
                              Therefore, q

Example: Can a conclusion be reached from these two statements?

    A.   All swimmers are athletes.
          All athletes are scholars.

In "if-then" form, these would be:
    If you are a swimmer, then you are an athlete.
    If you are an athlete, then you are a scholar.

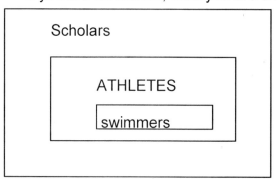

Clearly, if you are a swimmer, then you are also an athlete. This includes you in the group of scholars.

    B.   All swimmers are athletes.
          All wrestlers are athletes.

In "if-then" form, these would be:
    If you are a swimmer, then you are an athlete.
    If you are a wrestler, then you are an athlete.

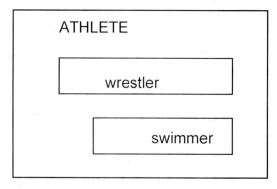

Clearly, if you are a swimmer or a wrestler, then you are also an athlete. This does NOT allow you to come to any other conclusions.

A swimmer may or may NOT also be a wrestler. Therefore, NO CONCLUSION IS POSSIBLE.

Suppose that these statements were given to you, and you were asked to try to reach a conclusion. The statements are:

Example: Determine whether statement A, B, C, or D can be deduced from the following:

(i) If John drives the big truck, then the shipment will be delivered.

(ii) The shipment will not be delivered.

  ⌄a. John does not drive the big truck.
   b. John drives the big truck.
   c. The shipment will not be delivered.
   d. None of the above conclusion is true.

Let p: John drives the big truck.
    q: The shipment is delivered.

statement (i) gives p → q, statement (ii) gives ~ q. This is the Law of Contraposition.

Therefore, the logical conclusion is ~p or "John does not drive the big truck". So the answer is response A.

Example: Given that:
(i)Peter is a Jet Pilot or Peter is a Navigator.
(ii)Peter is not a Jet Pilot

Determine which conclusion can be logically deduced.

   a. Peter is not a Navigator.
  ⌄b. Peter is a Navigator.
   c. Peter is neither a Jet Pilot nor a Navigator.
   d. None of the above is true.

Let p: Peter is a Jet Pilot
    q: Peter is a Navigator.

So we have p ∨ q from statement (i)
           ~p   from statement (ii)

So choose response B.

Try These:

What conclusion, if any, can be reached? Assume each statement is true, regardless of any personal beliefs.

1. If the Red Sox win the World Series, I will die.
   I died.

2. If an angle's measure is between 0° and 90°, then the angle is acute. Angle B is not acute.

3. Students who do well in geometry will succeed in college.
   Annie is doing extremely well in geometry.

4. Left-handed people are witty and charming.
   You are left-handed.

Question #1   The Red Sox won the World Series.
Question #2   Angle B is not between 0 and 90 degrees.
Question #3   Annie will do well in college.
Question #4   You are witty and charming.

Skill 1.2   Examine problems to determine missing information needed to solve them

Some problems do not contain enough information with which to solve them.

For example:

During one semester, a college student used 70 gallons of gas driving back and forth to visit her family. The total cost of gas was $225. What was the average number of gallons of gas used per trip?

This question cannot be answered because you do not know the number of trips the student made.

Skill 1.3 **Analyze a partial solution to a problem to determine an appropriate next step**

Example: A fish is 30 inches long. The head is as long as the tail. If the head was twice as long and the tail was its present length, then the body would be 18 inches long. How long is the body?

Partial solution: Let x represent the head.

$$2x + x + 18 = 30$$
$$3x = 12$$
$$x = 4$$

We now create an equation to solve for the body of the fish with y representing the body.

$$x + x + y = 30$$
$$2x + y = 30$$
$$\text{Substitute 4 for } x.$$
$$2(4) + y = 30$$
$$8 + y = 30$$
$$y = 22$$

In this example, we are able to substitute the partial solution to solve for the variable in the problem's actual question.

Example: How many squares must be added to a 10-by-10 square to create an 11-by-11 square?

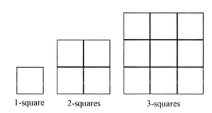

1-square   2-squares   3-squares

Partial solution: We determine that a 3-by-3 square has 5 more squares than a 2-by-2 square, which has 3 more squares than 1 square.

By examining the pattern, we see that we can answer the question by adding the dimension of the previous square (in this case, 10) to the dimension of the current square (in this case, 11) to answer the question. Twenty-one squares must be added to a 10-by-10 square to create an 11-by-11 square.

COMPETENCY 2.0   UNDERSTAND CONNECTIONS BETWEEN MATHEMATICAL REPRESENTATIONS AND IDEAS; AND USE MATHEMATICAL TERMS AND REPRESENTATIONS TO ORGANIZE, INTERPRET, AND COMMUNICATE INFORMATION.

Skill 2.1   Analyze data, and make inferences from two or more graphic sources (e.g., diagrams, graphs, equations)

To make a **bar graph** or a **pictograph**, determine the scale to be used for the graph. Then determine the length of each bar on the graph, or determine the number of pictures needed to represent each item of information. Be sure to include an explanation of the scale in the legend.

Example: A class had the following grades:
4 A's, 9 B's, 8 C's, 1 D, 3 F's.
Graph these on a bar graph and a pictograph.

Pictograph

Grade	Number of Students
A	☺☺☺☺
B	☺☺☺☺☺☺☺☺☺
C	☺☺☺☺☺☺☺☺
D	☺
F	☺☺☺

Bar graph

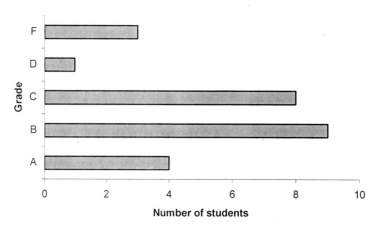

To make a **line graph**, determine appropriate scales for both the vertical and horizontal axes (based on the information to be graphed). Describe what each axis represents, and mark the scale periodically on each axis. Graph the individual points of the graph, and connect the points on the graph from left to right.

Example: Graph the following information using a line graph.

The number of National Merit finalists/school year

	90-91	91-92	92-93	93-94	94-95	95-96
Central	3	5	1	4	6	8
Wilson	4	2	3	2	3	2

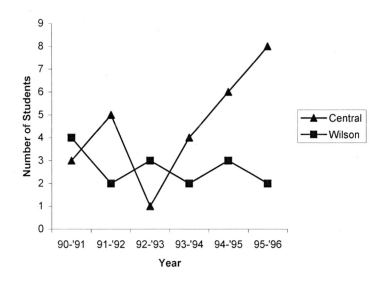

To make a **circle graph**, total all the information that is to be included on the graph. Determine the central angle to be used for each sector of the graph using the following formula:

$$\frac{\text{information}}{\text{total information}} \times 360° = \text{degrees in central} \sphericalangle$$

Lay out the central angles to these sizes, label each section, and include its percent.

Example: Graph this information on a circle graph:

Monthly expenses:

Rent, $400
Food, $150
Utilities, $75
Clothes, $75
Church, $100
Misc., $200

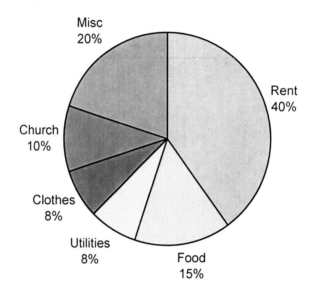

Scatter plots compare two characteristics of the same group of things or people and usually consist of a large body of data. They show how much one variable is affected by another. The relationship between the two variables is their **correlation**. The closer that the data points come to making a straight line when plotted, the closer the correlation.

Stem and leaf plots are visually similar to line plots. The **stems** are the digits in the greatest place value of the data values, and the **leaves** are the digits in the next greatest place values. Stem and leaf plots are best suited for small sets of data and are especially useful for comparing two sets of data. The following is an example using test scores:

4	9
5	4 9
6	1 2 3 4 6 7 8 8
7	0 3 4 6 6 6 7 7 7 8 8 8 8
8	3 5 5 7 8
9	0 0 3 4 5
10	0 0

Histograms are used to summarize information from large sets of data that can be naturally grouped into intervals. The vertical axis indicates **frequency** (the number of times any particular data value occurs), and the horizontal axis indicates data values or ranges of data values. The number of data values in any interval is the **frequency of the interval**.

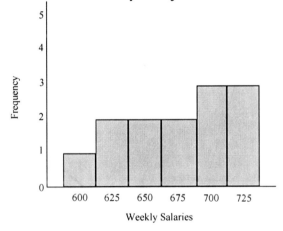

A **trend** line on a line graph shows the correlation between two sets of data. A trend may show positive correlation (both sets of data get bigger together) negative correlation (one set of data gets bigger while the other gets smaller), or no correlation.

An **inference** is a statement which is derived from reasoning. When reading a graph, inferences help with interpretation of the data that is being presented. From this information, a **conclusion** and even **predictions** about what the data actually means are possible.

Example: Katherine and Tom were both doing poorly in math class. Their teacher had a conference with each of them in November. The following graph shows their math test scores during the school year.

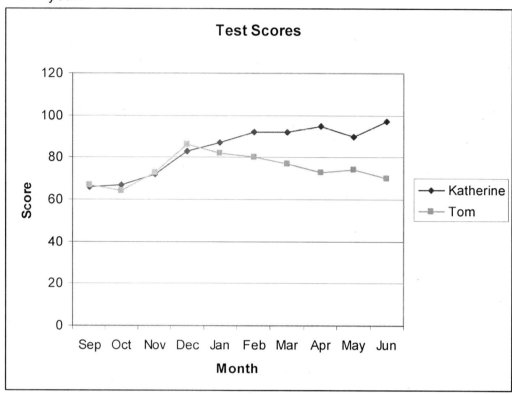

What kind of trend does this graph show?

This graph shows that there is a positive trend in Katherine's test scores and a negative trend in Tom's test scores.

What inferences can you make from this graph?

We can infer that Katherine's test scores rose steadily after November. Tom's test scores spiked in December, but then began to fall again and became negatively trended.

What conclusion can you draw based upon this graph?

We can conclude that Katherine took her teacher's meeting seriously and began to study in order to do better on the exams. It seems as though Tom tried harder for a bit, but his test scores eventually slipped back down to the level where he began.

Skill 2.2   **Restate a problem related to a concrete situation in mathematical terms**

Example: The YMCA wants to sell raffle tickets to raise $32,000. If they must pay $7,250 in expenses and prizes out of the money collected from the tickets, then how many tickets worth $25 each must they sell?

Let x = number of tickets sold
Then $25x$ = total money collected for x tickets

Total money minus expenses is greater than $32,000.

$25x - 7250 = 32,000$
$25x = 39350$
$x = 1570$

If they sell 1,570 tickets, they will raise $32,000.

For more examples see Skill 3.5.

Skill 2.3   **Use mathematical modeling/multiple representations to present, interpret, communicate, and connect mathematical information and relationships selecting an appropriate graph or table summarizing information presented in another form (e.g., a newspaper excerpt)**

See Skill 2.1.

COMPETENCY 3.0   APPLY KNOWLEDGE OF NUMERICAL, GEOMETRIC, AND ALGEBRAIC RELATIONSHIPS IN PROBLEM SOLVING AND MATHEMATICAL CONTEXTS.

Skill 3.1   Represent and use numbers in a variety of equivalent forms (e.g., integer, fraction, decimal, percent)

Rational numbers can be expressed as the ratio of two integers, $\frac{a}{b}$ where $b \neq 0$, for example $\frac{2}{3}$, $-\frac{4}{5}$, $5 = \frac{5}{1}$.

The rational numbers include integers, fractions and mixed numbers, terminating and repeating decimals. Every rational number can be expressed as a repeating or terminating decimal and can be shown on a number line.

Integers are positive and negative whole numbers and zero.
    ...-6, -5, -4, -3, -2, -1, 0, 1, 2, 3, 4, 5, 6, ...

Whole numbers are natural numbers and zero.
    0, 1, 2, 3, ,4 ,5 ,6 ...

Natural numbers are the counting numbers.
    1, 2, 3, 4, 5, 6, ...

Irrational numbers are real numbers that cannot be written as the ratio of two integers. These are infinite non-repeating decimals.
    <u>Examples</u>: $\sqrt{5}$ = 2.2360.., pi =∏ = 3.1415927...

A **fraction** is an expression of numbers in the form x/y, where x is the numerator and y is the denominator, which cannot be zero.

Example: $\dfrac{3}{7}$ 3 is the numerator; 7 is the denominator

If the fraction has common factors for the numerator and denominator, divide both by the common factor to reduce the fraction to its lowest form.

Example:

$$\frac{13}{39} = \frac{1 \times 13}{3 \times 13} = \frac{1}{3}$$ Divide by the common factor 13

A **mixed** number has an integer part and a fractional part.

Example: $2\frac{1}{4}, \ ^{-}5\frac{1}{6}, \ 7\frac{1}{3}$

Percent = per 100 (written with the symbol %). Thus $10\% = \dfrac{10}{100} = \dfrac{1}{10}$.

Decimals = deci = part of ten. To find the decimal equivalent of a fraction, use the denominator to divide the numerator, as shown in the following example.

Example: Find the decimal equivalent of $\dfrac{7}{10}$.

Since 10 cannot divide into 7 evenly

$$\frac{7}{10} = 0.7$$

The **exponent form** is a shortcut method to write repeated multiplication. Basic form: b^{n}, where b is called the base, and n is the exponent. b and n are both real numbers. b^{n} implies that the base b is multiplied by itself n times.

Examples: $3^{4} = 3 \times 3 \times 3 \times 3 = 81$

$2^{3} = 2 \times 2 \times 2 = 8$

$(^{-}2)^{4} = (^{-}2) \times (^{-}2) \times (^{-}2) \times (^{-}2) = 16$

$^{-}2^{4} = ^{-}(2 \times 2 \times 2 \times 2) = ^{-}16$

Key exponent rules:

For 'a' nonzero, and 'm' and 'n' real numbers:

1) $a^{m} \cdot a^{n} = a^{(m+n)}$ Product rule

2) $\dfrac{a^{m}}{a^{n}} = a^{(m-n)}$ Quotient rule

3) $\dfrac{a^{-m}}{a^{-n}} = \dfrac{a^{n}}{a^{m}}$

When 10 is raised to any power, the exponent tells the numbers of zeroes in the product.

Example: $10^7 = 10,000,000$

Caution: Unless the negative sign is inside the parentheses and the exponent is outside the parentheses, the sign is not affected by the exponent.

$(^-2)^4$ implies that -2 is multiplied by itself 4 times.

$^-2^4$ implies that 2 is multiplied by itself 4 times, then the answer is negated.

Scientific notation is a more convenient method for writing very large and very small numbers. It employs two factors. The first factor is a number between 1 and 10. The second factor is a power of 10. This notation is a "shorthand" for expressing large numbers (like the weight of 100 elephants) or small numbers (like the weight of an atom in pounds).

Recall that:

$10^n = (10)^n$ Ten multiplied by itself n times.

$10^0 = 1$ Any nonzero number raised to power of zero is 1.

$10^1 = 10$

$10^2 = 10 \times 10 = 100$

$10^3 = 10 \times 10 \times 10 = 1000$ (kilo)

$10^{-1} = 1/10$ (deci)

$10^{-2} = 1/100$ (centi)

$10^{-3} = 1/1000$ (milli)

$10^{-6} = 1/1,000,000$ (micro)

Example: Write 46,368,000 in scientific notation.

1)   Introduce a decimal point and decimal places.
46,368,000 = 46,368,000.0000

2)   Make a mark between the two digits that give a number between -9.9 and 9.9.
4 ∧ 6,368,000 .0000

3)   Count the number of digit places between the decimal point and the mark. This number is the 'n'-the power of ten.

So, $46,368,000 = 4.6368 \times 10^7$

Example: Write 0.00397 in scientific notation.

1)   Decimal place is already in place.

2)   Make a mark between 3 and 9 to get a one number between -9.9 and 9.9.

3)   Move decimal place to the mark (3 hops).

$0.003 \wedge 97$

Motion is to the right, so n of 10^n is negative.

Therefore, $0.00397 = 3.97 \times 10^{-3}$.

Converting decimals, fractions and percents

A **decimal** can be converted to a **percent** by multiplying by 100, or merely moving the decimal point two places to the right. A **percent** can be converted to a **decimal** by dividing by 100, or moving the decimal point two places to the left.

Examples: 0.375 = 37.5%
0.7 = 70%
0.04 = 4 %
3.15 = 315 %
84% = 0.84
3 % = 0.03
60% = 0.6
110% = 1.1
$\frac{1}{2}$ % = 0.5% = 0.005

A **percent** can be converted to a **fraction** by placing it over 100 and reducing to simplest terms.

Example: Convert 0.056 to a fraction.

Multiplying 0.056 by $\frac{1000}{1000}$ to get rid of the decimal point:

$$0.056 \times \frac{1000}{1000} = \frac{56}{1000} = \frac{7}{125}$$

Example: Find 23% of 1000.

$$= \frac{23}{100} \times \frac{1000}{1} = 23 \times 10 = 230$$

Example: Convert 6.25% to a decimal and to a fraction.

$$6.25\% = 0.0625 = 0.0625 \times \frac{10000}{10000} = \frac{625}{10000} = \frac{1}{16}$$

An example of a type of problem involving fractions is the conversion of recipes. For example, if a recipe serves 8 people, and we want to make enough to serve only 4, then we must determine how much of each ingredient to use. The conversion factor, the number we multiply each ingredient by, is:

$$\text{Conversion Factor} = \frac{\text{Number of Servings Needed}}{\text{Number of Servings in Recipe}}$$

Example: Consider the following recipe.

3 cups flour
½ tsp. baking powder
2/3 cups butter
2 cups sugar
2 eggs

If the above recipe serves 8, how much of each ingredient do we need to serve only 4 people?

First, determine the conversion factor.

$$\text{Conversion Factor} = \frac{4}{8} = \frac{1}{2}$$

Next, multiply each ingredient by the conversion factor.

3 x ½ =	1 ½ cups flour
½ x ½ =	¼ tsp. baking powder
2/3 x ½ = 2/6 =	1/3 cups butter
2 x ½ =	1 cup sugar
2 x ½ =	1 egg

Skill 3.2   **Apply operational algorithms to add, subtract, multiply and divide fractions, decimals, and integers**

Properties are rules that apply for addition, subtraction, multiplication, or division of real numbers. These properties are:

Commutative: You can change the order of the terms or factors as follows.

For addition: $a + b = b + a$
For multiplication: $ab = ba$

Since addition is the inverse operation of subtraction, and multiplication is the inverse operation of division, no separate laws are needed for subtraction and division.

Example: $5 + \,^-8 = \,^-8 + 5 = \,^-3$

Example: $^-2 \times 6 = 6 \times \,^-2 = \,^-12$

Associative: You can regroup the terms as you like.

For addition: $a + (b + c) = (a + b) + c$
For multiplication: $a(bc) = (ab)c$

This rule does not apply for division and subtraction.

Example: $(^-2 + 7) + 5 = \,^-2 + (7 + 5)$
$\qquad\quad 5 + 5 \;=\; ^-2 + 12 \;= 10$

Example: $(3 \times \,^-7) \times 5 \;=\; 3 \times (^-7 \times 5)$
$\qquad\quad ^-21 \times 5 = 3 \times \,^-35 = \,^-105$

Identity: Finding a number so that when added to a term results in that number (additive identity); finding a number such that when multiplied by a term results in that number (multiplicative identity).

For addition: $a + 0 = a$ (zero is additive identity)
For multiplication: $a \cdot 1 = a$ (one is multiplicative)

Example: $17 + 0 = 17$

Example: $^-34 \times 1 = \,^-34$
The product of any number and one is that number.

Inverse: Finding a number such that when added to the number it results in zero; or when multiplied by the number results in 1.

For addition: $a + (-a) = 0$
For multiplication: $a \cdot (1/a) = 1$

$(-a)$ is the additive inverse of a; $(1/a)$, also called the reciprocal, is the multiplicative inverse of a.

Example: $25 + {}^-25 = 0$

Example: $5 \times \frac{1}{5} = 1$ The product of any number and its reciprocal is one.

Distributive: This technique allows us to operate on terms within a parentheses without first performing operations within the parentheses. This is especially helpful when terms within the parentheses cannot be combined.

$a (b + c) = ab + ac$

Example: $6 \times ({}^-4 + 9) = (6 \times {}^-4) + (6 \times 9)$
$6 \times 5 = {}^-24 + 54 = 30$

To multiply a sum by a number, multiply each addend by the number, then add the products.

Addition of whole numbers

Example: At the end of a day of shopping, a shopper had $24 remaining in his wallet. He spent $45 on various goods. How much money did the shopper have at the beginning of the day?

The total amount of money the shopper started with is the sum of the amount spent and the amount remaining at the end of the day.

$$\begin{array}{r} 24 \\ + \ \ 45 \\ \hline 69 \end{array}$$ → The original total was $69.

Example: A race took the winner 1 hr. 58 min. 12 sec. on the first half of the race and 2 hr. 9 min. 57 sec. on the second half of the race. How much time did the entire race take?

$$\begin{array}{r}
1 \text{ hr. } 58 \text{ min. } 12 \text{ sec.} \\
+ \ 2 \text{ hr. } \ 9 \text{ min. } 57 \text{ sec.} \\
\hline
3 \text{ hr. } 67 \text{ min. } 69 \text{ sec.}
\end{array}$$ Add these numbers

$$\begin{array}{r}
+ \ 1 \text{ min } -60 \text{ sec.} \\
\hline
\end{array}$$ Change 60 seconds to 1 min.

$$\begin{array}{r}
3 \text{ hr. } 68 \text{ min. } \ 9 \text{ sec.} \\
+ \ 1 \text{ hr.} -60 \text{ min.} \qquad . \\
\hline
4 \text{ hr. } \ 8 \text{ min. } \ 9 \text{ sec.}
\end{array}$$ Change 60 minutes to 1 hr.

4 hr. 8 min. 9 sec. ←final answer

Subtraction of Whole Numbers

Example: At the end of his shift, a cashier has $96 in the cash register. At the beginning of his shift, he had $15. How much money did the cashier collect during his shift?

The total collected is the difference of the ending amount and the starting amount.

$$\begin{array}{r}
96 \\
- \ 15 \\
\hline
81
\end{array}$$ → The total collected was $81.

Multiplication of whole numbers

Multiplication is one of the four basic number operations. In simple terms, multiplication is the addition of a number to itself a certain number of times. For example, 4 multiplied by 3 is the equal to 4 + 4 + 4 or 3 + 3 + 3 +3. Another way of conceptualizing multiplication is to think in terms of groups. For example, if we have 4 groups of 3 students, then the total number of students is 4 multiplied by 3. We call the solution to a multiplication problem the product.

The basic algorithm for whole number multiplication begins with aligning the numbers by place value, with the number containing more places on top.

$$\begin{array}{r}
172 \\
\times \ \ 43 \\
\hline
\end{array}$$ → Note that we placed 122 on top because it has more places than 43 does.

Next, we multiply the ones' place of the second number by each place value of the top number sequentially.

$$\begin{array}{r}
(2) \\
172 \\
\times \ \ \ 43 \\
\hline
516
\end{array}$$ {3 x 2 = 6, 3 x 7 = 21, 3 x 1 = 3}
Note that we had to carry a 2 to the hundreds' column because 3 x 7 = 21. Note also that we add, not multiply, carried numbers to the product.

Next, we multiply the number in the tens' place of the second number by each place value of the top number sequentially. Because we are multiplying by a number in the tens' place, we place a zero at the end of this product.

```
      (2)
      172
x      43  ──→  {4 x 2 = 8, 4 x 7 = 28, 4 x 1 = 4}
      516
     6880
```

Finally, to determine the final product we add the two partial products.

```
      172
x      43
      516
  +  6880
     7396  ──→  The product of 172 and 43 is 7396.
```

Example: A student buys 4 boxes of crayons. Each box contains 16 crayons. How many total crayons does the student have?

The total number of crayons is 16 x 4.

```
      16
x      4  ──→
      64      Total number of crayons equals 64.
```

Division of whole numbers

Division, the inverse of multiplication, is another of the four basic number operations. When we divide one number by another, we determine how many times we can multiply the divisor (number divided by) before we exceed the number we are dividing (dividend). For example, 8 divided by 2 equals 4 because we can multiply 2 four times to reach 8 (2 x 4 = 8 or 2 + 2 + 2 + 2 = 8). Using the grouping conceptualization we used with multiplication, we can divide 8 into 4 groups of 2 or into 2 groups of 4. We call the answer to a division problem the quotient.

If the divisor does not divide evenly into the dividend, then we express the leftover amount either as a remainder or as a fraction with the divisor as the denominator. For example, 9 divided by 2 equals 4 with a remainder of 1 or 4 ½.

The basic algorithm for division is long division. We start by representing the quotient as follows.

$$14\overline{)293}$$ → 14 is the divisor, and 293 is the dividend.

This represents $293 \div 14$.

Next, we divide the divisor into the dividend starting from the left.

$$\begin{array}{r} 2 \\ 14\overline{)293} \end{array}$$ → 14 divides into 29 two times with a remainder.

Next, we multiply the partial quotient by the divisor, subtract this value from the first digits of the dividend, and bring down the remaining dividend digits to complete the number.

$$\begin{array}{r} 2 \\ 14\overline{)293} \\ -28 \\ \hline 13 \end{array}$$ → $2 \times 14 = 28$, $29 - 28 = 1$, and bringing down the 3 yields 13.

Finally, we divide again (the divisor into the remaining value) and repeat the preceding process. The number left after the subtraction represents the remainder.

$$\begin{array}{r} 20 \\ 14\overline{)293} \\ -28 \\ \hline 13 \\ -0 \\ \hline 13 \end{array}$$ → The final quotient is 20 with a remainder of 13. We can also represent this quotient as 20 13/14.

Example: Each box of apples contains 24 apples. How many boxes must a grocer purchase to supply a group of 252 people with one apple each?

The grocer needs 252 apples. Because he must buy apples in groups of 24, we divide 252 by 24 to determine how many boxes he needs to buy.

$$\begin{array}{r} 10 \\ 24\overline{)252} \\ -24 \\ \hline 12 \\ -0 \\ \hline 12 \end{array}$$ → The quotient is 10 with a remainder of 12.

Thus, the grocer needs 10 boxes plus 12 more apples. Therefore, the minimum number of boxes the grocer can purchase is 11.

Example: At his job, John gets paid $20 for every hour he works. If John made $940 in a week, how many hours did he work?

This is a division problem. To determine the number of hours John worked, we divide the total amount made ($940) by the hourly rate of pay ($20). Thus, the number of hours worked equals 940 divided by 20.

$$
\begin{array}{r}
47 \\
20\overline{)940} \\
\underline{-80} \\
140 \\
\underline{-140} \\
0
\end{array}
$$

→ 20 divides into 940, 47 times with no remainder.

John worked 47 hours.

Addition and Subtraction of Decimals

When adding and subtracting decimals, we align the numbers by place value as we do with whole numbers. After adding or subtracting each column, we bring the decimal down, placing it in the same location as in the numbers added or subtracted.

Example: Find the sum of 152.3 and 36.342.

$$
\begin{array}{r}
152.300 \\
+\quad 36.342 \\
\hline
188.642
\end{array}
$$

Note that we placed two zeroes after the final place value in 152.3 in order to clarify the column addition.

Example: Find the difference of 152.3 and 36.342.

$$
\begin{array}{r}
2\ 9\ 10 \\
152.300 \\
-\quad 36.342 \\
\hline
58
\end{array}
\qquad \longrightarrow \qquad
\begin{array}{r}
(4)11(12) \\
152.300 \\
-\quad 36.342 \\
\hline
115.958
\end{array}
$$

Note how we borrowed to subtract from the zeroes in the hundredths' and thousandths' place of 152.300.

Multiplication of Decimals

When multiplying decimal numbers, we multiply exactly as with whole numbers and place the decimal moving in from the left the total number of decimal places contained in the two numbers multiplied. For example, when multiplying 1.5 and 2.35, we place the decimal in the product 3 places in from the left (3.525).

Example: Find the product of 3.52 and 4.1.

$$
\begin{array}{r}
3.52 \\
\times \ 4.1 \\
\hline
352 \\
+ \ 14080 \\
\hline
14432
\end{array}
$$

→ Note that there are 3 total decimal places in the two numbers.

→ We place the decimal 3 places in from the left.

Thus, the final product is 14.432.

Example: A shopper has 5 one-dollar bills, 6 quarters, 3 nickels, and 4 pennies in his pocket. How much money does he have?

$$5 \times \$1.00 = \$5.00$$

$$
\begin{array}{ccc}
 & 3 & \\
\$0.25 & \$0.05 & \$0.01 \\
\times \ \ 6 & \times \ \ 3 & \times \ \ 4 \\
\hline
\$1.50 & \$0.15 & \$0.04
\end{array}
$$

Note the placement of the decimals in the multiplication products. Thus, the total amount of money in the shopper's pocket is:

$$
\begin{array}{r}
\$5.00 \\
1.50 \\
0.15 \\
+ \ 0.04 \\
\hline
\$6.69
\end{array}
$$

Division of Decimals

When dividing decimal numbers, we first remove the decimal in the divisor by moving the decimal in the dividend the same number of spaces to the right. For example, when dividing 1.45 into 5.3 we convert the numbers to 145 and 530 and perform normal whole number division.

Example: Find the quotient of 5.3 divided by 1.45.
Convert to 145 and 530.

Divide.

$$
\begin{array}{r}
3 \\
145{\overline{\smash{\big)}\,530}} \\
\underline{- \ 435} \\
95
\end{array}
$$
→
$$
\begin{array}{r}
3.65 \\
145{\overline{\smash{\big)}\,530.00}} \\
\underline{- \ 435} \\
950 \\
\underline{- \ 870} \\
800
\end{array}
$$
→ Note that we insert the decimal to continue division.

Because one of the numbers divided contained one decimal place, we round the quotient to one decimal place. Thus, the final quotient is 3.7.

Operating with Percents

Example: 5 is what percent of 20?

This is the same as converting $\frac{5}{20}$ to % form.

$$\frac{5}{20} \times \frac{100}{1} = \frac{5}{1} \times \frac{5}{1} = 25\%$$

Example: There are 64 dogs in the kennel. 48 are collies. What percent are collies?

Restate the problem.   48 is what percent of 64?
Write an equation. $48 = n \times 64$
Solve. $\frac{48}{64} = n$

$n = \frac{3}{4} = 75\%$

75% of the dogs are collies.

Example: The auditorium was filled to 90% capacity. There were 558 seats occupied. What is the capacity of the auditorium?

Restate the problem.   90% of what number is 558?
Write an equation. $0.9n = 558$
Solve. $n = \frac{558}{.9}$
                          $n = 620$

The capacity of the auditorium is 620 people.

Example: A pair of shoes costs $42.00. Sales tax is 6%. What is the total cost of the shoes?

Restate the problem.   What is 6% of 42?
Write an equation. $n = 0.06 \times 42$
Solve. $n = 2.52$

Add the sales tax to the cost. $42.00 + $2.52 = $44.52

The total cost of the shoes, including sales tax, is $44.52.

Addition and subtraction of fractions

<u>Key Points</u>

1. You need a common denominator in order to add and subtract reduced and improper fractions.

Example: $\dfrac{1}{3}+\dfrac{7}{3}=\dfrac{1+7}{3}=\dfrac{8}{3}=2\dfrac{2}{3}$

Example: $\dfrac{4}{12}+\dfrac{6}{12}-\dfrac{3}{12}=\dfrac{4+6-3}{12}=\dfrac{7}{12}$

2. Adding an integer and a fraction of the <u>same</u> sign results directly in a mixed fraction.

Example: $2+\dfrac{2}{3}=2\dfrac{2}{3}$

Example: $^-2-\dfrac{3}{4}=^-2\dfrac{3}{4}$

3. Adding an integer and a fraction with different signs involves the following steps.

-get a common denominator
-add or subtract as needed
-change to a mixed fraction if possible

Example: $2-\dfrac{1}{3}=\dfrac{2\times3-1}{3}=\dfrac{6-1}{3}=\dfrac{5}{3}=1\dfrac{2}{3}$

Example: Add $7\dfrac{3}{8}+5\dfrac{2}{7}$

Add the whole numbers; add the fractions; and combine the two results:

$7\dfrac{3}{8}+5\dfrac{2}{7}=(7+5)+(\dfrac{3}{8}+\dfrac{2}{7})$

$=12+\dfrac{(7\times3)+(8\times2)}{56}$ (LCM of 8 and 7)

$=12+\dfrac{21+16}{56}=12+\dfrac{37}{56}=12\dfrac{37}{56}$

Example: Perform the operation.

$$\frac{2}{3} - \frac{5}{6}$$

We first find the LCM of 3 and 6 which is 6.

$$\frac{2 \times 2}{3 \times 2} - \frac{5}{6} \rightarrow \frac{4-5}{6} = \frac{^-1}{6} \qquad \text{(Using method A)}$$

Example: $^-7\frac{1}{4} + 2\frac{7}{8}$

$$^-7\frac{1}{4} + 2\frac{7}{8} = (^-7 + 2) + (\frac{^-1}{4} + \frac{7}{8})$$

$$= (^-5) + \frac{(^-2 + 7)}{8} = (^-5) + (\frac{5}{8})$$

$$= (^-5) + \frac{5}{8} = \frac{^-5 \times 8}{1 \times 8} + \frac{5}{8} = \frac{^-40 + 5}{8}$$

$$= \frac{^-35}{8} = ^-4\frac{3}{8}$$

Divide 35 by 8 to get 4, remainder 3.

Caution: Common error would be

$$^-7\frac{1}{4} + 2\frac{7}{8} = ^-7\frac{2}{8} + 2\frac{7}{8} = ^-5\frac{9}{8} \qquad \text{Wrong.}$$

It is correct to add -7 and 2 to get -5, but adding $\frac{2}{8} + \frac{7}{8} = \frac{9}{8}$

is wrong. It should have been $\frac{^-2}{8} + \frac{7}{8} = \frac{5}{8}$. Then,

$$^-5 + \frac{5}{8} = ^-4\frac{3}{8} \quad \text{as before.}$$

Multiplication of fractions

Using the following example: $3\dfrac{1}{4} \times \dfrac{5}{6}$

1. Convert each number to an improper fraction.

$$3\dfrac{1}{4} = \dfrac{(12+1)}{4} = \dfrac{13}{4}$$ $\dfrac{5}{6}$ is already in reduced form.

2. Reduce (cancel) common factors of the numerator and denominator if they exist.

$$\dfrac{13}{4} \times \dfrac{5}{6}$$ No common factors exist.

3. Multiply the numerators by each other and the denominators by each other.

$$\dfrac{13}{4} \times \dfrac{5}{6} = \dfrac{65}{24}$$

4. If possible, reduce the fraction back to its lowest term.

$\dfrac{65}{24}$ Cannot be reduced further.

5. Convert the improper fraction back to a mixed fraction by using long division.

$$\dfrac{65}{24} = 24\overline{)65} \quad \begin{array}{r} 2 \\ \underline{48} \\ 17 \end{array} \qquad = 2\dfrac{17}{24}$$

Summary of sign changes for multiplication:

a. $(+) \times (+) = (+)$

b. $(-) \times (+) = (-)$

c. $(+) \times (-) = (-)$

d. $(-) \times (-) = (+)$

Example: $7\dfrac{1}{3} \times \dfrac{5}{11} = \dfrac{22}{3} \times \dfrac{5}{11}$ Reduce like terms (22 and 11)

$$= \dfrac{2}{3} \times \dfrac{5}{1} = \dfrac{10}{3} = 3\dfrac{1}{3}$$

Example: $^{-}6\dfrac{1}{4} \times \dfrac{5}{9} = \dfrac{^{-}25}{4} \times \dfrac{5}{9}$

$$= \dfrac{^{-}125}{36} = {}^{-}3\dfrac{17}{36}$$

Example: $\dfrac{^{-}1}{4} \times \dfrac{^{-}3}{7}$ Negative times a negative equals positive.

$$= \dfrac{1}{4} \times \dfrac{3}{7} = \dfrac{3}{28}$$

Division of fractions:

1. Change mixed fractions to improper fractions.

2. Change the division problem to a multiplication problem by using the reciprocal of the number after the division sign.

3. Find the sign of the final product.

4. Cancel if common factors exist between the numerator and the denominator.

5. Multiply the numerators together and the denominators together.

6. Change the improper fraction to a mixed number.

Example: $3\dfrac{1}{5} \div 2\dfrac{1}{4} = \dfrac{16}{5} \div \dfrac{9}{4}$

$$= \dfrac{16}{5} \times \dfrac{4}{9}$$ Reciprocal of $\dfrac{9}{4}$ is $\dfrac{4}{9}$.

$$= \dfrac{64}{45} = 1\dfrac{19}{45}$$

Example:

$$7\frac{3}{4} \div 11\frac{5}{8} = \frac{31}{4} \div \frac{93}{8}$$

$$= \frac{31}{4} \times \frac{8}{93} \qquad \text{Reduce like terms.}$$

$$= \frac{1}{1} \times \frac{2}{3} = \frac{2}{3}$$

Example:

$$\left(-2\frac{1}{2}\right) \div 4\frac{1}{6} = \frac{^-5}{2} \div \frac{25}{6}$$

$$= \frac{^-5}{2} \times \frac{6}{25} \qquad \text{Reduce like terms.}$$

$$= \frac{^-1}{1} \times \frac{3}{5} = \frac{^-3}{5}$$

Example:

$$\left(-5\frac{3}{8}\right) \div \left(\frac{^-7}{16}\right) = \frac{^-43}{8} \div \frac{^-7}{16}$$

$$= \frac{^-43}{8} \times \frac{^-16}{7} \qquad \text{Reduce like terms.}$$

$$= \frac{43}{1} \times \frac{2}{7} \qquad \text{Negative times a negative equals a positive.}$$

$$= \frac{86}{7} = 12\frac{2}{7}$$

Skill 3.3   **Use scales and ratios to interpret maps and models**

A **ratio** is a comparison of 2 numbers. If a class had 11 boys and 14 girls, then the ratio of boys to girls could be written one of 3 ways:

$$11:14 \quad \text{or} \quad 11 \text{ to } 14 \quad \text{or} \quad \frac{11}{14}$$

The ratio of girls to boys is:

$$14:11, \quad 14 \text{ to } 11 \quad \text{or} \quad \frac{14}{11}$$

Ratios can be reduced when possible. A ratio of 12 cats to 18 dogs would reduce to 2:3, 2 to 3 or $2/3$.

Note: Read ratio questions carefully. Given a group of 6 adults and 5 children, the ratio of children to the entire group would be 5:11.

Students need to understand that ratios and proportions are used to create scale models of real-life objects, to understand the principles of ratio and proportion, and to understand how to calculate scale using ratio and proportion.

Scaled drawings (maps, blueprints, and models) are used in many real-world situations. Architects make blueprints and models of buildings. These drawings and models are then used by the contractors to build the buildings. Engineers make scaled drawings of bridges, machine parts, roads, airplanes, and many other things. Maps of the world, countries, states, roads, etc. are scaled drawings. Landscape designers use scale drawings and models of plants, decks, and other structures to show how they should be placed around a house or other building. Models of cars, boats, and planes made from kits are scaled. Automobile engineers construct models of cars before the actual assembly is done. Many museum exhibits are actually scaled models because the real size of the items displayed would be too large.

Examples of real-world problems that students might solve using scaled drawings include:

- reading road maps and determining the distance between locations by using the map scale,

- creating a scaled drawing (floor plan) of their classroom to determine the best use of space,

- creating an 8 ½" x 11" representation of a quilt to be pieced together, or

- drawing a blueprint of their rooms and creating a model from it.

Skill 3.4 **Use geometric concepts and formulas to solve**
estimating the surface area of a floor to determi
approximate cost of floor covering)

The **perimeter** of any polygon is the sum of the lengths of the sid

The **area** of a polygon is the number of square units covered by th

FIGURE	AREA FORMULA	PERIMETER FORMULA
Rectangle	LW	$2(L+W)$
Triangle	$\dfrac{1}{2}bh$	$a+b+c$
Parallelogram	bh	sum of lengths of sides
Trapezoid	$\dfrac{1}{2}h(a+b)$	sum of lengths of sides

Perimeter

Example: A farmer has a piece of land shaped as shown below. He wishes
to fence this land at an estimated cost of $25 per linear foot. What
is the total cost of fencing this property to the nearest foot.

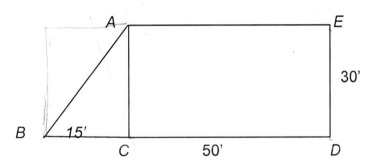

From the right triangle ABC, AC = 30 and BC = 15.

Since $(AB) = (AC)^2 + (BC)^2$
$(AB) = (30)^2 + (15)^2$

So $\sqrt{(AB)^2} = AB = \sqrt{1125} = 33.5410$ feet

To the nearest foot AB = 34 feet.
Perimeter of the piece of land is $= AB + BC + CD + DE + EA$

= 34 + 15 + 50 + 30 + 50 = 179 feet

cost of fencing = $25 x 179 = $4, 475.00

ea

Area is the space that a figure occupies. Example:

Example: What will be the cost of carpeting a rectangular office that measures 12 feet by 15 feet if the carpet costs $12.50 per square yard?

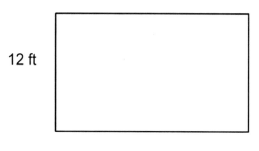

12 ft

15 ft

The problem is asking you to determine the area of the office. The area of a rectangle is *length x width = A*
Substitute the given values in the equation $A = lw$

$A = (12 \text{ ft.})(15 \text{ ft.})$

$A = 180 \text{ ft.}$

The problem asked you to determine the cost of carpet at $12.50 per square yard.

First, you need to convert 180 ft.^{2} into yards^2.

1 yd. = 3 ft.
   (1 yard)(1 yard) = (3 feet)(3 feet)
   1 yd^2 = 9 ft 2

Hence, $\underline{180 \text{ ft}^2}$ $\underline{1 \text{ yd}^2}$ $\underline{20}$
       1 $=$ 9 ft^2 $=$ 1 $= 20 \text{ yd}^2$

The carpet cost $12.50 per square yard; thus the cost of carpeting the office described is $12.50 x 20 = $250.00.

Example: Find the area of a parallelogram whose base is 6.5 cm and the height of the altitude to that base is 3.7 cm.

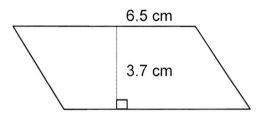

6.5 cm

3.7 cm

$A_{parallelogram} = bh$

$$= (3.7)(6.5)$$
$$= 24.05 \text{ cm}^2$$

Example: Find the area of this triangle.

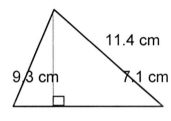

11.4 cm

9.3 cm   7.1 cm

16.8 cm

$A_{triangle} = \frac{1}{2}bh$

$$= 0.5\,(16.8)\,(7.1)$$
$$= 59.64 \text{ cm}^2$$

Example: Find the area of this trapezoid.

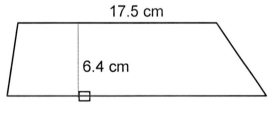

17.5 cm

6.4 cm

23.7 cm

The area of a trapezoid equals one-half the sum of the bases times the altitude.

$A_{trapezoid} = \frac{1}{2}h(b_1 + b_2)$

$$= 0.5\,(6.4)\,(17.5 + 23.7)$$
$$= 131.84 \text{ cm}^2$$

round a circle is the **circumference**. The ratio of the
to the diameter is represented by the Greek letter pi. $\Pi \sim 3.14$

ence of a circle is found by the formula $C = 2\Pi r$ or $C = \Pi d$
radius of the circle and d is the diameter.

The **area** of a circle is found by the formula $A = \Pi r^2$.

Example: Find the circumference and area of a circle whose radius is 7
            meters.

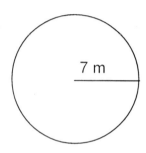

7 m

C = 2Πr $A = \Pi r^2$
= 2(3.14)(7)   = 3.14(7)(7)
= 43.96 m   = 153.86 m^2

Volume and **Surface area** are computed using the following formulas:

FIGURE	VOLUME	TOTAL SURFACE AREA
Right Cylinder	$\pi r^2 h$	$2\pi rh + 2\pi r^2$
Right Cone	$\dfrac{\pi r^2 h}{3}$	$\pi r\sqrt{r^2 + h^2} + \pi r^2$
Sphere	$\dfrac{4}{3}\pi r^3$	$4\pi r^2$
Rectangular Solid	LWH	$2LW + 2WH + 2LH$

FIGURE	LATERAL AREA	TOTAL AREA	VO
Regular Pyramid	1/2Pl	1/2Pl+B	1/3Bh

P = Perimeter
h = height
B = Area of Base
l = slant height

Example: What is the volume of a shoe box with a length of 35 cms, a width of 20 cms, and a height of 15 cms?

Volume of a rectangular solid
= Length x Width x Height
= 35 x 20 x 15
= 10500 cm^3

Example: A water company is trying to decide whether to use traditional cylindrical paper cups or to offer conical paper cups since both cost the same. The traditional cups are 8 cm wide and 14 cm high. The conical cups are 12 cm wide and 19 cm high. The company will use the cup that holds the most water.

Draw and label a sketch of each.

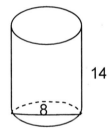

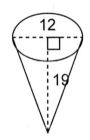

$V = \pi r^2 h$ $V = \dfrac{\pi r^2 h}{3}$ 1. write formula

$V = \pi(4)^2(14)$ $V = \dfrac{1}{3}\pi(6)^2(19)$ 2. substitute

$V = 703.717$ cm^3 $V = 716.283$ cm^3 3. solve

The choice should be the conical cup since its volume is more.

Example: How much material is needed to make a basketball that has a diameter of 15 inches? How much air is needed to fill the basketball?

Draw and label a sketch:

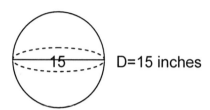 D=15 inches

Total surface area	Volume	
$TSA = 4\pi r^2$	$V = \dfrac{4}{3}\pi r^3$	1. write formula
$= 4\pi(7.5)^2$	$= \dfrac{4}{3}\pi(7.5)^3$	2. substitute
$= 706.858 \text{ in}^2$	$= 1767.1459 \text{ in}^3$	3. solve

Skill 3.5 **Solve problems using algebraic concepts and formulas (e.g., calculating wages based on sales commission)**

Procedure for solving algebraic equations

Example: $3(x + 3) =^- 2x + 4$ Solve for x.
1) Expand to eliminate all parentheses.

$3x + 9 =^- 2x + 4$

2) Multiply each term by the LCD to eliminate all denominators.

3) Combine like terms on each side when possible.

4) Use the properties to put all variables on one side and all constants on the other side.

$\rightarrow 3x + 9 - 9 =^- 2x + 4 - 9$ (subtract nine from both sides)
$\rightarrow 3x =^- 2x - 5$
$\rightarrow 3x + 2x =^- 2x + 2x - 5$ (add 2x to both sides)
$\rightarrow 5x =^- 5$
$\rightarrow \dfrac{5x}{5} = \dfrac{^-5}{5}$ (divide both sides by 5)

$$\rightarrow x = ^{-}1$$

Example: Mark and Mike are twins. Three times Mark's age plus four equals four times Mike's age minus 14. How old are the boys?

Since the boys are twins, their ages are the same. "Translate" the English into Algebra. Let x = their age

$$3x + 4 = 4x - 14$$

$$18 = x$$

The boys are each 18 years old.

Example: The Simpsons went out for dinner. All four of them ordered the aardvark steak dinner. Bert paid for the four meals and included a tip of $12 for a total of $84.60. How much was an aardvark steak dinner?

Let x = the price of one aardvark dinner.
So $4x$ = the price of four aardvark dinners.

$$4x + 12 = 84.60$$
$$4x = 72.60$$
$$x = \$18.50 \text{ for each dinner.}$$

Example: A pair of shoes costs $42.00. Sales tax is 6%. What is the total cost of the shoes?

Restate the problem.	What is 6% of 42?
Write an equation.	$n = 0.06 \times 42$
Solve.	$n = 2.52$

Add the sales tax to the cost. $42.00 + \$2.52 = \$44.52$

The total cost of the shoes, including sales tax, is $44.52.

Example: A class wants to take a field trip from New York City to Albany to visit the capital. The trip is approximately 160 miles. If they will be traveling at 50 miles per hour, then how long will it take for them to get there (assuming traveling at a steady rate)?

Set up the equation as a proportion and solve:

$$\frac{160 \text{ miles}}{x \text{ hours}} = \frac{50 \text{ miles}}{1 \text{ hour}}$$

(160 miles)(1 hour) = (50 miles) (x hours)

160 = 50x

x = 3.2 hours

Example: A salesman drove 480 miles from Pittsburgh to Hartford. The next day he returned the same distance to Pittsburgh in half an hour less time than his original trip took because he increased his average speed by 4 mph. Find his original speed.

Since distance = rate x time then time = $\dfrac{\text{distance}}{\text{rate}}$

original time − 1/2 hour = shorter return time

$$\frac{480}{x} - \frac{1}{2} = \frac{480}{x+4}$$

Multiplying by the LCD of $2x(x+4)$, the equation becomes:

$$480\big[2(x+4)\big] - 1\big[x(x+4)\big] = 480(2x)$$

$$960x + 3840 - x^2 - 4x = 960x$$

$$x^2 + 4x - 3840 = 0$$

$$(x+64)(x-60) = 0$$

$x = 60$ 60 mph is the original speed

                          64 mph is the faster return speed

Skill 3.6 **Apply appropriate algebraic equations to the solution of problems (e.g., determining the original price of a sale item given the rate of discount)**

Example: There are 64 dogs in the kennel. 48 are collies. What percent are collies?

Restate the problem. 48 is what percent of 64?
Write an equation. $48 = n \times 64$
Solve. $\frac{48}{64} = n$

$n = \frac{3}{4} = 75\%$

75% of the dogs are collies.

Example: The auditorium was filled to 90% capacity. There were 558 seats occupied. What is the capacity of the auditorium?

Restate the problem. 90% of what number is 558?
Write an equation. $0.9n = 558$
Solve. $n = \frac{558}{.9}$

$n = 620$

The capacity of the auditorium is 620 people.

COMPETENCY 4.0   UNDERSTAND MAJOR CONCEPTS, PRINCIPLES, AND THEORIES IN SCIENCE AND TECHNOLOGY; AND USE THAT UNDERSTANDING TO ANALYZE PHENOMENA IN THE NATURAL WORLD AND TO INTERPRET INFORMATION PRESENTED IN ILLUSTRATED OR WRITTEN FORM

Branches of science

Science is composed of a number branches:

Life science has the following branches:

Biology is the study of plants and animals.

Botany is the branch of biology that deals with plants, and **Zoology** is the branch that is about animals.

Ecology is the study of the relationship of the organisms to their environment and **Human Health** is that branch of Biology dealing with the health and well being of human beings.

Physical Science has two branches:

Chemistry is the study of the structure and make up of matter and the changes matter undergoes.

Physics is the branch of that deals with energy and matter and how they interact.

Earth science deals with earth or one or more of its parts.

Astronomy is the science of the heavenly bodies and of their sizes, motions, and composition.

Geology deals with the history of the history of the earth and its life, especially as recorded in rocks.

Meteorology deals with atmosphere, weather and weather forecasting.

Oceanography is the study of oceans.

LIFE SCIENCE

Animal cells – begin with a discussion of the nucleus as a round body inside the cell. It controls the cell's activities. The nuclear membrane contains threadlike structures called chromosomes. The genes are units that control cell activities found in the nucleus. The cytoplasm has many structures in it. Vacuoles contain the food for the cell. Other vacuoles contain waste materials. Animal cells differ from plant cells because they have cell membranes.

Plant cells – have cell walls. A cell wall differs from cell membranes. The cell membrane is very thin and is a part of the cell. The cell wall is thick and is a nonliving part of the cell. Chloroplasts are bundles of chlorophyll.

Single cells – A single celled organism is called a **protist.** When you look under a microscope, you can see the animal-like protists known as **protozoans.** They do not have chloroplasts. They are usually classified by the way they move for food. Amoebas engulf other protists by flowing around and over them. The paramecium has a hair-like structures like tiny oars that allow it to move back and forth searching for food. The euglena is an example of a protozoan that moves with a tail-like structure called a flagellum.

Plant-like protists have cell walls and float in the ocean. **Bacteria** are the simplest protists. A bacterial cell is surrounded by a cell wall, but there is no nucleus inside the cell. Most bacteria do not contain chlorophyll, so they do not make their own food. The classification of bacteria is by shape. Cocci are round, bacilli are rod-shaped, and spirilla are spiral shaped.

Structure of a Cell

1. Nucleus - The brain of the cell. The nucleus contains:

> **chromosomes**- DNA, RNA ane proteins tightly coiled to conserve space while providing a large surface area.
> **chromatin** - loose structure of chromosomes. Chromosomes are called chromatin when the cell is not dividing.
> **nucleoli** - where ribosomes are made. These are seen as dark spots in the nucleus.
> **nuclear membrane** - contains pores which let RNA out of the nucleus. The nuclear membrane is continuous with the endoplasmic reticulum, which allows the membrane to expand or shrink if needed.

2. Ribosomes - the site of protein synthesis. Ribosomes may be free floating in the cytoplasm or attached to the endoplasmic reticulum. There may be up to a half a million ribosomes in a cell, depending on how much protein is made by the cell.

3. Endoplasmic Reticulum - These are folded and provide a large surface area. They are the "roadway" of the cell and allow for transport of materials. The lumen of the endoplasmic reticulum helps to keep materials out of the cytoplasm and headed in the right direction. The endoplasmic reticulum is capable of building new membrane material. There are two types:

Smooth Endoplasmic Reticulum - contain no ribosomes on their surface.

Rough Endoplasmic Reticulum - contain ribosomes on their surface. This form of ER is abundant in cells that make many proteins, like in the pancreas, which produces many digestive enzymes.

4. Golgi Complex or Golgi Apparatus - This structure is stacked to increase surface area. The Golgi Complex functions to sort, modify, and package molecules that are made in other parts of the cell. These molecules are either sent out of the cell or to other organelles within the cell.

5. Lysosomes - found mainly in animal cells. These contain digestive enzymes that break down food, substances not needed, viruses, damaged cell components, and, eventually, the cell itself. It is believed that lysosomes are responsible for the aging process.

6. Mitochondria - large organelles that make ATP to supply energy to the cell. Muscle cells have many mitochondria because they use a great deal of energy. The folds inside the mitochondria are called cristae. They provide a large surface where the reactions of cellular respiration occur. Mitochondria have their own DNA and are capable of reproducing themselves if a greater demand is made for additional energy. Mitochondria are found only in animal cells.

7. Plastids - found in photosynthetic organisms only. They are similar to the mitochondria due to their double-membrane structure. They also have their own DNA and can reproduce if increased capture of sunlight becomes necessary. There are several types of plastids:

> **Chloroplasts** - green, function in photosynthesis. They are capable of trapping sunlight.

> **Chromoplasts** - make and store yellow and orange pigments; they provide color to leaves, flowers and fruits.

> **Amyloplasts** - store starch and are used as a food reserve. They are abundant in roots like potatoes.

8. Cell Wall - found in plant cells only, it is composed of cellulose and fibers. It is thick enough for support and protection, yet porous enough to allow water and dissolved substances to enter. Cell walls are cemented to each other.

9. Vacuoles - hold stored food and pigments. Vacuoles are very large in plants. This allows them to fill with water in order to provide turgor pressure. Lack of turgor pressure causes a plant to wilt.

10. Cytoskeleton - composed of protein filaments attached to the plasma membrane and organelles. They provide a framework for the cell and aid in cell movement. They constantly change shape and move about. Three types of fibers make up the cytoskeleton:

> **Microtubules** - largest of the three; make cilia and flagella for locomotion. Flagella grow from a basal body. Some examples are sperm cells and tracheal cilia. Centrioles are also composed of microtubules. They form the spindle fibers that pull the cell apart into two cells during cell division. Centrioles are not found in the cells of higher plants.

> **Intermediate Filaments** - they are smaller than microtubules but larger than microfilaments. They help the cell to keep its shape.

> **Microfilaments** - smallest of the three, they are made of actin and small amounts of myosin (like in muscle cells). They function in cell movement such as cytoplasmic streaming, endocytosis, and amoeboid movement. This structure pinches the two cells apart after cell division, forming two cells.

Taxonomy and classification of bacteria, protists, and fungi

Carolus Linnaeus is known as the father of taxonomy. **Taxonomy** is the science of classification. Linnaeus based his system on morphology (study of structure). Later on, evolutionary relationships (phylogeny) were also used to sort and group species. The modern classification system uses binomial nomenclature. This consists of a two-word name for every species. The genus is the first part of the name, and the species is the second part.

Species are defined by the ability to successfully reproduce with members of their own kind.

Kingdom Monera - bacteria and blue-green algae, prokaryotic, having no true nucleus, unicellular.

Kingdom Protista - eukaryotic, unicellular, some are photosynthetic, some are consumers.

Kingdom Fungi - eukaryotic, multicellular, absorptive consumers, contain a chitin cell wall.

Bacteria are classified according to their morphology (shape). **Bacilli** are rod shaped, **cocci** are round, and **spirillia** are spiral shaped. The **gram stain** is a staining procedure used to identify bacteria. Gram-positive bacteria pick up the stain and turn purple. Gram-negative bacteria do not pick up the stain and are pink in color. Microbiologists use methods of locomotion, reproduction, and the food-gathering to classify protista.

Vertebrates

Vertebrates are animals with a vertebral column. These are complex living organisms. In order to understand them, it is important to discuss their life processes.

Skeletal System - The skeletal system functions to provide support. Vertebrates have an endoskeleton, with muscles attached to bones. Skeletal proportions are controlled by area-to-volume relationships. Body size and shape is limited due to the forces of gravity. Surface area is increased to improve efficiency in all organ systems.

Muscular System – Its function is for movement. There are three types of muscle tissue. Skeletal muscle is voluntary. These muscles are attached to bones. Smooth muscle is involuntary. It is found in organs and enables functions such as digestion and respiration. Cardiac muscle is a specialized type of smooth muscle.

Nervous System - The neuron is the basic unit of the nervous system. It consists of an axon, which carries impulses away from the cell body; the dendrite, which carries impulses toward the cell body; and the cell body, which contains the nucleus. Synapses are spaces between neurons. Chemicals called neurotransmitters are found close to the synapse. The myelin sheath, composed of Schwann cells, covers the neurons and provides insulation.

Digestive System - The function of the digestive system is to break down food and to absorb it into the blood stream where it can be delivered to all cells of the body for use in cellular respiration. As animals evolved, digestive systems changed from simple absorption to a system with a separate mouth and anus, allowing the animal to become independent of a host.

Respiratory System - This system functions in the gas exchange of oxygen (needed) and carbon dioxide (waste). It delivers oxygen to the bloodstream and picks up carbon dioxide for release out of the body. Simple animals diffuse gases from and to their environment. Gills allow aquatic animals to exchange gases in a fluid medium by removing dissolved oxygen from the water. Lungs maintain a fluid environment for gas exchange in terrestrial animals.

Circulatory System - The function of the circulatory system is to carry oxygenated blood and nutrients to all cells of the body and to return with carbon dioxide waste to be expelled from the lungs. Animals evolved from an open system to a closed system with vessels leading to and from the heart.

Viruses

Viruses are neither living nor non-living things, and yet they have some characteristics of both. Viruses are difficult to classify. Some important features of viruses are:listed below:

They can be seen only under the electron microscope. There are many shapes of viruses, but these three are the most prominent - round, rod shaped, and many sided. A virus consists of a chromosome-like part surrounded by a protein coat. The chromosome-like part carries the hereditary material. Viruses are not made of cell parts. The unique feature of viruses is that they are able to reproduce only inside a living organism, and this is the trait they share with living organisms.

Viral diseases have been fought through the use of vaccination, where a small amount of the virus is introduced so that the immune system is able to recognize it later and to fight it off. Antibodies are more quickly manufactured when the host has had prior exposure. Viruses are difficult to treat because antibiotics are ineffective against them. That is why doctors do not usually prescribe antibiotics for those who have a cold or the flu, common viral infections.

ECOLOGY

Ecology is the study of organisms, where they live, and their interactions with the environment. A **population** is a group of the same species in a specific area. A **community** is a group of populations residing in the same area. Communities that are ecologically similar in regards to temperature, rainfall, and the species that live there are called **biomes**. Specific biomes include:

Marine - covers 75% of the earth. This biome is organized by the depth of the water. The intertidal zone is from the tide line to the edge of the water. The littoral zone is from the water's edge to the open sea. It includes coral reef habitats and is the most densely populated area of the marine biome. The open-sea zone is divided into the epipelagic zone and the pelagic zone. The epipelagic zone receives more sunlight and has a larger number of species. The ocean floor is called the benthic zone and is populated with bottom feeders.

Tropical Rain Forest - temperature is constant (25 degrees C) and rainfall exceeds 200 cm. per year. Located around the area of the equator, the rain forest has abundant, diverse species of plants and animals.

Savanna - temperatures range from 0-25 degrees C depending on the location. Rainfall is from 90 to 150 cm per year. Plants include shrubs and grasses. The savanna is a transitional biome between the rain forest and the desert.

Desert - temperatures range from 10-38 degrees C. Rainfall is under 25 cm per year. Plant species include xerophytes and succulents. Lizards, snakes, and small mammals are common animals.

Temperate Deciduous Forest - temperature ranges from -24 to 38 degrees C. Rainfall is between 65 to 150 cm per year. Deciduous trees are common, as well as deer, bear, and squirrels.

Taiga - temperatures range from -24 to 22 degrees C. Rainfall is between 35 to 40 cm per year. Taiga is located very north and very south of the equator, getting close to the poles. Plant life includes conifers and plants that can withstand harsh winters. Animals include weasels, mink, and moose.

Tundra - temperatures range from -28 to 15 degrees C. Rainfall is limited, ranging from 10 to 15 cm per year. The tundra is located even further north and south than the taiga. Common plants include lichens and mosses. Animals include polar bears and musk ox.

Polar or Permafrost - temperature ranges from -40 to 0 degrees C. It rarely gets above freezing. Rainfall is below 10 cm per year. Most water is bound up as ice. Life is limited.

Succession - Succession is an orderly process of replacing a community that has been damaged or beginning one where no life previously existed. Primary succession occurs after a community has been totally wiped out by a natural disaster or where life never existed before, as in a flooded area. Secondary succession takes place in communities that were once flourishing but were disturbed by some source, either man or nature, but were not totally stripped. A climax community is a community that is established and flourishing.

HUMAN HEALTH

Structure and function of organs and systems of the human body.

Skeletal System - The skeletal system functions provides support. Vertebrates have an endoskeleton, with muscles attached to bones. Skeletal proportions are controlled by area to volume relationships. Body size and shape are limited due to the forces of gravity. Surface area is increased to improve efficiency in all organ systems.

The **axial skeleton** consists of the bones of the skull and vertebrae. The **appendicular skeleton** consists of the bones of the legs, arms, tail, and shoulder girdle. Bone is a connective tissue. Parts of the bone include compact bone, which gives strength; spongy bone, which contains red marrow to make blood cells; yellow marrow in the center of long bones, which stores fat cells; and the periosteum, which is the protective covering on the outside of the bone.

A **joint** is defined as a place where two bones meet. Joints enable movement. **Ligaments** attach bone to bone. **Tendons** attach bones to muscles.

Muscular System - Functions in movement. There are three types of muscle tissue. Skeletal muscle is voluntary. These muscles are attached to bones. Smooth muscle is involuntary. It is found in organs and enables functions such as digestion and respiration. Cardiac muscle is a specialized type of smooth muscle and is found in the heart. Muscles can only contract; therefore they work in antagonistic pairs to allow back and forward movement. Muscle fibers are made of groups of myofibrils themselves made of groups of sarcomeres. Actin and myosin are proteins which make up the sarcomere.

Physiology of muscle contraction - A nerve impulse strikes a muscle fiber. This causes calcium ions to flood the sarcomere. Calcium ions allow ATP to expend energy. The myosin fibers creep along the actin, causing the muscle to contract. Once the nerve impulse has passed, calcium is pumped out, and the contraction ends.

Nervous System - The neuron is the basic unit of the nervous system. It consists of an axon, which carries impulses away from the cell body; the dendrite, which carries impulses toward the cell body; and the cell body, which contains the nucleus. Synapses are spaces between neurons. Chemicals called neurotransmitters are found close to the synapse. The myelin sheath, composed of Schwann cells, covers the neurons and provides insulation.

Physiology of the nerve impulse - Nerve action depends on depolarization and an imbalance of electrical charges across the neuron. A polarized nerve has a positive charge outside the neuron. A depolarized nerve has a negative charge outside the neuron. Neurotransmitters turn off the sodium pump, which results in depolarization of the membrane. This wave of depolarization (as it moves from neuron to neuron) carries an electrical impulse. This is actually a wave of opening and closing gates that allows for the flow of ions across the synapse. Nerves have an action potential. There is a threshold of the level of chemicals that must be met or exceeded in order for muscles to respond. This is called the "all or none" response.

The **reflex arc** is the simplest nerve response. The brain is bypassed. When a stimulus (like touching a hot stove) occurs, sensors in the hand send the message directly to the spinal cord. This stimulates motor neurons that contract the muscles to move the hand.

Voluntary nerve responses involve the brain. Receptor cells send the message to sensory neurons which lead to association neurons. The message is taken to the brain. Motor neurons are stimulated, and the message is transmitted to effector cells which cause the end effect.

Organization of the Nervous System - The somatic nervous system is controlled consciously. It consists of the central nervous system (brain and spinal cord) and the peripheral nervous system (nerves that extend from the spinal cord to the muscles). The autonomic nervous system is unconsciously controlled by the hypothalamus of the brain. Smooth muscles, the heart, and digestion are some processes controlled by the autonomic nervous system. The sympathetic nervous system works opposite of the parasympathetic nervous system. For example, if the sympathetic nervous system stimulates an action, the parasympathetic nervous system would end that action.

Neurotransmitters - these are chemicals released by exocytosis. Some neurotransmitters stimulate, while others inhibit, action.

Acetylcholine - the most common neurotransmitter; it controls muscle contraction and heartbeat. The enzyme acetylcholinesterase breaks it down to end the transmission.

PHYSICAL SCIENCE

Science may be defined as a body of knowledge that is systematically derived from study, observations, and experimentation. Its goal is to identify and establish principles and theories which may be applied to solve problems. Pseudoscience, on the other hand, is a belief that is not supported by such methods. There is no scientific methodology or application. Some of the more classic examples of pseudoscience include witchcraft, alien encounters, or any topics that are explained by hearsay.

Science uses the metric system because it is accepted worldwide and allows easier comparison among experiments done by scientists around the world. Learn the following basic units and prefixes:

> **meter** - measure of length
> **liter** - measure of volume
> **gram** - measure of mass

deca-(meter, liter, gram) = 10X the base unit	**deci** = 1/10 the base unit
hecto-(meter, liter, gram)= 100X the base unit	**centi** = 1/100 the base
kilo-(meter, liter, gram) = 1000X the base unit	**milli** = 1/1000 the base

CHEMISTRY

The **phase of matter** (solid, liquid, or gas) is identified by its shape and volume. A **solid** has a definite shape and volume. A **liquid** has a definite volume, but no shape. A **gas** has no shape or volume because it will spread out to occupy the entire space of whatever container it is in.

Energy is the ability to cause change in matter. Applying heat to a frozen liquid changes it from solid back to liquid. Continue heating it, and it will boil and give off steam, a gas.

Evaporation is the change in phase from liquid to gas. **Condensation** is the change in phase from gas to liquid.

An **atom** is a nucleus surrounded by a cloud with moving electrons.

The **nucleus** is the center of the atom. The positive particles inside the nucleus are called **protons.** The mass of a proton is about 2,000 times that of the mass of an electron. The number of protons in the nucleus of an atom is called the **atomic number**. All atoms of the same element have the same atomic number.

Neutrons are another type of particle in the nucleus. Neutrons and protons have about the same mass, but neutrons have no charge. Neutrons were discovered because scientists observed that not all atoms in neon gas have the same mass. They had identified isotopes. **Isotopes** of an element have the same number of protons in the nucleus, but have different masses. Neutrons explain the difference in mass. They have mass but no charge.

The mass of matter is measured against a standard mass such as the gram. Scientists measure the mass of an atom by comparing it to that of a standard atom. The result is relative mass. The **relative mass** of an atom is its mass expressed in terms of the mass of the standard atom. The isotope of the element carbon is the standard atom. It has six (6) neutrons and is called carbon-12. It is assigned a mass of 12 atomic mass units (amu). Therefore, the **atomic mass unit (amu)** is the standard unit for measuring the mass of an atom. It is equal to the mass of a carbon atom.

The **mass number** of an atom is the sum of its protons and neutrons. In any element, there is a mixture of isotopes, some having slightly more or slightly fewer protons and neutrons. The **atomic mass** of an element is an average of the mass numbers of its atoms.

Mass number =   # protons + # neutrons (p + n)
Atomic mass = average mass, usually not a whole number

Each atom has an equal number of electrons (negative) and protons (positive). Therefore, atoms are neutral. Electrons orbiting the nucleus occupy energy levels that are arranged in order and the electrons tend to occupy the lowest energy level available. A **stable electron arrangement** is an atom that has all of its electrons in the lowest possible energy levels.

Some basic chemical reactions:

There are four kinds of chemical reactions:

In a **composition reaction**, two or more substances combine to form a compound.

A + B → AB
i.e. silver and sulfur yield silver dioxide

In a **decomposition reaction**, a compound breaks down into two or more simpler substances.

AB → A + B
i.e. water breaks down into hydrogen and oxygen

In a **single replacement reaction**, a free element replaces an element that is part of a compound.

A + BX → AX + B
i.e. iron plus copper sulfate yields iron sulfate plus copper

In a **double replacement reaction**, parts of two compounds replace each other. In this case, the compounds seem to switch partners.

AX + BY → AY + BX
i.e. sodium chloride plus mercury nitrate yields sodium nitrate plus mercury chloride

PHYSICS

Work is done on an object when an applied force moves through a distance.

Power is the work done divided by the amount of time that it took to do it. (Power = Work / time)

Simple machines.

1. Inclined plane
2. Lever
3. Wheel and axle
4. Pulley

Sound waves

The **pitch** of a sound depends on the **frequency** that the ear receives. High-pitched sound waves have high frequencies. High notes are produced by an object that is vibrating at a greater number of times per second than one that produces a low note.

The **intensity** of a sound is the amount of energy that crosses a unit of area in a given unit of time. The loudness of the sound is subjective and depends upon the effect on the human ear. Two tones of the same intensity but different pitches may appear to have different loudness. The intensity level of sound is measured in decibels. Normal conversation is about 60 decibels. A power saw is about 110 decibels.

The **amplitude** of a sound wave determines its loudness. Loud sound waves have large amplitudes. The larger the sound wave, the more energy is needed to create the wave.

An oscilloscope is useful in studying waves because it gives a picture of the wave that shows the crest and trough of the wave. **Interference** is the interaction of two or more waves that meet. If the waves interfere constructively, the crest of each one meets the crests of the others. They combine into a crest with greater amplitude. As a result, you hear a louder sound. If the waves interfere destructively, then the crest of one meets the trough of another. They produce a wave with lower amplitude that produces a softer sound.

If you have two tuning forks that produce different pitches, then one will produce sounds of a slightly higher frequency. When you strike the two forks simultaneously, you may hear beats. **Beats** are a series of loud and soft sounds. This is because when the waves meet, the crests combine at some points and produce loud sounds. At other points, they nearly cancel each other out and produce soft sounds.

Light Waves

The electromagnetic spectrum is measured in frequency (f) in hertz and wavelength (λ) in meters. The frequency times the wavelength of every electromagnetic wave equals the speed of light (3.0×10^9 meters/second).

Roughly, the range of wavelengths of the electromagnetic spectrum is:

	f	λ
Radio waves	$10^{5} - 10^{-1}$ hertz	$10^{3} - 10^{9}$ meters
Microwaves	$10^{-1} - 10^{-3}$ hertz	$10^{9} - 10^{11}$ meters
Infrared radiation	$10^{-3} - 10^{-6}$ hertz	$10^{11.2} - 10^{14.3}$ meters
Visible light	$10^{-6.2} - 10^{-6.9}$ hertz	$10^{14.3} - 10^{15}$ meters
Ultraviolet radiation	$10^{-7} - 10^{-9}$ hertz	$10^{15} - 10^{17.2}$ meters
X-Rays	$10^{-9} - 10^{-11}$ hertz	$10^{17.2} - 10^{19}$ meters
Gamma Rays	$10^{-11} - 10^{-15}$ hertz	$10^{19} - 10^{23.25}$ meters

Radio waves are used for transmitting data. Common examples are television, cell phones, and wireless computer networks. Microwaves are used to heat food and deliver Wi-Fi service. Infrared waves are utilized in night-vision goggles. Visible light we are all familiar with because the human eye is most sensitive to this wavelength range. UV light causes sunburns and would be even more harmful if most of it were not captured in the Earth's ozone layer. X-rays aid us in the medical field, and gamma rays are most useful in the field of astronomy.

Electrostatics is the study of stationary electric charges. A plastic rod that is rubbed with fur or a glass rod that is rubbed with silk will become electrically charged and will attract small pieces of paper. The charge on the plastic rod rubbed with fur is negative, and the charge on glass rod rubbed with silk is positive.

Electrically charged objects share these characteristics:

1. Like charges repel one another.
2. Opposite charges attract each other.
3. Charge is conserved. A neutral object has no net change. If the plastic rod and fur are initially neutral, then, when the rod becomes charged by the fur, a negative charge is transferred from the fur to the rod. The net negative charge on the rod is equal to the net positive charge on the fur.

Materials through which electric charges can easily flow are called **conductors**. Metals which are good conductors include silicon and boron. On the other hand, an **insulator** is a material through which electric charges do not move easily, if at all. An example of an insulator would be non-metal elements of the periodic table. A simple device used to indicate the existence of a positive or negative charge is called an **electroscope**. An electroscope is made up of a conducting knob, and attached to it are very lightweight conducting leaves usually made of foil (gold or aluminum). When a charged object touches the knob, the leaves push away from each other because like charges repel. It is not possible to tell whether if the charge is positive or negative.

Charging by induction:

Touch the knob with a finger while a charged rod is nearby. The electrons will be repulsed and flow out of the electroscope through the hand. If the hand is removed while the charged rod remains close, the electroscope will retain the charge.

When an object is rubbed with a charged rod, the object will take on the same charge as the rod. However, charging by induction gives the object the opposite charge as that of the charged rod.

Grounding charge:

Charge can be removed from an object by connecting it to the earth through a conductor. The removal of static electricity by conduction is called **grounding**.

An **electric circuit** is a path along which electrons flow. A simple circuit can be created with a dry cell, wire, a bell, or a light bulb. When all are connected, the electrons flow from the negative terminal, through the wire to the device, and back to the positive terminal of the dry cell. If there are no breaks in the circuit, the device will work. The circuit is closed. Any break in the flow will create an open circuit and cause the device to shut off.

The device (bell, bulb) is an example of a **load**. A load is a device that uses energy. Suppose that you also add a buzzer so that the bell rings when you press the buzzer button. The buzzer is acting as a **switch**. A switch is a device that opens or closes a circuit. Pressing the buzzer makes the connection complete, and the bell rings. When the buzzer is not engaged, the circuit is open, and the bell is silent.

A **series circuit** is one where the electrons have only one path along which they can move. When one load in a series circuit goes out, the circuit is open. An example of this is a set of Christmas tree lights that is missing a bulb. None of the bulbs will work.

A **parallel circuit** is one where the electrons have more than one path to move along. If a load goes out in a parallel circuit, the other load will still work because the electrons can still find a way to continue moving along the path.

When an electron goes through a load, it does work and, therefore, loses some of its energy. The measure of how much energy is lost is called the **potential difference**. The potential difference between two points is the work needed to move a charge from one point to another.

Potential difference is measured in a unit called the volt. **Voltage** is potential difference. The higher the voltage, the more energy the electrons have. This energy is measured by a device called a voltmeter. To use a voltmeter, place it in a circuit parallel with the load you are measuring.

Current is the number of electrons per second that flow past a point in a circuit. Current is measured with a device called an ammeter. To use an ammeter, put it in series with the load you are measuring.

As electrons flow through a wire, they lose potential energy. Some is changed into heat energy because of resistance. **Resistance** is the ability of the material to oppose the flow of electrons through it. All substances have some resistance, even if they are good conductors, such as copper. This resistance is measured in units called **ohms**. A thin wire will have more resistance than a thick one because it will have less room for electrons to travel. In a thicker wire, there will be more possible paths for the electrons to flow through. Resistance also depends upon the length of the wire. The longer the wire, the more resistance it will have.

Potential difference, resistance, and current form a relationship know as **Ohm's Law**. Current **(I)** is measured in amperes and is equal to potential difference **(V)** divided by resistance **(R)**.

$$I = V / R$$

If you have a wire with resistance of 5 ohms and a potential difference of 75 volts, then you can calculate the current by

I = 75 volts / 5 ohms
I = 15 amperes

A current of 10 or more amperes will cause a wire to get hot. 22 amperes is about the maximum for a house circuit. Anything above 25 amperes can start a fire.

Magnetism

Magnets have a north pole and a south pole. Like poles repel, and opposing poles attract. A **magnetic field** is the space around a magnet where its force will affect objects. The closer you are to a magnet, the stronger the force. As you move away, the force becomes weaker.

Some materials act as magnets, and some do not. This is because magnetism is a result of electrons in motion. The most important motion in this case is the spinning of the individual electrons. Electrons spin in pairs in opposite directions in most atoms. Each spinning electron has the magnetic field that it creates canceled out by the electron that is spinning in the opposite direction.

In an atom of iron, there are four unpaired electrons. The magnetic fields of these are not canceled out. Their fields add up to make a tiny magnet. There fields exert forces on each other setting up small areas in the iron called **magnetic domains** where atomic magnetic fields line up in the same direction.

You can make a magnet out of an iron nail by stroking the nail in the same direction repeatedly with a magnet. This causes poles in the atomic magnets in the nail to be attracted to the magnet. The tiny magnetic fields in the nail line up in the direction of the magnet. The magnet causes the domains pointing in its direction to grow in the nail. Eventually, one large domain results, and the nail becomes a magnet.

A bar magnet has a north pole and a south pole. If you break the magnet in half, each piece will have a north and south pole.
Earth has a magnetic field. In a compass, a tiny, lightweight magnet is suspended and will line its south pole up with the North Pole magnet of Earth.

A magnet can be made out of a coil of wire by connecting the ends of the coil to a battery. When the current goes through the wire, the wire acts in the same way that a magnet does, it is called an **electromagnet**. The poles of the electromagnet will depend upon which way the electric current runs. An electromagnet can be made more powerful in three ways:

1. Make more coils.
2. Put an iron core (nail) inside the coils.
3. Use more battery power.

EARTH SCIENCE

Astronomy

There are eight established planets in our solar system; Mercury, Venus, Earth, Mars, Jupiter, Saturn, Uranus, and Neptune. Pluto was an established planet in our solar system, but, since the summer of 2006, its status has been being reconsidered. The planets are divided into two groups based on distance from the sun. The inner planets include Mercury, Venus, Earth, and Mars. The outer planets include Jupiter, Saturn, Uranus, and Neptune.

Mercury -- the closest planet to the sun. Its surface has craters and rocks. The atmosphere is composed of hydrogen, helium, and sodium. Mercury was named after the Roman messenger god.

Venus -- has a slow rotation when compared to Earth. Venus and Uranus rotate in opposite directions from the other planets. This opposite rotation is called retrograde rotation. The surface of Venus is not visible due to the extensive cloud cover. The atmosphere is composed mostly of carbon dioxide. Sulfuric acid droplets in the dense cloud cover give Venus a yellow appearance. Venus has a greater greenhouse effect than observed on Earth. The dense clouds and carbon dioxide trap heat. Venus was named after the Roman goddess of love.

Earth -- considered a water planet (70% of its surface covered by water). Gravity holds the masses of water in place. The different temperatures observed on earth allow for the different states (solid, liquid, gas) of water to exist. The atmosphere is composed mainly of oxygen and nitrogen. Earth is the only planet that is known to support life.

Mars -- the surface of Mars contains numerous craters, active and extinct volcanoes, ridges, and valleys with extremely deep fractures. Iron oxide found in the dusty soil makes the surface seem rust colored and the skies seem pink in color. The atmosphere is composed of carbon dioxide, nitrogen, argon, oxygen, and water vapor. Mars has polar regions with ice caps composed of water. Mars has two satellites. Mars was named after the Roman war god.

Jupiter -- largest planet in the solar system. Jupiter has 16 moons. The atmosphere is composed of hydrogen, helium, methane, and ammonia. There are white-colored bands of clouds, indicating rising gas, and dark colored bands of clouds, indicating descending gases. The gas movement is caused by heat from the energy emitted by Jupiter's core. Jupiter has a Great Red Spot that is thought to be a hurricane type cloud. Jupiter has a strong magnetic field.

Saturn -- the second largest planet in the solar system. Saturn has rings of ice, rock, and dust particles circling it. Saturn's atmosphere is composed of hydrogen, helium, methane, and ammonia. Saturn has 20 plus satellites. Saturn was named after the Roman god of agriculture.

Uranus -- the second largest retrograde-revolution planet in the solar system. Uranus is a gaseous planet. It has 10 dark rings and 15 satellites. Its atmosphere is composed of hydrogen, helium, and methane. Uranus was named after the Greek god of the heavens.

Neptune -- another gaseous planet, with an atmosphere consisting of hydrogen, helium, and methane. Neptune has 3 rings and 2 satellites. Neptune was named after the Roman sea god because its atmosphere is the same color as the seas.

Pluto -- once considered the smallest planet in the solar system; its status as a planet is being reconsidered. Pluto's atmosphere probably contains methane, ammonia, and frozen water. Pluto has 1 satellite. Pluto revolves around the sun every 250 years. Pluto was named after the Roman god of the underworld.

Comets, asteroids, and meteors.
Astronomers believe that rocky fragments that never formed into a planet, **asteroids**, may be remnants from the birth of the solar system. They are found in the region between Mars and Jupiter.

Comets are masses of frozen gases, cosmic dust, and small rocky particles. Astronomers think that most comets originate in a dense comet cloud beyond Pluto. Comets consist of a nucleus, a coma, and a tail. A comet's tail always points away from the sun. The most famous comet, **Halley's Comet,** is named after the person who first discovered it in 240 B.C. It returns to the skies near Earth every 75 to 76 years.

Meteoroids are composed of particles of rock and metal of various sizes. When a meteoroid travels through the earth's atmosphere, friction causes its surface to heat up, and it begins to burn. A burning meteoroid falling through the earth's atmosphere is called a **meteor** (also known as a "shooting star").

Meteorites are meteors that strike the earth's surface. A physical example of a meteorite's impact on Earth's surface can be seen in Arizona. The Barringer Crater is a huge meteor crater. There are many other meteor craters throughout the world.

Geology - defines basic three layers of crust, mantle, and core, Types of rocks igneous, sedimentary, and metamorphic,

Types of rocks:

Three major types of rocks are - sedimentary, metamorphic, and igneous.

When fluid sediments are transformed into solid sedimentary rocks, the process is known as **lithification**. One very common process affecting sediments is compaction, in which the weights of overlying materials compress and compact the deeper sediments. The compaction process leads to cementation. **Cementation** is when sediments are converted to sedimentary rock.

Igneous rocks can be classified according to their texture, their composition, and the way they formed.

Molten rock is called magma. When molten rock pours out onto the surface of Earth, it is called lava.

As magma cools, the elements and compounds begin to form crystals. The slower the magma cools, the larger the crystals grow. Rocks with large crystals are said to have a coarse-grained texture. Granite is an example of a coarse grained rock. Rocks that cool rapidly before any crystals can form have a glassy texture, such as obsidian, also commonly known as volcanic glass.

Metamorphic rocks are formed by high temperatures and great pressures. The process by which the rocks undergo these changes is called metamorphism. The outcome of metamorphic changes include deformation by extreme heat and pressure, compaction, destruction of the original characteristics of the parent rock, bending and folding while in a plastic stage, and the emergence of completely new and different minerals due to chemical reactions with heated water and dissolved minerals.

Metamorphic rocks are classified into two groups, **foliated** (leaf like) rocks and **unfoliated** rocks. Foliated rocks consist of compressed, parallel bands of minerals which give the rocks a striped appearance. Examples of such rocks include slate, schist, and gneiss. Unfoliated rocks are not banded, and examples of such include quartzite, marble, and anthracite rocks.

Minerals are natural, non-living solids with a definite chemical composition and a crystalline structure. **Ores** are minerals or rock deposits that can be mined for a profit. **Rocks** are earthen materials made of one or more minerals. A **Rock Facies** is a rock group that differs from comparable rocks (as in composition, age, or fossil content).

Meteorology - weather, layers of the atmosphere, water 70% of earth surface. cloud types.

El Niño refers to a sequence of changes in the ocean and atmospheric circulation across the Pacific Ocean. The water around the equator is unusually hot every two-to-seven years. Trade winds normally blow east to west across the equatorial latitudes, piling warm water into the western Pacific. A huge mass of heavy thunderstorms usually forms in the area and produces vast currents of rising air that displace heat toward a magnetic pole. This helps create the strong, mid-latitude jet streams. The world's climate patterns are disrupted by this change in location of thunderstorm activity.

Relative humidity is the actual amount of water vapor in a certain volume of air compared to the maximum amount of water vapor this air could hold at a given temperature.

Types of storms

A **thunderstorm** is a brief, local storm produced by the rapid upward movement of warm, moist air within a cumulo-nimbus cloud. Thunderstorms always produce lightning and thunder and are accompanied by strong wind gusts and heavy rain or hail.

A severe storm with swirling winds that may reach speeds of hundreds of km per hour is called a **tornado**. Such a storm is also referred to as a "twister". The sky is covered by large cumulo-nimbus clouds and violent thunderstorms; a funnel-shaped swirling cloud may extend downward from a cumulo-nimbus cloud and reach the ground. Tornadoes are storms that leave a narrow path of destruction on the ground.

A swirling, funnel-shaped cloud that extends downward and touches a body of water is called a **waterspout.**

Hurricanes are storms that develop when warm, moist air carried by trade winds rotates around a low-pressure "eye". A large, rotating, low-pressure system accompanied by heavy precipitation and strong winds is called a tropical cyclone (better known as a hurricane). In the Pacific region, a hurricane is called a typhoon.

Storms that occur only in the winter are known as blizzards or ice storms. A **blizzard** is a storm with strong winds, blowing snow, and frigid temperatures. An **ice storm** consists of falling rain that freezes when it strikes the ground, covering everything with a layer of ice.

Air masses moving toward or away from Earth's surface are called air currents. Air moving parallel to Earth's surface is called **wind**. Weather conditions are generated by winds and air currents carrying large amounts of heat and moisture from one part of the atmosphere to another. Wind speeds are measured by instruments called anemometers.

The wind belts in each hemisphere consist of convection cells that encircle Earth like belts. There are three major wind belts on Earth: (1) Trade Winds (2) Prevailing Westerlies, and (3) Polar Easterlies. Wind-belt formation depends on the differences in air pressures that develop in the Doldrums, the Horse Latitudes, and the Polar Regions. The Doldrums surround the equator. Within this belt, heated air usually rises straight up into Earth's atmosphere. The Horse Latitudes are regions of high barometric pressure with calm and light winds, and the Polar Regions contain cold dense air that sinks to Earth's surface.

Winds caused by local temperature changes include sea breezes and land breezes.

Sea breezes are caused by the unequal heating of the land and an adjacent, large body of water. Land heats up faster than water. The movement of cool ocean air toward the land is called a sea breeze. Sea breezes usually begin blowing about mid-morning and cease about sunset.

A breeze that blows from the land to the ocean or a large lake is called a **land breeze.**

Monsoons are huge wind systems that cover large geographic areas and that reverse direction seasonally. The monsoons of India and Asia are examples of these seasonal winds. They alternate wet and dry seasons. As denser, cooler air over the ocean moves inland, a steady seasonal wind called a summer or wet monsoon is produced.

Cloud types

Cirrus clouds - White and feathery; high in the sky.

Cumulus – thick, white, fluffy.

Stratus – layers of clouds cover most of the sky.

Nimbus – heavy, dark clouds that represent thunderstorm clouds.

Variation on the clouds mentioned above.

Cumulo-nimbus

Strato-nimbus

The air temperature at which water vapor begins to condense is called the **dew point.**

Oceanography

Seventy percent of the earth's surface is covered with saltwater and is termed the hydrosphere. The mass of this saltwater is about 1.4×10^{24} grams. The ocean waters continuously circulate among different parts of the hydrosphere. There are seven major oceans: the North Atlantic Ocean, South Atlantic Ocean, North Pacific Ocean, South Pacific Ocean, Indian Ocean, Arctic Ocean, and the Antarctic Ocean.

Pure water is a combination of the elements hydrogen and oxygen. These two elements make up about 96.5% of ocean water. The remaining portion is made up of dissolved solids. The concentration of these dissolved solids determines the water's salinity.

Salinity is the number of grams of these dissolved salts in 1,000 grams of sea water. The average salinity of ocean water is about 3.5%. In other words, one kilogram of sea water contains about 35 grams of salt. Sodium Chloride or salt (NaCl) is the most abundant of the dissolved salts. The dissolved salts also include smaller quantities of magnesium chloride, magnesium and calcium sulfates, and traces of several other salt elements. Salinity varies throughout the world's oceans; the total salinity of the oceans varies from place to place and also varies with depth. Salinity is low near river mouths, where the ocean mixes with fresh water,; and salinity is high in areas of high evaporation rates.

COMPETENCY 5.0   **UNDERSTAND THE HISTORICAL DEVELOPMENT AND CULTURAL CONTEXTS OF MATHEMATICS, SCIENCE, AND TECHNOLOGY; THE RELATIONSHIPS AND COMMON THEMES THAT CONNECT MATHEMATICS, SCIENCE, AND TECHNOLOGY; AND THE IMPACT OF MATHEMATICS, SCIENCE, AND TECHNOLOGY ON HUMAN SOCIETIES**

The combination of science, mathematics, and technology comprises scientific endeavor and makes science useful. It is impossible to study science on its own without the support of other disciplines like mathematics, technology, geology, and physics.

Science is tentative. By definition, it is searching for information by making educated guesses. It must be replicable. Another scientist must be able to achieve the same results under the same conditions at a later time. The term empirical means that it must be assessed through tests and observations. Science changes over time. Science is limited by the available technology. An example of this would be the relationship of the discovery of the cell and the invention of the microscope. As our technology improves, more hypotheses will become theories and, possibly, laws. Science is also limited by the data that is able to be collected. Data may be interpreted differently on different occasions. Science's limitations result in explanations changing as new technologies emerge. New technologies gather previously unavailable data and enable us to build upon current theories with new information.

Ancient history followed the **Geocentric Theory**, which was displaced by the **Heliocentric Theory** developed by Copernicus, Ptolemy, and Kepler. Newton's laws of motion were based on mass, force, and acceleration; and state that the force of gravity between any two objects in the universe depends upon their mass and distance. These laws are still widely used today. In the 20th century, Albert Einstein was the most outstanding scientist because of his work on relativity, which led to his theory that 'E=mc squared.' Early in the 20th century, Alfred Wegener proposed his theory of continental drift, stating that continents moved away from the super continent, Pangaea. This theory was accepted in the 1960s when more evidence was collected. John Dalton and Lavosier made significant contributions in the field of atoms and matter. The Curies and Ernest Rutherford contributed greatly to the studies of radioactivity and of the splitting of atom, which have lot of practical applications. Charles Darwin proposed his theory of evolution, and Gregor Mendel's experiments on peas helped us to understand heredity. The most significant improvement was the industrial revolution in Britain, in which science was applied practically to increase productivity. However, it also introduced a number of social problems, like child labor.

The nature of science mainly consists of three important things:

1. The scientific world view

This includes some very important assumptions, for instance, it is possible to understand this highly organized world and its complexities with the help of technology. Scientific ideas are subject to change. After repeated experiments, a theory is established, but this theory could be changed in the future. Only laws that occur naturally do not change. Scientific knowledge may not be discarded, but is modified – e.g., Albert Einstein didn't discard the Newtonian principles, but modified them in his theory of relativity. Also, science can't answer all of our questions. We can't find answers to questions related to our beliefs, moral values, and our norms.

2. Scientific inquiry

Scientific inquiry starts with a simple question. This simple question leads to information gathering, an educated guess otherwise known as a hypothesis. To prove the hypothesis, an experiment has to be conducted, which yields data and leads to a conclusion. All experiments must be repeated at least twice to get reliable results. Thus, scientific inquiry leads to new knowledge or verifies established theories. Science requires empirical proof or evidence. Science is dependent on accuracy, not bias or prejudice. In science, there is no place for preconceived ideas or premeditated results. By using their senses and modern technology, scientists aim at getting reliable information. Science is a combination of logic and imagination. A scientist needs to think, to imagine, and to reason. Science explains, reasons, and predicts. These three are interwoven and are inseparable. While reasoning is absolutely important for science, there should be no bias or prejudice. Science is not authoritarian because it has been shown that scientific authority can be wrong. No one can determine or make decisions for others on any issue.

3. Scientific enterprise

Science is a complex activity involving various people and places. A scientist may work alone or in a laboratory, classroom, or, for that matter, anywhere. Mostly it is a group activity requiring cooperation, communication of results or findings, consultations, discussions, etc. Science demands a high degree of communication to the governments, funding authorities, and to the public.

Bias

Scientific research can be biased in the choice of what data to consider, in the reporting or recording of the data, and/or in how the data are interpreted. Scientists may be influenced by their nationality, sex, ethnic origin, age, or political convictions. For example, when studying a group of animals, male scientists may focus on the social behavior of the males and typical male characteristics.

Although bias related to the investigator, the sample, the method, or the instrument may not be completely avoidable in every case, it is important to know the possible sources of bias and how bias could affect the evidence. Moreover, scientists need to be attentive to possible bias in their own work and that of other scientists.

Objectivity may not always be attained. However, one precaution that may be taken to guard against undetected bias is to have many different investigators or groups of investigators working on a project. By different, it is meant that the groups are made up of various nationalities, ethnic origins, ages, and political convictions and composed of both males and females. It is also important to note one's aspirations and to make sure to be truthful to the data even when grants, promotions, and notoriety are at risk.

The importance of verifiable evidence and peer review in science

Science is a process of checks and balances. It is expected that scientific findings will be challenged and, in many cases, retested. Often, one experiment will be the beginning point for another. While bias does exist, the use of controlled experiments and an awareness on the part of the scientist can go far toward ensuring a sound experiment. Even if the science is well done, it may still be questioned. It is through this continual search that hypotheses are made into theories and sometimes become laws. It is also through this search that new information is discovered.

Common scientific concepts and themes that link and unify science fields

The following are the concepts and processes generally recognized as common to all scientific disciplines:

Systems, order, and organization
Evidence, models, and explanation
Constancy, change, and measurement
Evolution and equilibrium
Form and function

Because the natural world is so complex, the study of science involves the **organization** of items into smaller groups based on interaction or interdependence. These groups are called **systems**. Examples of organization are the periodic table of elements and the five-kingdom classification scheme for living organisms. Examples of systems are the solar system, cardiovascular system, Newton's laws of force and motion, and the laws of conservation.

Order refers to the behavior and measurability of organisms and events in nature. The arrangement of planets in the solar system and the life cycle of bacterial cells are examples of order.

Scientists use **evidence** and **models** to form **explanations** of natural events. Models are miniaturized representations of a larger event or system. Evidence is anything that furnishes proof.

Constancy and **change** describe the observable properties of natural organisms and events. Scientists use different systems of **measurement** to observe change and constancy. For examples, the freezing and melting points of given substances and the speed of sound are constant under constant conditions. Growth, decay, and erosion are all examples of natural change.

Evolution is the process of change over a long period of time. While biological evolution is the most common example, one can also classify technological advancement, changes in the universe, and changes in the environment as evolution.

Equilibrium is the state of balance between opposing forces of change. Homeostasis and ecological balance are examples of equilibrium.

Form and **function** are properties of organisms and systems that are closely related. The function of an object usually dictates its form, and the form of an object usually facilitates its function. For example, the form of the heart (e.g. muscle, valves) allows it to perform its function of circulating blood through the body.

Systems

Groups of related organs are organ systems. Organ systems consist of organs working together to perform a common function. The commonly recognized organ systems of animals include the reproductive system, nervous system, circulatory system, respiratory system, lymphatic system (immune system), endocrine system, urinary system, muscular system, digestive system, integumentary system, and skeletal system. In addition, organ systems are interconnected, and a single system rarely works alone to complete a task.

One obvious example of the interconnectedness of organ systems is the relationship between the circulatory and respiratory systems. As blood circulates through the organs of the circulatory systems, it is re-oxygenated in the lungs of the respiratory system. Another example is the influence of the endocrine system on other organ systems. Hormones released by the endocrine system greatly influence processes of many organ systems, including the nervous and reproductive systems.

In addition, bodily response to infection is a coordinated effort of the lymphatic (immune system) and circulatory systems. The lymphatic system produces specialized immune cells, filters out disease-causing organisms, and removes fluid waste from in and around tissue. The lymphatic system utilizes capillary structures of the circulatory system and interacts with blood cells in a coordinated response to infection.

The pituitary gland and hypothalamus respond to varying levels of hormones by increasing or decreasing production and secretion of glandular products. High levels of a hormone cause down-regulation of the production and secretion pathways, while low levels of a hormone cause up-regulation of the production and secretion pathways.

"Fight or flight" refers to the human body's response to stress or danger. Briefly, as a response to an environmental stressor, the hypothalamus releases a hormone that acts on the pituitary gland, triggering the release of another hormone, adrenocorticotropin (ACTH), into the bloodstream. ACTH then signals the adrenal glands to release the hormones cortisol, epinephrine, and norepinephrine. These three hormones act to ready the body to respond to a threat by increasing blood pressure and heart rate, speeding reaction time, diverting blood to the muscles, and releasing glucose for use by the muscles and brain. The stress-response hormones also inhibit growth, development, and other non-essential functions. Cortisol completes the fight-or-flight feedback loop by acting on the hypothalamus to stop hormonal production after the threat has passed.

Finally, the muscular and skeletal systems are closely related. Skeletal muscles attach to the bones of the skeleton and drive movement of the body.

Scientific Models

The model is a basic element of the scientific method. Many things in science are studied with models. A model is any simplification or substitute for what we are actually studying, attempting to understand, or making predictions about. A model is a substitute, but it is similar to what it represents. We encounter models at every step of our daily living. The Periodic Table of the elements is a model chemists use for predicting the properties of the elements. Physicists use Newton's laws to predict how objects will interact, such as planets and spaceships. In geology, the continental drift model predicts the past positions of continents. Samples, ideas, and methods are all examples of models. At every step of scientific study, models are extensively used. The primary activity of the hundreds of thousands of US scientists is to produce new models, resulting in tens of thousands of scientific papers published per year.

Types of models:

* **Scale models**: some models are basically downsized or enlarged copies of their target systems, like the models of protein and DNA.

* **Idealized models**: An idealization is a deliberate simplification of something complicated with the objective of making it easier to understand. Some examples are frictionless planes, point masses, isolated systems, etc.

* **Analogical models**: standard examples of analogical models are the billiard model of a gas, the computer model of the mind, or the liquid-drop model of the nucleus.

*** Phenomenological models**: These are usually defined as models that are independent of theories.

*** Data models**: Corrected, rectified, regimented, and, in many instances, idealized versions of the data that we gained from immediate observation (raw data).

*** Theory models**: Any structure is a model if it represents an idea (theory). An example of this is a flow chart, which summarizes a set of ideas.

Uses of models:

1. Models are crucial for understanding the structure and function of processes in science.
2. Models help us to visualize the organs/systems they represent, just like putting a face to a person.
3. Models are very useful to predict and foresee future events, like hurricanes.

Limitations:

1. Though models are every useful to us, they can never replace the real things.
2. Models are not exactly like the real items that they represent.
3. Caution must be exercised before presenting the models to the class because they may not be accurate.
4. It is the responsibility of educators to analyze models critically for proportion, content value, and other important data.
5. One must be careful about the representation style. This style differs from person to person.

Interrelationships among science and other disciplines

Math, science, and technology have common themes in how they are applied and understood. All three use models, diagrams, and graphs to simplify a concept for analysis and interpretation. Patterns observed in these systems lead to predictions based on these observations. Another common theme among these three systems is equilibrium. **Equilibrium** is a state in which forces are balanced, resulting in stability. Static equilibrium is stability due to a lack of changes, and dynamic equilibrium is stability due to a balance between opposite forces.

The fundamental relationship between the natural and social sciences is the use of the scientific method and the rigorous standards of proof that both disciplines require. This emphasis on organization and evidence separates the sciences from the arts and humanities. Natural science, particularly biology, is closely related to social science, the study of human behavior. Biological and environmental factors often dictate human behavior, and accurate assessment of behavior requires a sound understanding of biological factors.

Concepts and methods common to science and technology

Biological science is closely connected to technology and the other sciences and greatly impacts society and everyday life. Scientific discoveries often lead to technological advances; conversely, technology is often necessary for scientific investigation, and advances in technology often expand the reach of scientific discoveries. In addition, biology and the other scientific disciplines share several unifying concepts and processes that help unify the study of science. Finally, because biology is the science of living systems, biology directly impacts society and everyday life.

Science and technology, while distinct concepts, are closely related. Science attempts to investigate and explain the natural world, while technology attempts to solve human adaptation problems. Technology often results from the application of scientific discoveries, and advances in technology can increase the impact of scientific discoveries. For example, Watson and Crick used science to discover the structure of DNA, and their discovery led to many biotechnological advances in the manipulation of DNA. These technological advances greatly influenced the medical and pharmaceutical fields. The success of Watson and Crick's experiments, however, was dependent on the technology available. Without the necessary technology, the experiments would have failed.

The combination of biology and technology has improved the human standard of living in many ways. However, the negative impact of increasing human life expectancy, resulting overpopulation of the environment, is problematic. In addition, advances in biotechnology (e.g. genetic engineering, cloning) introduce ethical dilemmas that society must consider. Biologists use a variety of tools and technologies to perform tests, collect and display data, and analyze relationships. Examples of commonly used tools include computer-linked probes, spreadsheets, and graphing calculators.

Biologists use computer-linked probes to measure various environmental factors, including temperature, dissolved oxygen, pH, ionic concentration, and pressure. The advantage of computer-linked probes, as compared to more traditional observational tools, is that the probes automatically gather data and present them in an accessible format. This property of computer-linked probes eliminates the need for constant human observation and manipulation.

Biologists use spreadsheets to organize, analyze, and display data. For example, conservation ecologists use spreadsheets to model population growth and development, apply sampling techniques, and create statistical distributions to analyze relationships. Spreadsheet use simplifies data collection and manipulation and allows for the presentation of data in a logical and understandable format.

Graphing calculators are another technology with many applications in biology. For example, biologists use algebraic functions to analyze growth, development, and other natural processes. Graphing calculators can manipulate algebraic data and create graphs for analysis and observation. In addition, biologists use the matrix function of graphing calculators to model problems in genetics. The use of graphing calculators simplifies the creation of graphical displays, including histograms, scatter plots, and line graphs. Biologists can also transfer data and displays to computers for further analysis. Finally, biologists connect computer-linked probes, used to collect data, to graphing calculators to ease the collection, transmission, and analysis of data.

Key events in the history of science, and the science contributions of people from a variety of social and ethnic backgrounds

The history of biology follows man's understanding of the living world from the earliest recorded history to modern times. Though the concept of biology as a field of science arose only in the 19th century, its origins could be traced back to the ancient Greeks (Galen and Aristotle).

During the Renaissance and Age of Discovery, renewed interest in the rapidly increasing number of known organisms generated considerable interest in biology.

Andreas Vesalius (1514-1564) was a Belgian anatomist and physician whose dissections of the human body and resulting descriptions of it helped to correct misconceptions of the day. The books Vesalius wrote on anatomy were the most accurate and comprehensive anatomical texts of time.

Anton van Leeuwenhoek is known as the father of microscopy. In the 1650s, Leeuwenhoek began making tiny lenses that gave magnifications up to 300x. He was the first to see and describe bacteria, yeast plants, and the microscopic life found in water. Over the years, light microscopes have advanced to produce greater clarity and magnification. The scanning electron microscope (SEM) was developed in the 1950s. Instead of light, a beam of electrons passes through the specimen. Scanning electron microscopes have a resolution about one thousand times greater than light microscopes. The disadvantage of the SEM is that the chemical and physical methods used to prepare the sample result in the death of the specimen.

Carl Von Linnaeus (1707-1778), a Swedish botanist, physician, and zoologist, is well known for his contributions in ecology and taxonomy. Linnaeus is famous for his binomial system of nomenclature in which each living organism has two names, genus and species. He is considered the father of modern ecology and taxonomy.

In the late 1800s, Pasteur discovered the role of microorganisms in the cause of disease, pasteurization, and the rabies vaccine. Koch took his observations one step further by postulating that specific diseases were caused by specific pathogens. **Koch's postulates** are still used as guidelines in the field of microbiology. They state that the same pathogen must be found in every diseased person, the pathogen must be isolated and grown in culture, the disease must be induced in experimental animals from the culture, and the same pathogen must be isolated from the experimental animal.

In the 18th century, many fields of science, like botany, zoology and geology, began to evolve as scientific disciplines in the modern sense.

In the 20th century, the rediscovery of Mendel's work led to the rapid development of genetics by Thomas Hunt Morgan and his students.

DNA structure was another key event in biological study. In the 1950s, James Watson and Francis Crick discovered the structure of a DNA molecule, the double helix. This structure made it possible to explain DNA's ability to replicate and control the synthesis of proteins.

Following the cracking of the genetic code, biology has largely split between organismal biology-consisting of ecology, ethology, systematics, paleontology, evolutionary biology, developmental biology, and other disciplines that deal with whole organisms or group of organisms; and the disciplines related to molecular biology, which include cell biology, biophysics, biochemistry, neuroscience, and immunology.

The use of animals in biological research has expedited many scientific discoveries. Animal research has allowed scientists to learn more animal biological systems, including the circulatory and reproductive systems. One significant use of animals is for the testing of drugs, vaccines, and other products (such as perfumes and shampoos) before use or consumption by humans. There are significant pros and cons of animal research. The debate about the ethical treatment of animals has been ongoing since the introduction of animals to research. Many people believe the use of animals in research is cruel and unnecessary. Animal use is federally and locally regulated. The purpose of the Institutional Animal Care and Use Committee (IACUC) is to oversee and evaluate all aspects of an institution's animal care and use program.

The influence of social and cultural factors on science and technology

Curiosity is the heart of science. Maybe this is why so many diverse people are drawn to it. In the area of zoology one of the most recognized scientists is Jane Goodall. Miss Goodall is known for her research with chimpanzees in Africa. Jane has spent many years abroad conducting long-term studies of chimp interactions and returns from Africa to lecture and provide information about Africa, the chimpanzees, and her institute located in Tanzania.

In the area of chemistry, we recognize Dorothy Crowfoot Hodgkin. She studied at Oxford and won the Nobel Prize of Chemistry in 1964 for identifying the shape of vitamin B 12.

Have you ever heard of Florence Nightingale? She was a true person living in the 1800's, and she shaped the nursing profession. Florence was born into wealth and shocked her family by choosing to study health reforms for the poor in lieu of attending the expected social events. Florence studied nursing in Paris and became involved in the Crimean war. The British lacked supplies, and the secretary of war asked for Florence's assistance. She earned her nickname walking the floors at night checking on patients and writing letters to British officials demanding supplies.

In 1903 the Nobel Prize in Physics was jointly awarded to three individuals: Marie Curie, Pierre Curie, and Becquerel. Marie was the first woman ever to receive this prestigious award. In addition, she received the Nobel Prize in chemistry in 1911, making her the only person to receive two Nobel awards in science. Ironically, her cause of death, in 1934, was overexposure to radioactivity, the area of research for which she was so respected.

Neil Armstrong is an American icon. He will always be symbolically linked to our aeronautics' program. This astronaut and naval aviator is known for being the first human to set foot on the Moon.

Sir Alexander Fleming was a pharmacologist from Scotland who isolated the antibiotic penicillin from a fungus in 1928. Flemming also noted that bacteria developed resistance whenever too little penicillin was used or when it was used for too short a period, a key problem we still face today.

It is important to realize that many of the most complex scientific questions have been answered in a collaborative form. The human genome project is a great example of research conducted and shared by multiple countries world wide.

It is also interesting to note that, because of differing cultural beliefs, some cultures may allow areas of research that other cultures may be unlikely to examine.

Society and culture are very closely related. They are, in fact, closely intertwined. Together, they have influenced every aspect of the human life. Science and technology are no exception to this.

Let us examine **the influence of social and cultural factors on science** first, and then we will see their effect on technology.

The influence of social and cultural factors on science is profound. In a way, we can say that society has changed the face of science by absorbing scientific innovations. Science has always been a big part of society. The difference is that, in ancient societies, people did not realize that it was science, but took it as a part of their lives. In the modern society, everything has a label and a name, so people are aware of science and other disciplines.

Societies have had trouble accepting science, especially where the science exposed some cultural aspects as myths. There was a big dilemma concerning whether or not to accept the proven facts provided by scientific investigations or to cling to cultural norms. This went on for centuries. It took a long time for societies to accept scientific facts and to leave some of the cultural practices behind or to modify them. At the same time, we must give full credit to cultural practices which have some scientific basis, but are sometimes connected to religion and taken more seriously by believers than by the population at large. We can conclude that there are two factors - one is cultural practices by societies which are scientifically based, and the second one is cultural practices which have no scientific foundation (myths and superstitions). A society's progress depends on distinguishing between these two. Some indigenous societies suffered when they were not quick to adjust since their cultures were very ancient and the people found it difficult to accept new challenges and to adapt to changes. At the same time, ancient cultures like the Chinese, Egyptian, Greek, Asian, and Indian had well developed science that was recorded in their ancient writings.

Let's take a look at **the effect of society and culture on technology.** If we compare science to a volcano, technology is like lava spewing out of the volcano. This was the scenario in the last few centuries in terms of rapid strides in the development of technology. Technology greatly influenced society and culture, and, at the same time, science and culture exercised their influence on technology. It is like a two-way street.

It became extremely difficult for some societies to come to terms with technological advances. Even today, some cultures are not using modern technology, but, at the same time, they are using technology in principle - using simple machines for farming rather than using complex machines like tractors. Other cultures have so readily adapted to technology that lives are intertwined with it--intertwined so much that we are utilize the computer, television, microwave, dishwasher, washing machine, cell phone, etc. on a daily basis. It is surprising to realize that we began with no technology and now are enslaved to it. Cultures that are not in tune with modern technology are falling behind. It is often argued that to live without technology yields peace of mind, serenity, and happiness; but the downside is that valuable opportunities in this age of communication are thus lost.

Positive contributions of technology are that it revolutionized education, medicine, communication, travel, etc. The world has seemed to shrink in that we don't seem as far apart and we have means to stay connected. As a result of this technology, man is exploring space, which used to be elusive and as distant as the planets themselves.

When we take a critical look at these facts, we have to commend societies for trying to keep their own cultures, as culture is a very important aspect of humanity. We also need to appreciate cultures that accepted or incorporated science and technology.

Differences between ethical and unethical uses of science

To understand scientific ethics, we need to have a clear understanding of ethics. Ethics is defined as a system of public, general rules for guiding human conduct (Gert, 1988). The rules are general because they are supposed to apply to all people at all times, and they are public because they are not secret codes or practices.

Philosophers have given a number of moral theories to justify moral rules, which range from utilitarianism (a theory of ethics that prescribes the quantitative maximization of good consequences for a population). It is a form of consequentialism. This theory was proposed by Mozi, a Chinese philosopher who lived during BC 471-381), Kantianism (a theory proposed by Immanuel Kant, a German philosopher who lived during 1724-1804, which ascribes intrinsic value to rational beings and is the philosophical foundation of contemporary human rights) to social contract theory (a view of the ancient Greeks which states that the person's moral and or political obligations are dependent upon a contract or agreement between them to form society).

The following are some of the guiding principles of scientific ethics:

1. Scientific Honesty: not to commit fraud or fabricate or misinterpret data for personal gain
2. Caution: to avoid errors and sloppiness in all scientific experimentation
3. Credit: give credit where credit is due and not to copy
4. Responsibility: only to report reliable information to the public and not to mislead in the name of science
5. Freedom: freedom to criticize old ideas, to question new research, and to conduct research.

Many more principles could be added to this list. Though these principles seem straightforward and clear, it is very difficult to put them into practice since they could be interpreted in more ways than one. Nevertheless, it is not an excuse for scientists to overlook these guiding principles of scientific ethics.

Scientists are expected to show good conduct in their scientific pursuits. Conduct here refers to all aspects of scientific activity, including experimentation, testing, education, data evaluation, data analysis, data storing, peer review, government funding, the staff, etc.

The common ethical code described above could be applied to many areas, including science. When the general code is applied to a particular area of human life, it then becomes an institutional code. Hence, scientific ethics is an institutional code of conduct that reflects the chief concerns and goals of science.

To discuss scientific ethics, we can look at natural phenomena like rain. Rain, in the normal sense, is extremely useful to us, and it is absolutely important that there is a water cycle. When rain gets polluted with acid, it becomes acid rain. Here lies the ethical issue of releasing all these pollutants into the atmosphere. Should the scientists communicate the whole truth about acid rain or withhold some information because it may alarm the public. There are many issues like this. Whatever may be the case; scientists are expected to be honest and forthright with the public.

The effects of scientific and technological developments on the environment, human biology, society, and culture

In the last century, the advances in the fields of science and technology were amazing and have changed the lives of human beings forever. Life styles were greatly affected, and the society experienced dramatic changes. People started to take science and technology very seriously. The advances in these two interrelated fields are no longer the domain of the few elite and sophisticated. The average person started to use the advances in the field of technology in their daily lives. Because of this, the societal structure is changing rapidly to the extent that even young children are using technology.

With any rapid change, there are always good and poor things associated with it. Caution and care are the two words we need to associate with these giant strides in technology. At the same time, we need high technology in our lives, and we can't afford not to make use of these developments and reap the benefits for the good of humanity.

Our environment, human biology, society at large, and our culture are being affected. Let us take each point and examine very carefully the effects of science and technology on the above.

1. Environment:

The environment is constantly and rapidly undergoing tremendous changes.

The positive effects include ability to predict hurricanes; measuring changes in radioactivity present in our environment; the remedial measures for that problem; predicting the levels of gases like carbon monoxide, carbon dioxide, and other harmful gases; various estimates like the green house effect, ozone layer, and UV radiation; to name a few. With the help of modern technology, it is possible to know their quantities and to monitor, plan, and implement measures to deal with them. Even with the most advanced technology available to us, it is impossible to go back to the clean, green earth, since man has made marks on it in a negative way. It is possible to a limited extent to alleviate the problem, but it is impossible to eradicate it.

The negative aspects of the effect of technology on our environment are numerous. The first and foremost is pollution of various kinds - water, air, noise etc. There are the greenhouse effect, the indiscriminate use of fertilizers, the spraying of pesticides, the use of various additives to our food, deforestation, unprecedented exploitation of non-renewable energy resources, to name a few. As we discussed earlier, it is not possible to solve these problems with money and human resources; but educating the society and making people aware of these negative aspects will go a long way. For example, as teachers, we need to educate students about using natural resources cautiously and trying to save those resources, and we also need to teach them that little steps in the right direction will go a long way (e.g., car pooling, not wasting paper, whenever possible, to walk). It is important to teach students to have trees if they have space or at least to have house plants because they improve the quality of air we breath.

2. Human biology:

The strides science and technology have made have lasting effects on human biology. A few examples are organ transplants, in-vitro fertilization, cloning, new drugs, new understanding of various diseases, cosmetic surgery, reconstructive surgery, use of computers in operations, lasers in medicine, forensic science, etc. These changes have made lasting difference to the humanity.

As always there are pros and cons to these changes.

The positive aspects are that people with organ transplants have renewed hope. Their life spans are increased, and their quality of life has improved with the use of technology such as pace makers. Couples who experienced infertility are having babies now. Corrective and cosmetic surgeries are giving new confidence to patients. Glasses to correct vision problems are being replaced slowly by laser surgery.

The negative aspects are paternity issues arising out of in-vitro fertilization, some medical blunders, the indiscriminate use of corrective and cosmetic surgery, older mothers, and young orphans, etc.

3. Society:

Society is not the same as it used to be even 25 years ago. The use of technology has changed our patterns of life style, our behavior, our ethical and moral thinking, and our economy and career opportunities.

The positive effects are the economy booming due to the high-tech industry, more career opportunities for people to select from among, raising of standard of living, prolonged life with quality, closeness even though we are separated by thousands of kilometers/miles, quicker and faster communication, etc. The computer has contributed a lot to these changes. Normal household chores are being done by machines, giving relief through a cost-effective and time-saving means for upkeep of kitchen and home.

The negative aspects are far reaching. The breakdown in family structure could be attributed partly to high tech. Family meals and family togetherness are being replaced by gadgets. Some would argue that, as a result of this, our young people are becoming insecure, indirectly affecting their problem-solving skills. Young people are becoming increasingly vulnerable due to internet programs, including chat rooms and online pornography. There must be stringent measures to protect our younger generation from internet predators. The effects of various high-tech gadgets, like the microwave, are not entirely positive.

Constant game playing utilizing new technology (Gameboy, Xbox) encourage a sedentary lifestyle and childhood obesity.

4. Culture:

This is a very sensitive, yet very important, issue. Those above listed factors are affecting the culture of people.

The positive aspects are that technology is uniting us to a certain extent (e.g., it is possible to communicate with a person of any culture even when we are not seeing them face to face). It makes business and personal communication much easier over long distances. Some people were not comfortable with communicating with other cultures, since they were used to closed societies, but e-mail has changed that. When we all use the same pieces of technology, we understand each other better, and a common ground is established. Internet can definitely boast of some successful marriages which are cross-cultural. Sharing opinions and information has been enhanced.

With modern technology, travel is changing the way we think and career opportunities. It is helping us to know other cultures, different ways of doing the same thing, and the positive values of other cultures.

The negative aspects include declining moral and ethical values as increased awareness is allowing for a new wave of thinking. Care must be exercised how much of our past culture we are willing to trade for the modern. Positive aspects of any culture must be guarded carefully and passed on to generations to come.

On the whole, we can safely conclude that science and technology are part of our lives, and we must always exercise caution and be careful when we are adapting to new ideas and new thinking. It is possible that awareness and incorporation of other cultural practices will make us a better nation, which our founding fathers envisioned and dreamed of.

The relationships between personal choices and health

While genetics plays an important role in health, human behaviors can greatly affect short- and long-term health both positively and negatively. Behaviors that negatively affect health include smoking, excessive alcohol consumption, substance abuse, and poor eating habits. Behaviors that positively affect health include good nutrition and regular exercise.

Smoking negatively affects health in many ways. First, smoking decreases lung capacity, causes persistent coughing, and limits the ability to engage in strenuous physical activity. In addition, the long-term affects are even more damaging. Long-term smoking can cause lung cancer, heart disease, and emphysema (a lung disease).

Alcohol is the most abused legal drug. Excessive alcohol consumption has both short- and long-term negative effects. Drunkenness can lead to reckless behavior and distorted judgment that can cause injury or death. In addition, extreme alcohol abuse can cause alcohol poisoning resulting in immediate death. Long-term alcohol abuse is also extremely hazardous. The potential effects of long-term alcohol abuse include liver cirrhosis, heart problems, high blood pressure, stomach ulcers, and cancer.

The abuse of illegal substances can also negatively affect health. Commonly abused drugs include cocaine, heroin, opiates, methamphetamines, and marijuana. Drug abuse can cause immediate death or injury and, if used for a long time, can cause many physical and psychological health problems.

A healthy diet and regular exercise are the cornerstones of a healthy lifestyle. A diet rich in whole grains, fruits, vegetables, polyunsaturated fats, and lean protein and low in saturated fat and sugar can positively affect overall health. Such diets can reduce cholesterol levels, lower blood pressure, and help manage body weight. Conversely, diets high in saturated fat and sugar can contribute to weight gain, heart disease, strokes, and cancer.

Finally, regular exercise has both short- and long-term health benefits. Exercise increases physical fitness and improves energy levels, overall body function, and mental well-being. Long-term, exercise helps protect against chronic diseases, maintains healthy bones and muscles, helps maintain a healthy body weight, and strengthens the body's immune system.

Evaluating various sources of scientific information

Because people often attempt to use scientific evidence in support of political or personal agendas, the ability to evaluate the credibility of scientific claims is a necessary skill in today's society. In evaluating scientific claims made in the media, public debates, and advertising, one should follow several guidelines.

First, scientific, peer-reviewed journals are the most accepted source for information on scientific experiments and studies. One should carefully scrutinize any claim that does not reference peer-reviewed literature.

Second, the media and those with an agenda to advance (advertisers and politicians) often overemphasize the certainty and importance of experimental results. One should question any scientific claim that sounds fantastic or overly certain.

Finally, knowledge of experimental design and of the scientific method is important in evaluating the credibility of studies. For example, one should look for the inclusion of control groups and the presence of data to support the given conclusions.

COMPETENCY 6.0   UNDERSTAND AND APPLY SKILLS, PRINCIPLES, AND PROCEDURES ASSOCIATED WITH INQUIRY AND PROBLEM SOLVING IN THE SCIENCES

Scientific investigation is a very important part of science. Scientific investigation consists of a number of steps designed to solve a problem. This is important because it helps in solving scientific problems and in gathering new information. Scientists start with a problem and solve it in an orderly fashion called the scientific method. This is made up of a series of steps, which, when applied properly, solve scientific problems. The key to the success of this method lies in minimizing human prejudice. As human beings, we tend to have bias. The steps consist of identifying the problem, gathering information, formulating a hypothesis, experimental design, interpreting data, and drawing conclusions.

The first step in a science investigation is identifying the problem. As we observe, we notice interesting things that arouse our curiosity. We ask ourselves the basic questions of enquiry – how, why, what, when, which and where. The two most important questions are how and why. We can classify observations into two types. The first is qualitative, which we describe in words. No mention of numbers or quantities is made – the water is very hot, the solution is sour. The second type is quantitative, where numbers and quantities are used. This more precise: mass = 125 kg., distance = 500 km.

The second step is gathering information. As much information as possible is collected from various sources like the internet, books, journals, knowledgeable people, and newspapers. This lays a solid foundation for formulating a hypothesis.

The third step is hypothesizing. This is making statement about the problem with the knowledge acquired using the two important words, 'if' and 'when'. The next step is designing an experiment. Before this is done, we need to identify the control, the constants, the independent variables and the dependent variable.

For beginners, the simplest investigation would be to manipulate only one variable at a time. In this way, the experiment doesn't get too complicated and is easier to handle. The control has to be identified, and then the variable which can effect the outcome of the results. For an experiment to be authentic and reliable, constants have to be identified and kept constant throughout the experiment. Finally, the dependent variable, which is dependent on the independent variable, has to be identified. The dependent variable is the factor that is being measured in an experiment – e.g. height of plant, number of leaves, etc. For an experiment to be valid and useful, it should be completed in an appropriate time frame. The results are noted carefully. At the end of the experiment, the data have to be analyzed and searched for patterns. Any science investigation has to be repeated at least twice to get reproducible results. After the analysis, conclusions must be drawn based on the data.

In order to draw conclusions, we need to study the data on hand. The data tell us whether or not the hypothesis is correct. If the hypothesis is not correct, another hypothesis has to be formulated, and a new experiment has to be done.

If the hypothesis is tested and the results are repeated in further experimentation, then a theory could be formulated. A theory is a hypothesis that is tested repeatedly by different scientists and has yielded the consistent results. A theory has more validity because it can be used to predict future events.

Scientific inquiries should end in formulating an explanation or model. Models can be physical, conceptual, and/or mathematical. Drawing conclusions generates significant discussion and arguments. There may be several possible explanations for any given sets of results: not all of them are reasonable. Carefully consideration of the data leads to a reasonable conclusion. The conclusion needs to be backed up by scientific criteria.

After the conclusion is drawn, the final step is communication. In this age, much emphasis is put on the method of communication. The conclusions must be communicated by clearly describing the information using accurate data, visual presentations like graphs (bar/line/pie), tables/charts, diagrams, artwork, and other appropriate media, like power point presentation. Modern technology should be used whenever possible. The method of communication must suit a given audience.

Written communication is as important as oral communication. This is essential for submitting research papers to scientific journals, newspapers, other magazines etc.

Characteristics and uses of various types of scientific investigations

Scientific investigations come in all sizes and forms. One can conduct a simple survey of a population by interviewing a small sample with the hope of gaining an understanding of the entire population. This method is often used by medical and pharmaceutical companies and may include a questionnaire that asks about health and lifestyle. Ecologists use field observations. Like the medical questionnaire, they incorporate small sample sizes to gain a better understanding of a larger group. For example, they may document one animal to determine its migratory patterns, or they may place cameras in one area to capture footage of a roaming animal or pack. Ecologists study an area and all of the organisms within it, but they often limit sampling size and use a representative of the population. Whenever possible, a scientist would prefer to conduct controlled experiments. This can happen most readily in a laboratory, and is nearly impossible to achieve in nature. In a controlled experiment, only one variable is manipulated at one time, and a control, or normal variable under normal conditions, is always present. This control group gives scientists something to compare the variable against. It tells them what would normally have happened under the experimental conditions had they not altered/introduced the variable.

An experiment is proposed and performed with the sole objective of testing a hypothesis. When evaluating an experiment, it is important to first look at the question it was supposed to answer. How logically did the experiment flow from there? How many variables existed (it is best to only test one variable at a time)? You discover a scientist conducting an experiment with the following characteristics. He has two rows each set up with four stations. The first row has a piece of tile as the base at each station. The second row has a piece of linoleum as the base at each station. The scientist has eight eggs and is prepared to drop one over each station. What is he testing? He is trying to answer whether or not the egg is more likely to break when dropped over one material as opposed to the other. His hypothesis might have been: The egg will be less likely to break when dropped on linoleum. This is a simple experiment. If the experiment was more complicated, or for example, conducted on a microscopic level, one might want to examine the appropriateness of the instruments utilized and their calibration.

Properly collecting data yields information that appropriately answers the original question. For example, one wouldn't try use a graduated cylinder to measure mass, nor would one use a ruler to measure a microscopic item. Utilizing appropriate measuring devices, using proper units, and careful mathematics will provide strong results. Carefully evaluating and analyzing the data creates a reasonable conclusion. The conclusion needs to be backed up by scientific criteria, then, finally, communicated to the audience.

The use of appropriate methods, tools, and technologies for gathering, recording, processing, analyzing, and evaluating data and for communicating the results of scientific investigations

The procedure used to obtain data is important to the outcome. Experiments consist of **controls** and **variables**. A control is the experiment run under normal conditions. The variable includes a factor that is changed. In biology, the variable may be light, temperature, pH, time, etc. The differences in tested variables may be used to make a prediction or to form a hypothesis. Only one variable should be tested at a time. One would not alter both the temperature and pH of the experimental subject.

An **independent variable** is one that is changed or manipulated by the researcher. This could be the amount of light given to a plant or the temperature at which bacteria is grown. The **dependent variable** is that which is influenced by the independent variable.

Measurements may be taken in different ways. There is an appropriate measuring device for each aspect of biology. A graduated cylinder is used to measure volume. A balance is used to measure mass. A microscope is used to view microscopic objects. A centrifuge is used to separate two or more parts in a liquid sample. The list goes on, but you get the point. For each variable, there is an appropriate way to measure it. The internet and teaching guides are virtually unlimited resources for laboratory ideas. You should be imparting to the students the importance of the method with which they conduct the study, the resource they use to do so, the concept of double checking their work, and the use of appropriate units.

Biologists use a variety of tools and technologies to perform tests, to collect and display data, and to analyze relationships. Examples of commonly used tools include computer-linked probes, spreadsheets, and graphing calculators.

Biologists use computer-linked probes to measure various environmental factors, including temperature, dissolved oxygen, pH, ionic concentration, and pressure. The advantage of computer-linked probes, as compared to more traditional observational tools, is that the probes automatically gather data and present it in an accessible format. This property of computer-linked probes eliminates the need for constant human observation and manipulation.

Biologists use spreadsheets to organize, analyze, and display data. For example, conservation ecologists use spreadsheets to model population growth and development, to apply sampling techniques, and to create statistical distributions in order to analyze relationships. Spreadsheet use simplifies data collection and manipulation and allows the presentation of data in a logical and understandable format.

Graphing calculators are another technology with many applications to biology. For example, biologists use algebraic functions to analyze growth, development, and other natural processes. Graphing calculators can manipulate algebraic data and create graphs for analysis and observation. In addition, biologists use the matrix function of graphing calculators to model problems in genetics. The use of graphing calculators simplifies the creation of graphical displays, including histograms, scatter plots, and line graphs. Biologists can also transfer data and displays to computers for further analysis. Finally, biologists connect computer-linked probes used to collect data to graphing calculators to ease the collection, transmission, and analysis of data.

Appropriate methods and criteria for organizing and displaying data

The type of graphic representation used to display observations depends on the data that is collected. **Line graphs** are used to compare different sets of related data or to predict data that has not yet been measured. An example of a line graph would be comparing the rate of activity of different enzymes at varying temperatures. A **bar graph** or **histogram** is used to compare different items and to make comparisons based on this data. An example of a bar graph would be comparing the ages of children in a classroom. A **pie chart** is useful when organizing data as part of a whole. A good use for a pie chart would be displaying the percent of time students spend on various after-school activities.

As noted before, the independent variable is controlled by the experimenter. This variable is placed on the x-axis (horizontal axis). The dependent variable is influenced by the independent variable and is placed on the y-axis (vertical axis). It is important to choose the appropriate units for labeling the axes. It is best to take the largest value to be plotted and to divide it by the number of blocks, rounding to the nearest whole number.

Precision, accuracy, and error

Accuracy is the degree of conformity of a measurement of some quantity to its actual (true) value. Precision, also called reproducibility or repeatability, is the degree to which further measurements or calculations will show the same or similar results.

Accuracy is the degree of veracity; while precision is the degree of reproducibility.

The best analogy to explain accuracy and precision is the target comparison.

Repeated measurements are compared to arrows that are fired at a target. Accuracy describes the closeness of arrows to the bull's eye at the target center. Arrows that strike closer to the bull's eye are considered more accurate.

All experimental uncertainty is due to either random errors or systematic errors.

Random errors are statistical fluctuations in the measured data due to the precision limitations of the measurement device. Random errors usually result from the experimenter's inability to take the same measurement in exactly the same way to get exactly the same number.

Sample Test: Scientific, Mathematical, and Technological Processes

1. $\left(\dfrac{-4}{9}\right) + \left(\dfrac{-7}{10}\right) =$

   A. $\dfrac{23}{90}$

   B. $\dfrac{-23}{90}$

   C. $\dfrac{103}{90}$

   D. $\dfrac{-103}{90}$

2. $(5.6) \times (-0.11) =$

   A. -0.616

   B. 0.616

   C. -6.110

   D. 6.110

3. $0.74 =$

   A. $\dfrac{74}{100}$

   B. 7.4%

   C. $\dfrac{33}{50}$

   D. $\dfrac{74}{10}$

4. 303 is what percent of 600?

   A. 0.505%

   B. 5.05%

   C. 505%

   D. 50.5%

5. An item that sells for $375 is put on sale at $120. What is the percent of decrease?

   A. 25%

   B. 28%

   C. 68%

   D. 34%

6. A car gets 25.36 miles per gallon. The car has been driven 83,310 miles. What is a reasonable estimate for the number of gallons of gas used?

   A. 2,087 gallons

   B. 3,000 gallons

   C. 1,800 gallons

   D. 164 gallons

7. The owner of a rectangular piece of land 40 yards in length and 30 yards in width wants to divide it into two parts. She plans to join two opposite corners with a fence, as shown in the diagram below. The cost of the fence will be approximately $25 per linear foot. What is the estimated cost for the fence?

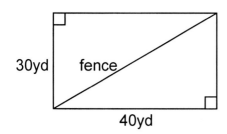

A. $1,250

B. $62,500

C. $5,250

D. $3,750

8. What is the area of a square whose side is 13 feet?

A. 169 feet

B. 169 square feet

C. 52 feet

D. 52 square feet

9. The trunk of a tree has a 2.1 meter radius. What is its circumference?

A. 2.1π square meters

B. 4.2π meters

C. 2.1π meters

D. 4.2π square meters

10. $\dfrac{7}{9}+\dfrac{1}{3}\div\dfrac{2}{3}=$

A. $\dfrac{5}{3}$

B. $\dfrac{3}{2}$

C. 2

D. $\dfrac{23}{18}$

11. Choose the statement that is true for all real numbers.

  A. $a = 0, b \neq 0$, then $\dfrac{b}{a}$ = undefined.

  B. $^-(a + (^-a)) = 2a$

  C. $2(ab) =^- (2a)b$

  D. $^-a(b + 1) = ab - a$

12. If $4x - (3 - x) = 7(x - 3) + 10$, then

  A. $x = 8$

  B. $x = -8$

  C. $x = 4$

  D. $x = -4$

13. Given the formula $d = rt$, (where d = distance, r = rate, and t = time), calculate the time required for a vehicle to travel 585 miles at a rate of 65 miles per hour.

  A.   8.5 hours

  B.   6.5 hours

  C.   9.5 hours

  D.   9 hours

14. What is the area of this triangle?

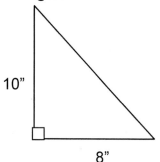

10"

8"

  A.   80 square inches

  B.   20 square inches

  C.   40 square inches

  D.   30 square inches

15. It takes five equally skilled people nine hours to shingle Mr. Joe's roof. Let t be the time required for only 3 of these men to do the same job. Select the correct statement of the given condition.

  A. $\dfrac{3}{5} = \dfrac{9}{t}$

  B. $\dfrac{9}{5} = \dfrac{3}{t}$

  C. $\dfrac{5}{9} = \dfrac{3}{t}$

  D. $\dfrac{14}{9} = \dfrac{t}{5}$

16. In a sample of 40 full-time employees at a particular company, 35 were also holding down a part-time job requiring at least 10 hours/week. If this proportion holds for the entire company of 25,000 employees, how many full-time employees at this company are actually holding down a part-time job of at least 10 hours per week.

A. 714

B. 625

C. 21,875

D. 28,571

17. The following chart shows the yearly average number of international tourists visiting Palm Beach for 1990-1994. How may more international tourists visited Palm Beach in 1994 than in 1991?

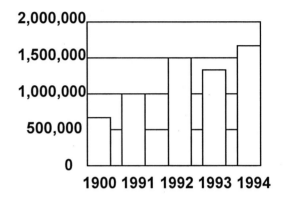

A. 100,000

B. 600,000

C. 1,600,000

D. 8,000,000

18. What is the mode of the data in the following sample?

9, 10, 11, 9, 10, 11, 9, 13

A. 9

B. 9.5

C. 10

D. 11

19. Consider the graph of the distribution of the length of time it took individuals to complete an employment form.

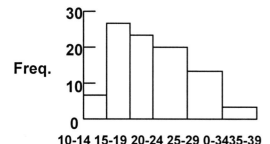

Freq.

10-14 15-19 20-24 25-29 0-3435-39

Minutes

Approximately how many individuals took fewer than 15 minutes to complete the employment form?

A.   35
B.   28
C.   7
D.   4

20. Solve for x.

$$3x - \frac{2}{3} = \frac{5x}{2} + 2$$

A. $5\frac{1}{3}$

B. $\frac{17}{3}$

C.   2

D. $\frac{16}{2}$

21. When is a hypothesis formed?

A. Before the data is taken.

B. After the data is taken.

C. After the data is analyzed.

D. Concurrent with graphing the data.

22. In an experiment measuring the growth of bacteria at different temperatures, what is the independent variable?

A. Number of bacteria.

B. Growth rate of bacteria.

C. Temperature.

D. Size of bacteria.

23. A scientist exposes mice to cigarette smoke and notes that their lungs develop tumors. Mice that were not exposed to the smoke do not develop as many tumors. Which of the following conclusions may be drawn from these results?

    I.   Cigarette smoke causes lung tumors.

    II.   Cigarette smoke exposure has a positive correlation with lung tumors in mice.

    III.   Some mice are predisposed to develop lung tumors.

    IV.   Mice are often a good model for humans in scientific research.

A. I and II only

B. II only

C. I , II, and III only

D. II and IV only

24. Which of the following types of rock are made from magma?

A. Fossils

B. Sedimentary

C. Metamorphic

D. Igneous

25. Which parts of an atom are located inside the nucleus?

A. Electrons and neutrons.

B. Protons and neutrons.

C. Protons only.

D. Neutrons only.

Answer Key: Scientific, Mathematical, and Technological Processes

1.	D
2.	A
3.	A
4.	D
5.	C
6.	B
7.	D
8.	B
9.	B
10.	D
11.	A
12.	C
13.	D
14.	C
15.	B
16.	C
17.	B
18.	A
19.	C
20.	A
21.	A
22.	C
23.	B
24.	D
25.	B

Answers with Rationale: Scientific, Mathematical, and Technological Processes

1. Find the LCD of $\dfrac{^-4}{9}$ and $\dfrac{^-7}{10}$. The LCD is 90, so you get

   $$\dfrac{^-40}{90} + \dfrac{^-63}{90} = \dfrac{^-103}{90}, \text{ which is answer } \mathbf{D}.$$

2. Simple multiplication. The answer will be negative because a positive times a negative is a negative number. $5.6 \times ^-0.11 = ^-0.616$, which is answer **A**.

3. $0.74 \rightarrow$ the 4 is in the hundredths place, so the answer is $\dfrac{74}{100}$, which is **A**.

4. Use x for the percent. $600x = 303$. $\dfrac{600x}{600} = \dfrac{303}{600} \rightarrow x = 0.505 = 50.5\%$, which is answer **D**.

5. Use $(1 - x)$ as the discount. $375x = 120$.
   $375(1 - x) = 120 \rightarrow 375 - 375x = 120 \rightarrow 375x = 255 \rightarrow x = 0.68 = 68\%$
   which is answer **C**.

6. Divide the number of miles by the miles per gallon to determine the approximate number of gallons of gas used.
   $$\dfrac{83310 \text{ miles}}{25.36 \text{ miles per gallon}} = 3285 \text{ gallons.} \text{ This is approximately 3000}$$
   gallons, which is answer **B**.

7. Find the length of the diagonal by using the Pythagorean theorem. Let x be the length of the diagonal.
   $$30^2 + 40^2 = x^2 \rightarrow 900 + 1600 = x^2$$
   $$2500 = x^2 \rightarrow \sqrt{2500} = \sqrt{x^2}$$
   $$x = 50 \text{ yards}$$
   Convert to feet. $\dfrac{50 \text{ yards}}{x \text{ feet}} = \dfrac{1 \text{ yard}}{3 \text{ feet}} \rightarrow 1500 \text{ feet}$
   It cost \$25.00 per linear foot, so the cost is (1500 ft)(\$25) = \$3750, which is answer **D**.

8. Area = length times width (lw).
   Length = 13 feet
   Width = 13 feet (square, so length and width are the same).
   Area = $13 \times 13 = 169$ square feet.
   Area is measured in square feet. So the answer is **B**.

9. Circumference is $2\pi r$, where r is the radius. The circumference is $2\pi 2.1 = 4.2\pi$ meters (not square meters because not measuring area), which is answer **B.**

10. First, do the division.
$$\frac{1}{3} \div \frac{2}{3} = \frac{1}{3} \times \frac{3}{2} = \frac{1}{2}$$
Add.
$$\frac{7}{9} + \frac{1}{2} = \frac{14}{18} + \frac{9}{18} = \frac{23}{18}, \text{ which is answer } \textbf{D.}$$

11. A is the correct answer because any number divided by 0 is undefined.

12. Solve for x.
The answer is **C.**

13. We are given d = 585 miles and r = 65 miles per hour and $d = rt$. Solve for t. $585 = 65t \rightarrow t = 9$ hours, which is answer **D.**

14. The area of a triangle is $\frac{1}{2}bh$.

$\frac{1}{2}x8x10 = 40$ square inches. The answer is **C.**

15. $\dfrac{9 \text{ hours}}{5 \text{ people}} = \dfrac{3 \text{ people}}{t \text{ hours}}$ The answer is **B.**

16. $\dfrac{35}{40}$ full time employees have a part time job also. Out of 25,000 full time employees, the number that have a part time job also is
$\dfrac{35}{40} = \dfrac{x}{25000} \rightarrow 40x = 875000 \rightarrow x = 21875$, so 21875 full time employees also have a part time job. The answer is **C.**

17. The number of tourists in 1991 was 1,000,000 and the number in 1994 was 1,600,000. Subtract to get a difference of 600,000, which is answer **B.**

18. The mode is the number that appears most frequently. 9 appears 3 times, which is more than the other numbers. Therefore the answer is **A.**

19. According to the chart, the number of people who took under 15 minutes is 7, which is answer **C.**

LIBERAL ARTS & SCIENCE TEST   92

20. $3x(6) - \dfrac{2}{3}(6) = \dfrac{5x}{2}(6) + 2(6)$ 6 is the LCD of 2 and 3

$18x - 4 = 15x + 12$

$18x = 15x + 16$

$3x = 16$

$x = \dfrac{16}{3} = 5\dfrac{1}{3}$ which is answer **A.**

21. A. A hypothesis is an educated guess made before undertaking an experiment. The hypothesis is then evaluated based on the observed data. Therefore, the hypothesis must be formed before the data is taken, not during or after the experiment. This is consistent only with answer (A).

22. C. To answer this question, recall that the independent variable in an experiment is the entity that is changed by the scientist in order to observe the effects (the dependent variable(s)). In this experiment, temperature is changed in order to measure growth of bacteria, so (C) is the answer. Note that answer (A) is the dependent variable and that neither (B) nor (D) is directly relevant to the question.

23. B. Although cigarette smoke has been found to cause lung tumors (and many other problems), this particular experiment shows only that there is a positive correlation between smoke exposure and tumor development in these mice. It may be true that some mice are more likely to develop tumors than others, which is why a control group of identical mice should have been used for comparison. Mice are often used to model human reactions, but this is as much due to their low financial and emotional cost as it is due to their being a "good model" for humans. Therefore, the answer must be (B).

24. D. Few fossils are found in metamorphic rock, and virtually none are found in igneous rocks. Igneous rocks are formed from magma, and magma is so hot that any organisms trapped by it are destroyed. Metamorphic rocks are formed by high temperatures and great pressures. When fluid sediments are transformed into solid sedimentary rocks, the process is known as lithification. The answer is (D).

25. B. Protons and neutrons are located in the nucleus; while electrons move around outside the nucleus. This is consistent only with answer (B).

COMPETENCY 7.0   UNDERSTAND THE INTERRELATEDNESS OF HISTORICAL, GEOGRAPHIC, CULTURAL, ECONOMIC, POLITICAL, AND SOCIAL ISSUES AND FACTORS.

Skill 7.1   Assess the likely effects of human activities or trends (described in written or graphic form) on the local, regional, or global environment.

A **population** is a group of people living within a certain geographic area. Populations are usually measured on a regular basis by census, which also measures age, economic, ethnic, and other data. Populations change over time due to many factors, and these changes can have significant impact on cultures.

When a population grows in size, it becomes necessary for it to either expand its geographic boundaries to make room for new people or to increase its density. Population density is simply the number of people in a population divided by some unit of geographic area in which they live. Cultures with a high population density are likely to have different ways of interacting with one another than those with a low density.

As a population grows, its economic needs change. More basic needs are required, and more workers are needed to produce them. If a population's production or purchasing power does not keep pace with its growth, its economy can be adversely affected. The age distribution of a population can impact the economy, too, if the number of young and old people who are not working is disproportionate to those who are. Growth in some areas may spur migration to other parts of a population's geographic region that are less densely populated. This redistribution of population also places demands on the economy because infrastructure is needed to connect these new areas to older population centers and land is put to new use.

Populations can grow (when the rate of birth is higher than the rate of death or by adding new people from other populations through **immigration)**. Immigration is often a source of societal change because people from other cultures bring their institutions and language to a new area. Immigration also impacts a population's educational and economic institutions because immigrants enter the workforce and place their children in schools.

Populations can also decline in number (when the death rate exceeds the birth rate or when people migrate to another area). War, famine, disease, and natural disasters can also dramatically reduce a population. The economic problems from population decline can be similar to those from over-population because economic demands may be higher than can be met. In extreme cases, a population may decline to the point that it can no longer perpetuate itself, and its members and their culture either disappear or are absorbed into another population.

When human and other population and migration patterns change; climate changes; or natural disasters disrupt the delicate balance of a habitat or an ecosystem; species either adapt or become extinct.

Floods, volcanoes, storms, and earthquakes can alter habitats. These changes can affect the species that exist within the habitats, either by causing extinction or by changing the environment in a way that will no longer support critical ecosystems. Inhabiting species, however, can also alter habitats, particularly through migration. Human civilization, population growth, and efforts to control the environment can have many negative effects on various habitats. Humans change their environments to suit their particular needs and interests. This can result in changes that result in the extinction of species or changes to the habitat itself. For example, deforestation damages the stability of mountain surfaces. One particularly devastating example is in the removal of the grasses of the Great Plains for agriculture. Tilling the ground and planting crops left the soil unprotected. Sustained drought dried out the soil into dust. When wind storms occurred, the topsoil was stripped away and blown all the way to the Atlantic Ocean.

Environmental and geographic factors have affected the pattern of **urban development** in the world. In turn, urban infrastructure and development patterns are interrelated factors.

The growth of urban areas is often linked to the advantages provided by geographic location. Before the advent of efficient overland routes of commerce such as railroads and highways, water provided the primary means of transportation of commercial goods. Most large American cities are situated along bodies of water. New York's major cities include Buffalo (on Lake Erie), Albany (on the Hudson River), and of course New York City (on a large harbor where two major rivers meet the Atlantic Ocean). Where water traffic was not provided for naturally, New Yorkers built a series of canals, including the Erie Canal, which sparked the growth of inland cities.

As transportation technology advanced, the supporting infrastructure was built to connect cities with one another and to connect remote areas to larger communities. The railroad, for example, allowed for the quick transport of agricultural products from rural areas to urban centers. This newfound efficiency not only further fueled the growth of urban centers, it changed the economy of rural America. Where once farmers had practiced only subsistence farming (growing enough to support one's own family), the new infrastructure meant that one could convert agricultural products into cash by selling them at market.

For urban dwellers, improvements in building technology and advances in transportation allowed for larger cities. Growth brought with it a new set of problems unique to each location. The bodies of water that had made the development of cities possible in their early days also formed natural barriers to growth. Further infrastructure in the form of bridges, tunnels, and ferry routes were needed to connect central urban areas with outlying communities.

As cities grew in population, living conditions became more crowded. As roads and bridges became better, and transportation technology improved, many people began to look outside the city for living space. Along with the development of these new suburbs came the infrastructure to connect them to the city in the form of commuter railroads and highways. In the case of New York City, which is situated mainly on islands, a mass-transit system became crucial early on to bring essential workers from outlying areas into the commercial centers.

The growth of suburbs had the effect in many cities of creating a type of economic segregation. Working-class people who could not afford new suburban homes and an automobile to carry them to and from work were relegated to closer, more densely populated areas. Frequently, these areas had to be passed through by those on their way to the suburbs, and rail lines and freeways sometimes bisected these urban communities. In the modern age, advancements in telecommunications' infrastructure may have an impact on urban growth patterns as information can pass instantly and freely between almost any two points on the globe, allowing access to some aspects of urban life to those in remote areas.

Natural resources are naturally occurring substances that are considered valuable in their natural form. A commodity is generally considered a natural resource when the primary activities associated with it are extraction and purification, as opposed to creation. Thus, mining, petroleum extraction, fishing, and forestry are generally considered natural-resource industries, while agriculture is not.

Natural resources are often classified into **renewable** and **non-renewable resources**. Renewable resources are generally living resources (fish, coffee, and forests, for example), which can restock (renew) themselves if they are not over-harvested. Renewable resources can restock themselves and be used indefinitely if they are properly managed. Once renewable resources are consumed at a rate that exceeds their natural rate of replacement, the standing stock will diminish and eventually run out. The rate of sustainable use of a renewable resource is determined by the replacement rate and amount of standing stock of that particular resource. Non-living renewable natural include soil, timber, oil, minerals, and other goods taken more or less as they are from Earth.

In recent years, the depletion of natural capital and attempts to move to sustainable development has been a major focus of development agencies. **Deforestation,** or clear cutting, is of particular concern in rainforest regions, which hold most of the Earth's natural biodiversity – irreplaceable, genetic, natural capital. Conservation of natural resources is the major focus of Natural Capitalism, environmentalism, the ecology movement, and Green parties. Some view this depletion as a major source of social unrest and conflicts in developing nations.

Environmental policy is concerned with the sustainability of Earth, of a region under the administration of some governing group, or of a local habitat. The concern of environmental policy is the preservation of the region, habitat or ecosystem. Because humans, both individually and in community, rely upon the environment to sustain human life, social and environmental policy must be mutually supportive. Because humans, both individually and in community, live Earth, draw upon Earth's natural resources, and affect the environment in many ways, environmental and social policy must be mutually supportive.

If modern societies have no understanding of the limitations upon natural resources or how their actions affect the environment and act without regard for the sustainability of Earth, it will become impossible for Earth to sustain human existence. At the same time, Earth's resources are necessary to support human welfare. Environmental policies must recognize that the planet is the home of humans and of other species, too.

In an age of **global warming**, unprecedented demand upon natural resources, and a shrinking planet, social and environmental policies must become increasingly interdependent if the planet is to continue to support life and human civilization.

Land use relates to the function of the land – what use is made of it. Use and development models are theories that attempt to inform the layout of urban areas, primarily in "more economically developed countries" or in "less economically developed countries".

Two primary land use models are generally applied to urban regions. These are: (1) The Burgess model (also called the concentric model), in which cities are seen to develop in a series of concentric circles with the central business district at the center, ringed by an industrial area, ringed by the low-class residential area, ringed by the middle-class residential area, and, finally, ringed by the high class residential area (often suburbs); and (2) The Hoyt model (also called the Sector Model), in which the central business district occupies a central area of a circle, with factories and industry occupying an elongated area that abuts the city center, and with the low-class residential area surrounding the industrial area, the middle class residential area forming a semi-circle toward the other side of the city center, and a small, upper-class residential sector extending from the city center out through the middle of the middle-class residential area.

Skill 7.2   Assess ways in which major transformations related to human work, thought, and belief have affected human society.

The classical civilization of **Greece,** based on the foundations already laid by such ancient groups as the Egyptians, Phoenicians, Minoans, and Mycenaeans, reached the highest levels of man's achievements. Among the more important contributions of Greece were the Greek alphabet (derived from the Phoenician letters) which formed the basis for the Roman and our present-day alphabets; extensive trading and colonization (resulting in the spread of the Greek civilization); the love of sports with emphasis on a sound body (leading to the tradition of the Olympic games); the rise of independent, strong city-states; the complete contrast between independent, freedom-loving Athens with its practice of pure democracy (direct, personal, active participation in government by qualified citizens) and rigid, totalitarian, militaristic Sparta; important accomplishments in drama, epic and lyric poetry, fables, myths centered around the many gods and goddesses, science, astronomy, medicine, mathematics, philosophy, art, architecture, and history; the conquests of Alexander the Great spreading Greek ideas to the areas he conquered and bringing to the Greek world many ideas from Asia; and, above all, the value of ideas, wisdom, curiosity, and the desire to learn as much as possible about the world.

Rome was the next and most successful of the ancient empires, building itself from one town that borrowed from its Etruscan neighbors into a worldwide empire stretching from the wilds of Scotland to the shores of the Middle East. Building on the principles of Hellenization, Rome imported and exported goods and customs galore, melding the production capabilities and the belief systems of all it conquered into a heterogeneous, yet distinctly Roman, civilization. Like no other empire before it, Rome conquered and absorbed those whom it conquered. Trade, religion, science, political structure—all these things were incorporated into the Roman Empire, benefiting the Empire's citizens.

The ancient civilization of **Rome** lasted approximately 1,000 years, including the periods of republic and empire, although its lasting influence on Europe and its history lasted much longer. There was a very sharp contrast between the curious, imaginative, inquisitive Greeks and the practical, simple, down-to-earth, no-nonsense Romans, who spread and preserved the ideas of ancient Greece and other culture groups. The contributions and accomplishments of the Romans are numerous, but their greatest included language, engineering, building, law, government, roads, trade, and the **Pax Romana**. Pax Romana was a long period of peace enabling free travel and trade, spreading people, cultures, goods, and ideas over a vast area of the known world. In the end, though, Rome grew too big to manage and its enemies too many to turn back. The sprawling nature of the Empire made it too big in the end to protect, and the heterogeneity dissolved into chaos and violence.

The official end of the **Roman Empire** came when Germanic tribes took over and controlled most of Europe. The five major tribes were the Visigoths, Ostrogoths, Vandals, Saxons, and Franks. In later years, the Franks successfully stopped the invasion of southern Europe by Muslims by defeating them under the leadership of Charles Martel at the Battle of Tours in 732 AD. Thirty-six years later, in 768 AD, the grandson of Charles Martel became King of the Franks and is known throughout history as Charlemagne. Charlemagne was a man of war unique in his respect for and encouragement of learning. He made great efforts to rule fairly and to ensure just treatment for his people.

The last century and a half has been a time of rapid and extensive change on almost every front. Notably, there has been a growing concern for human rights and civil rights. The end of imperialism and the liberation of former colonies and territorial holdings have created new nations and have increased communication and respect among the nations of the world. Democracy has grown; Communism has risen and almost fallen. Nations are no longer ruled by distant mother countries or their resident governors. But these freedoms have been won at great cost in human lives. Both political and individual freedoms have been won through struggle. Nationalism has risen and created new states, and nations have cultivated a national identity. Yet these individual nations have been brought into contact and cooperation in ways never before experienced in human history. Scientific and technological developments, new thinking in religion and philosophy, and new political and economic realities have combined to begin to create a global society that must now learn to define itself and learn how to cooperate and respect diversity in new ways.

The **Industrial Revolution**, which began in Great Britain and spread elsewhere, was the development of power-driven machinery (fueled by coal and steam) leading to the accelerated growth of industry, with large factories replacing homes and small workshops as work centers. The lives of people changed drastically, and a largely agricultural society changed to an industrial one. In Western Europe, the period of empire and colonialism began. The industrialized nations seized and claimed parts of Africa and Asia in an effort to control and provide the raw materials needed to feed the industries and machines in the "mother country". Later developments included power based on electricity and internal combustion, replacing coal and steam.

During the eighteenth and especially the nineteenth centuries, **nationalism** emerged as a powerful force in Europe and elsewhere in the world. Strictly speaking, nationalism was a belief in one's own nation, country, or people. The people of the European nations began to think in terms of a nation of people who had similar beliefs, concerns, and needs. This was partly a reaction to a growing discontent with the autocratic governments of the day and also just a general realization that there was more to life than the individual. People could feel a part of something like their nation, making themselves more than just an insignificant soul struggling to survive.

Nationalism precipitated several changes in government, most notably in France; it also brought large groups of people together, as with the unifications of Germany and Italy. What it didn't do, however, was to provide sufficient outlets for this sudden rise in national fervor. Especially in the 1700s and 1800s, European powers and peoples began looking to Africa and Asia in order to find colonies: rich sources of goods, trade, and cheap labor. Africa, especially, suffered at the hands of European imperialists bent on expanding their reach outside the borders of Europe. Asia suffered colonial expansion, most notably in India and Southeast Asia.

In **religion** and philosophy, there have been great changes as well. Religious interpretation tended to swing like a pendulum between the liberal and the conservative. By the end of the twenty-first century, however, the struggle for meaning and identity had resulted in a generalized conservative trend. This tendency can be seen in most religions yet today. Religion and philosophy are, to be sure, the means of self-definition and the understanding of one's place in the universe. Recent conservative trends, however, have had a polarizing effect. Issues of the relationship of church and state have arisen and been resolved in most countries during this period. Yet, at the same time, there has been an increasing effort to understand the religious beliefs of others, either to create new ways to define one's religion over and against other religions or as the basis of new attacks on the values and teachings of other religions. This same struggle resulted in the rise of the philosophical movement known as existentialism, as seen in the writings of Soren Kierkegaard, Karl Jaspers, and Jean-Paul Sartre.

The **Reformation** period consisted of two phases: the **Protestant Revolution** and the **Catholic Reformation**. The Protestant Revolution came about because of religious, political, and economic reasons. The religious reasons stemmed from abuses in the Catholic Church, including fraudulent clergy with their scandalous immoral lifestyles; the sale of religious offices, indulgences, and dispensations; different theologies within the Church; and frauds involving sacred relics.

The system of **feudalism** became a dominant feature of the economic and social system in Europe. It was a system of loyalty and protection. The strong protected the weak, who returned the favor with farm labor, military service, and loyalty. Life was lived out on a vast estate owned by a nobleman and his family called a "manor." It was a complete village supporting a few hundred people, mostly peasants. Improved tools and farming methods made life more bearable although most people never left the manor or traveled from their village during their lifetime. Feudalism was the organization of people based on the ownership of land by a **lord** or other **noble** who allowed individuals known as peasants or **serfs** to farm the land and to keep a portion of what they grew. The lord or noble, in return for the serfs' loyalty, offered them his protection. In practical effect, the serf was considered owned by his lord, with little or no rights at all. The lord's sole obligation to the serfs was to protect them so that they could continue to work for him (most, though not all, lords were men). This system would last for many centuries. In Russia it would last until the 1860s.

The end of the feudal manorial system was sealed by the outbreak and spread of the infamous **Black Death**, which killed over one-third of the total population of Europe. Those who survived and were skilled in any job or occupation were in demand, and many serfs or peasants found freedom and, for that time, a decidedly improved standard of living. Strong nation-states became powerful, and people developed a renewed interest in life and learning.

Sharpened skills; development of more sophisticated tools; commerce with other communities; and increasing knowledge of their environment; the resources available to them; and responses to the needs to share good, order community life and to protect their possessions from outsiders led to further division of labor and community development.

As trade routes developed and travel between cities became easier, trade led to specialization. Trade enabled a people to obtain the goods they desired in exchange for the goods they were able to produce. This, in turn, led to increased attention to refinements of technique and the sharing of ideas. The knowledge of a new discovery or invention provided knowledge and technology that increased the ability to produce goods for trade. As each community learned the value of the goods it produced and improved its ability to produce the goods in greater quantity, industry was born.

The **Agricultural Revolution**, initiated by the invention of the plow, led to a thoroughgoing transformation of human society by making large-scale agricultural production possible and facilitating the development of agrarian societies. During the period during which the plow was invented, the wheel, numbers, and writing were also invented. Coinciding with the shift from hunting wild game to the domestication of animals, this period was one of dramatic social and economic change.

Numerous changes in lifestyle and thinking accompanied the development of stable agricultural communities. Rather than gathering a wide variety of plants as hunter-gatherers, agricultural communities become dependent on a limited number of plants or crops. Subsistence became vulnerable to the weather and dependent upon planting and harvesting times. Agriculture also required a great deal of physical labor and the development of a sense of discipline. Agricultural communities become sedentary or stable in terms of location. This made the construction of dwellings appropriate. These tended to be built relatively close together, creating villages or towns. Stable communities also freed people from the need to carry everything with them while moving from hunting ground to hunting ground. This facilitated the invention of larger, more complex tools. As new tools were envisioned and developed, it began to make sense to have some specialization within the society.

The **Scientific Revolution** and the **Enlightenment** were two of the most important movements in the history of civilization, resulting in a new sense of self-examination and a wider view of the world than ever before. The Scientific Revolution was, above all, a shift in focus from **belief to evidence**. Scientists and philosophers wanted to see the proof, not just believe what other people told them. It was an exciting time if you were a forward-looking thinker.

A Polish astronomer, **Nicolaus Copernicus**, began the Scientific Revolution. He crystallized a lifetime of observations into a book that was published about the time of his death; in this book, Copernicus argued that the Sun, not Earth, was the center of a solar system and that other planets revolved around the Sun, not Earth. This flew in the face of established (read: Church-mandated) doctrine. The Church still wielded tremendous power at this time, including the power to banish people or sentence them to prison or even death. The Danish astronomer **Tycho Brahe** was the first to catalog his observations of the night sky, of which he made thousands. Building on Brahe's data, German scientist **Johannes Kepler** instituted his theory of planetary movement, embodied in his famous Laws of Planetary Movement. Using Brahe's data, Kepler also confirmed Copernicus's observations and argument that the Earth revolved around the Sun.

The most famous defender of this idea was **Galileo Galilei**, an Italian scientist who conducted many famous experiments in the pursuit of science. He is most well-known, however, for his defense of the heliocentric (sun-centered) idea.

Galileo died under house arrest, but his ideas didn't die with him. Picking up the baton was an English scientist named **Isaac Newton**, who became perhaps the most famous scientist of all. He is known as the discoverer of gravity and a pioneering voice in the study of optics (light), calculus, and physics.

More than any other scientist, Newton argued for (and proved) the idea of a mechanistic view of the world: You can see how the world works and prove how the world works through observation; if you can see these things with your own eyes, they must be so. Up to this time, people believed what other people told them.

The **Enlightenment** was a period of intense self-study that focused on ethics and logic. Scientists and philosophers questioned cherished truths, widely held beliefs, and their own sanity in an attempt to discover why the world worked—from within. "I think, therefore I am" was one of the famous sayings of that or any day. It was uttered by Rene Descartes, a French scientist-philosopher whose dedication to logic and the rigid rules of observation were a blueprint for the thinkers who came after him. One of the giants of the era was England's **David Hume**. A pioneer of the doctrine of empiricism, Hume was also a prime believer in the value of skepticism; in other words, he was naturally suspicious of things that other people told him to be true and constantly set out to discover the truth for himself. The Enlightenment thinker who might be the most famous is **Immanuel Kant** of Germany. He was both a philosopher and a scientist, and he took a definite scientific view of the world.

Also prevalent during the Enlightenment was the idea of the **social contract**, the belief that government existed because people wanted it to, that the people had an agreement with the government that they would submit to it as long as it protected them and didn't encroach on their basic human rights. This idea was first made famous by the Frenchman Jean-Jacques Rousseau but was also adopted by England's John Locke and America's Thomas Jefferson. **John Locke** was one of the most influential political writers of the seventeenth century and put great emphasis on human rights and advanced the belief that, when governments violate those rights, then people should rebel. He wrote the book "*Two Treatises of Government*" in 1690, which had tremendous influence on political thought in the American colonies and helped to shape the U.S. Constitution and Declaration of Independence.

The **Age of Exploration** actually had its beginnings centuries before exploration actually took place. The rise and spread of Islam in the seventh century and its subsequent control over the holy city of Jerusalem led to the European so-called holy wars, the Crusades, to free Jerusalem and the Holy Land from this control. Even though the Crusades were not a success, those who survived and returned to their homes and countries in Western Europe brought back with them new products such as silks, spices, perfumes, and new and different foods. Luxuries that were unheard of gave new meaning to colorless, drab, dull lives.

New ideas, new inventions, and new methods also went to Western Europe with the returning Crusaders and from these new influences was the intellectual stimulation which led to the period known as the Renaissance. The revival of interest in classical Greek art, architecture, literature, science, astronomy, and medicine; increased trade between Europe and Asia; and the invention of the printing press helped to push the spread of knowledge.

The word **Renaissance** literally means "rebirth," and the phenomenon signaled a rekindling of interest in the glory of ancient classical Greek and Roman civilizations. It was the period in human history marking the start of many ideas and innovations leading to our modern age. The Renaissance began in Italy, with many of its ideas starting in Florence, controlled by the infamous Medici family. Education, especially for some of the merchants, involved reading, writing, math, the study of law, and the writings of classical Greek and Roman writers.

Most famous are the Renaissance artists, first and foremost, Leonardo, Michelangelo, and Raphael, but also Titian, Donatello, and Rembrandt. All of these men pioneered a new method of painting and sculpture—that of portraying real events and real people as they really looked, not as the artists imagined them to be. One needs to look no further than Michelangelo's *David* to illustrate this.

Literature was a focus as well during the Renaissance. Humanists Petrarch, Boccaccio, Erasmus, and Sir Thomas More advanced the idea of being interested in life here on Earth and the opportunities it could bring, rather than constantly focusing on heaven and its rewards. The monumental works of Shakespeare, Dante, and Cervantes found their origins in these ideas as well as the ones that drove the painters and sculptors. All of these works, of course, owe much of their existence to the invention of the printing press, which occurred during the Renaissance.

The Renaissance changed music as well. No longer just a religious adjunct, music could be fun and composed for its own sake, to be enjoyed in fuller and more humanistic ways than in the Middle Ages. Musicians worked for themselves, rather than exclusively for the churches and so could command good money for their work, increasing their prestige. Science advanced considerably during the Renaissance, especially in the areas of physics and astronomy. Copernicus, Kepler, and Galileo led a Scientific Revolution in proving that Earth was round and certainly not perfect, an earth-shattering revelation to those who clung to medieval ideals of a geocentric, church-centered existence.

The **Industrial Revolution** of the eighteenth and nineteenth centuries resulted in even greater changes in human civilization and even greater opportunities for trade, increased production, and the exchange of ideas and knowledge.

The first phase of the Industrial Revolution (1750-1830) saw the mechanization of the textile industry; vast improvements in mining with the invention of the steam engine; and numerous improvements in transportation with the development and improvement of turnpikes, canals, and the railroad.

The second phase (1830-1910) resulted in vast improvements in a number of industries that had already been mechanized through such inventions as the Bessemer steel process and the invention of steam ships. New industries arose as a result of the new technological advances such as photography, electricity, and chemical processes. New sources of power were harnessed and applied, including petroleum and hydroelectric power. Precision instruments were developed and engineering was launched. It was during this second phase that the industrial revolution spread to other European countries, to Japan; and to the United States.

The direct results of the Industrial Revolution, particularly as they affected industry, commerce, and agriculture, included:
- Enormous increase in productivity.
- Huge increase in world trade.
- Specialization and division of labor.
- Standardization of parts and mass production.
- Growth of giant business conglomerates and monopolies.
- A new revolution in agriculture facilitated by the steam engine, machinery, chemical fertilizers, processing, canning, and refrigeration.

The political results included:
- Growth of complex government by technical experts.
- Centralization of government, including regulatory administrative agencies.
- Advantages to democratic development, including extension of franchise to the middle class and, later, to all elements of the population; mass education to meet the needs of an industrial society; and the development of media of public communication, including radio, television, and cheap newspapers.
- Dangers to democracy included the risk of manipulation of the media of mass communication; facilitation of dictatorial centralization and totalitarian control; subordination of the legislative function to administrative directives; efforts to achieve uniformity and conformity; and social impersonalization.

The economic results were numerous:
- The conflict between free trade and low tariffs and protectionism.
- The issue of free enterprise against government regulation.
- Struggles between labor and capital, including the trade-union movement.
- The rise of socialism.
- The rise of the utopian socialists.
- The rise of Marxian or scientific socialism.

The social results of the Industrial Revolution include:

- Increase of population, especially in industrial centers.
- Advances in science applied to agriculture, sanitation and medicine.
- Growth of great cities.
- Disappearance of the difference between city dwellers and farmers.
- Faster tempo of life and increased stress from the monotony of the work routine.
- The emancipation of women.
- The decline of religion.
- Rise of scientific materialism.
- Darwin's theory of evolution.

Things changed in the worlds of literature and art as well. The main development in the nineteenth century was **Romanticism**, an emphasis on emotion and the imagination that was a direct reaction to the logic and reason so stressed in the preceding Enlightenment. Famous Romantic authors include John Keats, William Wordsworth, Victor Hugo, and Johann Wolfgang von Goethe. The horrors of the Industrial Revolution gave rise to the very famous realists Charles Dickens, Fyodor Dostoevsky, Leo Tolstoy, and Mark Twain, who described life as they saw it, for better or for worse (and it was usually worse).

In Europe, Italy, and Germany, each was totally united into one nation from many smaller states. There were revolutions in Austria and Hungary, the Franco-Prussian War, the dividing of Africa among the strong European nations, interference and intervention of Western nations in Asia, and the breakup of Turkish dominance in the Balkans.

In Africa; France, Great Britain, Italy, Portugal, Spain, Germany, and Belgium controlled the entire continent except for Liberia and Ethiopia. In Asia and the Pacific Islands; only China, Japan, and present-day Thailand (Siam) kept their independence. The others were controlled by the strong European nations.

An additional reason for **European imperialism** was the harsh, urgent demand for the raw materials needed to fuel and feed the great Industrial Revolution. These resources were not available in the huge quantities so desperately needed, which necessitated (and rationalized) the partitioning of the continent of Africa and parts of Asia. In turn, these colonial areas would purchase the finished manufactured goods. Europe in the nineteenth century was a crowded place. Populations were growing, but resources were not. The peoples of many European countries were also agitating for rights as never before. To address these concerns, European powers began to look elsewhere for relief.

Skill 7.3   Infer aspects of a society's social structure or group interactions based on information presented in an excerpt.

Language is a primary way in which culture is passed between people of a society and from generation to generation. By examining the language used in an excerpt of dialogue or literature, one can make some general observations about a society and how its members interact.

Most languages have formal and informal ways of speaking and writing, for instance, in response to the relative social positions of the participants in a conversation. Examining how these forms are used in an excerpt can indicate the social standing of the speaker and the intended audience. Many languages use certain words to refer to other groups in a derogatory way. The use of these words can indicate cultural opinions and the social standing of various groups in relation to one another.

Skill 7.4   Analyze ways in which social, cultural, geographic, and economic factors influence inter-group relations and the formation of values, beliefs, and attitudes.

Socialization also takes place among adults who change their environment and are expected to adopt new behaviors. Joining the military, for example, requires a different type of dress and behavior than civilian culture. Taking a new job or going to a new school are other examples of situations where adults must re-socialize.

Two primary ways that socialization takes place are through positive and negative sanctions. Positive sanctions are rewards for appropriate or desirable behavior, and negative sanctions are punishments for inappropriate behavior. Recognition from peers and praise from a parent are examples of positive sanctions that reinforce expected social behaviors. Negative sanctions might include teasing by peers for unusual behavior or punishment by a parent.

Sanctions can be either formal or informal. Public awards and prizes are ways a society formally reinforces positive behaviors. Laws that provide for punishment of specific infractions are formal negative sanctions.

Sociologists have identified five different types of institutions around which societies are structured: family, education, government, religion, and economy. These institutions provide a framework for members of a society to learn about and participate in a society and allow for a society to perpetuate its beliefs and values for succeeding generations.

The **family** is the primary social unit in most societies. It is through the family that children learn the most essential skills for functioning in their society, such as language and appropriate forms of interaction. The family is connected to ethnicity, which is partly defined by a person's heritage.

Education is an important institution in a society because it allows for the formal passing on of a culture's collected knowledge. The institution of education is connected to the family because that is where a child's earliest education takes place. The United States has a public school system administered by the states that ensures a basic education and provides a common experience for most children.

A society's **governmental** institutions often embody its beliefs and values. Laws, for instance, reflect a society's values by enforcing its ideas of right and wrong. The structure of a society's government can reflect a society's ideals about the role of an individual. The American form of democracy emphasizes the rights of the individual, but, in return, expects individuals to respect the rights of others, including those of ethnic and political minorities.

Religion is frequently the institution from which springs a society's primary beliefs and values and can be closely related to other social institutions. Many religions have definite teachings on the structure and importance of the family, for instance. The U.S. Constitution guarantees the free practice of religion, which has led to a large number of denominations practicing in the U.S. today. Most Americans identify with Christian faiths.

A society's **economic** institutions define how an individual can contribute and receive economic reward. The United States has a capitalist economy driven by free enterprise. While this system allows for economic advancement for the individual, it can also produce areas of poverty and economic depression.

Skill 7.5 Assess the social or economic implications of political views presented in an excerpt.

A synthesis of information from multiple sources requires an understanding of the content chosen for the synthesis, first of all. Writers of syntheses will, no doubt, wish to incorporate their own ideas, particularly in any conclusions that are drawn, and show relationships to those of the chosen sources. That can only happen if writers have a firm grip on what others have said or written. The focus is not so much on documentary methods, but on techniques of critically examining and evaluating the ideas of others. Even so, careful documentation is extremely important in this type of presentation, particularly with regard to which particular edition is being read in the case of written sources; and date, location, etc., of online sources. The phrase "downloaded from such-and-such a website on such-and-such a date" is useful. If the conversation, interview, or speech is live; date, circumstances, and location must be indicated.

The purpose of a synthesis is to understand the works of others and to use that work in shaping a conclusion. Writers or speakers must clearly differentiate between the ideas that come from a source and their own ideas.

COMPETENCY 8.0   **UNDERSTAND PRINCIPLES AND ASSUMPTIONS UNDERLYING HISTORICAL OR CONTEMPORARY ARGUMENTS, INTERPRETATIONS, EXPLANATIONS, OR DEVELOPMENTS.**

Skill 8.1   **Infer the political principles illustrated in given situations or arguments.**

The Constitution of the United States is the fundamental law of the republic. It is a precise, formal, written document of the *extraordinary*, or *supreme*, type of constitution. The founders of the Union established it as the highest governmental authority. There is no national power superior to it. The foundations were so broadly laid as to provide for the expansion of national life and to make it an instrument which would last for all time. To maintain its stability, the framers created a difficult process for making any changes to it. No amendment can become valid until it is ratified by three-fourths of all of the states.

The Constitution binds the states in a governmental unity in everything that affects the welfare of all. At the same time, it recognizes the right of the people of each state to independence of action in matters that relate only to them. Since the Federal Constitution is the law of the land, all other laws must conform to it.

The debates conducted during the Constitutional Congress represent the issues and the arguments that led to the compromises in the final document. The debates also reflect the concerns of the Founding Fathers that the rights of the people be protected from abrogation by the government itself and the determination that no branch of government should have enough power to continually dominate the others. There is, therefore, a system of checks and balances.

The American nation was founded very much with the idea that the people would have a large degree of autonomy and liberty. The famous maxim "no taxation without representation" was a rallying cry for the Revolution, not only because the people didn't want to suffer the increasingly oppressive series of taxes imposed on them by the British Parliament, but also because the people could not in any way influence the lawmakers in Parliament in regard to those taxes. No American colonist had a seat in Parliament, and no American colonist could vote for members of Parliament.

One of the most famous words in the Declaration of Independence is "liberty," the pursuit of which all people should be free to attempt. That idea, that a people should be free to pursue their own course, even to the extent of making their own mistakes, has dominated political thought in the 200-plus years of the American republic.

Representation, the idea that a people elect—or even replace—their lawmakers was not a new idea, except in America. Residents of other British colonies did not have these rights, of course, and America was only a colony, according to the conventional wisdom of the British Government at the time. What the Sons of Liberty and other revolutionaries were asking for was to stand on an equal footing with the Mother Country. Along with the idea or representation comes the idea that key ideas and concepts can be deliberated and discussed, with, theoretically, everyone having a chance to voice their views. This applied to both lawmakers and the people who elected them. Lawmakers wouldn't just pass bills that became laws; rather, they would debate the particulars and go back and forth on the strengths and weaknesses of proposed laws before voting on them. Members of both houses of Congress had the opportunity to speak out on the issues, as did the people at large, who could contact their lawmakers and express their views. This idea ran very much counter to the experience that the Founding Fathers had before the Revolution—that of taxation without representation. The different branches of government were designed to serve as checks and balances on each other so that no particular branch could become too powerful. They each have their own specific powers.

Another key concept in the American ideal is **equality**, the idea that every person has the same rights and responsibilities under the law. The Great Britain that the American colonists knew was one of a stratified society, with social classes firmly in place. Not everyone was equal under the law or in the coffers; and it was clear for all to see that the more money and power a person had, the easier it was for that person to avoid things like serving in the army and being charged with a crime. The goal of the Declaration of Independence and of the Constitution was to provide equality for all who read those documents. The reality, though, was vastly different for large sectors of society, including women and non-white Americans.

Popular sovereignty grants citizens the ability to directly participate in their own government by voting and running for public office. This ideal is based on a belief of equality that holds that all citizens have an equal right to engage in their own governance and is established in the **United States Constitution**. The Constitution also contains a list of specific rights that citizens have and which the government cannot infringe upon. Popular sovereignty also allows for citizens to change the government if they feel it is necessary. This was the driving ideal behind the Declaration of Independence and is embodied in the governmental structure laid out in the Constitution.

Due process under the law was also a big concern of the founders. Various amendments protect the rights of people. Amendments five through eight protect citizens who are accused of crimes and are brought to trial. Every citizen has the right to due process of law, (due process was defined earlier as the government following the same fair rules for everyone brought to trial.) These rules include the right to a trial by an impartial jury, the right to be defended by a lawyer, and the right to a speedy trial. The last two amendments limit the powers of the federal government to those that are expressly granted in the Constitution, any rights not expressly mentioned in the Constitution, thus, belong to the states or to the people.

This feeds into the idea of basic opportunity. The so-called "American Dream" is that every individual has an equal chance to make his or her fortune in a new land and that the country that is the United States will welcome and even encourages that initiative. The system is based on individual freedom of choice. The history of the country is filled with stories of people who ventured to America and made their fortunes in the Land of Opportunity. Unfortunately, for anyone who wasn't a white male, that basic opportunity was sometimes a difficult thing to achieve.

Bill Of Rights - The first ten amendments to the United States Constitution deal with civil liberties and civil rights. They were written mostly by James Madison. They are in brief:

1. Freedom of Religion.
2. Right To Bear Arms.
3. Security from the quartering of troops in homes.
4. Right against unreasonable search and seizures.
5. Right against self-incrimination.
6. Right to trial by jury, right to legal council.
7. Right to jury trial for civil actions.
8. No cruel or unusual punishment allowed.
9. These rights shall not deny other rights the people enjoy.
10. Powers not mentioned in the Constitution shall be retained by the states or the people.

An amendment is a change or addition to the United States Constitution. Two-thirds of both houses of Congress are required to propose and then pass one. Or two-thirds of the state legislatures must call a convention to propose one, and then it must be ratified by three-fourths of the state legislatures. To date, there are only 27 Amendments to the Constitution that have passed. An amendment may be used to cancel out a previous one, such as the 18th Amendment (1919) known as Prohibition, canceled by the 21st Amendment (1933). Amending the United States Constitution is an extremely difficult thing to do.

An Amendment must start in Congress. One or more lawmakers propose it, and then each house votes on it in turn. The Amendment must have the support of two-thirds of each house separately in order to progress on its path into law. (It should be noted here that this two-thirds need be only two-thirds of a quorum, which is just a simple majority. Thus, it is theoretically possible for an amendment to be passed and to become law even though it has been approved by less than half of one or both houses.)

The final and most difficult step for an amendment is the ratification by state legislatures. A total of three-fourths of those must approve the amendment. Approval there requires only a simple majority, but the number of states that must approve the Amendment is 38. Hundreds of Amendments have been proposed through the years, but only 27 have become part of the Constitution.

A key element in some of those failures has been the time limit that Congress has the option to put on amendment proposals. A famous example of an amendment that got close but didn't reach the threshold before the deadline expired was the Equal Rights Amendment, which was proposed in 1972, but which couldn't muster enough support for passage even though its deadline was extended from seven to 10 years.

The first ten amendments are called the Bill of Rights and were approved at the same time, shortly after the Constitution was ratified. The 11th and 12th Amendments were ratified around the turn of the nineteenth century and, respectively, voided foreign suits against states and revised the method of presidential election. The 13th, 14th, and 15th Amendments were passed in succession after the end of the Civil War. Slavery was outlawed by the 13th Amendment. The 14th & 15th Amendments provided for equal protection and for voting rights, respectively, without consideration of skin color.

The first twentieth century amendment was Number 16, which provided for a federal income tax. Providing for direct election to the Senate was the 17th Amendment. Up till then, senators were appointed by state leaders, not elected by the public at large.

The 18th Amendment prohibited the use or sale of alcohol across the country. The long battle for voting rights for women ended in success with the passage of the nineteenth Amendment. The date for the beginning of terms for the President and the Congress was changed from March to January by the twentieth Amendment. With the 21st Amendment came the only instance in which an amendment was repealed. In this case, it was the 18th Amendment and its prohibition of alcohol consumption or sale.

The 22nd Amendment limited the number of terms that a President could serve to two. Presidents since George Washington had followed Washington's practice of not running for a third term; this changed in 1940 when Franklin D. Roosevelt ran for re-election a second time. He was re-elected that time and a third time, too, four years later. He didn't live out his fourth term, but he did convince Congress and most of the state legislatures that some sort of term limit should be put in place.

The little-known 23rd Amendment provided for representation of Washington, D.C., in the Electoral College. The 24th Amendment prohibited poll taxes, which people had had to pay in order to vote.

Presidential succession is the focus of the 25th Amendment, which provides a blueprint of what to do if the president is incapacitated or killed. The 26th Amendment lowered the legal voting age for Americans from 21 to 18. The final Amendment, the 27th, prohibits members of Congress from substantially raising their own salaries. This Amendment was one of twelve originally proposed in the late eighteenth century. Ten of those twelve became the Bill of Rights, and one has yet to become law.

Skill 8.2   Recognize assumptions that inform the positions taken by political parties.

Government ultimately began as a form of protection. A strong person, usually one of the best warriors or someone who had the support of many strong men, assumed command of a people or a city or a land. The power to rule those people rested in his hands. (The vast majority of rulers throughout history have been male.) Laws existed insofar as the pronouncements and decision of the ruler and were not, in practice, written down, leading to inconsistency. Religious leaders had a strong hand in governing the lives of people, and, in many instances, the political leader was also the primary religious figure.

First in Greece and then in Rome and then in other places throughout the world, the idea of government by more than one person or more than just a handful came to the fore. Even though more people were involved, the purpose of government hadn't changed. These governments still existed to keep the peace and to protect their people from encroachments by both inside and outside forces.

In the modern day, people are subject to **laws** made by many levels of government. Local governments, such as city and county entities, are allowed to pass ordinances covering certain local matters, such as property taxation, school districting, civil infractions, and business licensing. These local bodies have perhaps the least political power in the governmental hierarchy, but, being small and relatively accessible, they are often the level at which many citizens become directly involved with government. Funding for local governments often comes from property and sales taxes.

State governments in the United States are mainly patterned after the federal government, with an elected legislative body, a judicial system, and a governor who oversees the executive branch. Like the federal government, state governments derive their authority from **constitutions**. State legislation applies to all residents of that state, and local laws must conform. State government funding is frequently from state income tax and sales taxes.

The national or federal government of the United States derives its power from the US Constitution and has three branches, the legislative, executive, and judicial. The federal government exists to make national policy, to legislate matters that affect the residents of all states, and to settle matters between states. National income tax is the primary source for federal funding. The US Constitution also provides the federal government with the authority to make treaties and enter agreements with foreign countries, creating a body of international law. While there is no authoritative international government, organizations such as the United Nations, the European Union, and other smaller groups exist to promote economic and political cooperation between nations.

Populism is the philosophy that is concerned with the common-sense needs of average people. Populism often finds expression as a reaction against perceived oppression of the average people by the wealthy elite in society. The prevalent claim of populist movements is that they will put the people first. Populism is often connected with religious fundamentalism, racism, or nationalism. Populist movements claim to represent the majority of the people and call them to stand up to institutions or practices that seem detrimental to their well-being.

Populism flourished in the late nineteenth and early twentieth centuries. Several political parties were formed out of this philosophy, including the Greenback Party, the Populist Party, the Farmer-Labor Party, the Single Tax movement of Henry George, the Share Our Wealth movement of Huey Long, the Progressive Party, and the Union Party.

The tremendous change that resulted from the industrial revolution led to a demand for reform that would control the power wielded by big corporations. The gap between the industrial moguls and the working people was growing. This disparity between rich and poor resulted in a public outcry for reform at the same time that there was an outcry for governmental reform that would end the political corruption and elitism of the day.

The reforms initiated by these leaders and the spirit of Progressivism were far-reaching. Politically, many states enacted the initiative and the referendum. The adoption of the recall occurred in many states. Several states enacted legislation that would undermine the power of political machines. On a national level, the two most significant political changes were (1) the ratification of the 19th Amendment, which required that all U.S. Senators be chosen by popular election, and (2) the ratification of the 19th Amendment, which granted women the right to vote.

Skill 8.3   Analyze assumptions on which given U.S. policies are based.

The purposes and aims of social policy are to improve human welfare and to meet basic human needs within the society. Social policy addresses basic human needs for the sustainability of the individual and the society. The concerns of social policy, then, include food, clean water, shelter, clothing, education, health, and social security. Social policy is part of public policy, determined by the city, the state, the nation, or the multi-national organization responsible for human welfare in a particular region.

Environmental policy is concerned with the sustainability of Earth, of regions under the administration of some governing group, and of individual or local habitat. The concern of environmental policy is the preservation of the region, habitat, or ecosystem.

Because humans, both individually and in community, rely upon the environment to sustain human life, social and environmental policy must be mutually supportive. Because humans, both individually and in community, live upon the earth, draw upon the natural resources of the earth, and affect the environment in many ways, environmental and social policy must be mutually supportive.

If modern societies have no understanding of the limitations upon natural resources or of how their actions affect the environment and they act without regard for the sustainability of the earth, then it will become impossible for Earth to sustain human existence. At the same time, Earth's resources are necessary to support human welfare. Environmental policies must recognize that the planet is the home of humans and of other species, too.

For centuries, social policies, economic policies, and political policies have ignored the impact of human existence and human civilization upon the environment. Human civilization has disrupted the ecological balance, contributed to the extinction of animal and plant species, and destroyed ecosystems through uncontrolled harvesting. In an age of global warming, unprecedented demand upon natural resources, and a shrinking planet; social and environmental policies must become increasingly interdependent if the planet is to continue to support life and human civilization.

Competition for control of areas of Earth's surface is a common trait of human interaction throughout history. This competition has resulted in both destructive conflict and peaceful and productive cooperation. Societies and groups have sought control of regions of Earth's surface for a wide variety of reasons; including religion, economics, politics, and administration. Numerous wars have been fought through the centuries for the control of territory for each of these reasons. At the same time, groups of people, even whole societies, have peacefully worked together to establish boundaries around regions or territories that served specific purposes in order to sustain the activities that support life and social organization.

Individuals and societies have divided the earth's surface through conflict for a number of reasons:

The domination of peoples or societies, e.g., colonialism.
The control of valuable resources, e.g., oil.
The control of strategic routes, e.g., the Panama Canal.

Conflicts can be spurred by religion, political ideology, national origin, language, and race. Conflicts can result from disagreement over how land, ocean, or natural resources will be developed, shared, and used. Conflicts have resulted from trade, migration, and settlement rights. Conflicts can occur between small groups of people, between cities, between nations, between religious groups, and between multi-national alliances.

Today, the world is primarily divided by political/administrative interests into state sovereignties. A particular region is recognized to be controlled by a particular government, including its territory, population, and natural resources. The only area of Earth's surface that today is not defined by state or national sovereignty is Antarctica.

Alliances are developed among nations on the basis of political philosophy, economic concerns, cultural similarities, religious interests, or for military defense. Some of the most notable alliances today are:

- The United Nations
- The North Atlantic Treaty Organization
- The Caribbean Community
- The Common Market
- The Council of Arab Economic Unity
- The European Union

Large companies and multi-national corporations also compete for control of natural resources for manufacturing, development, and distribution.

Throughout human history, there have been conflicts on virtually every scale over the right to divide Earth according to differing perceptions, needs, and values. These conflicts have ranged from tribal conflicts to urban riots and civil, regional, and world wars. While these conflicts have traditionally centered on control of land surfaces, new disputes are beginning to arise over the resources of the oceans and space.

Skill 8.4   Recognize concepts and ideas underlying alternative interpretations of past events.

The world of social science research has never been so open to new possibilities. Where our predecessors were unable to tread for fear of exceeding the limits of the available data, data access and data transfer, analytic routines, or computing power; today's social scientists can advance with confidence. Where once social scientists of empirical bent struggled with punch cards, chattering computer terminals, and jobs disappearing into the black hole of remote mainframe processors, often never reappearing; we now enjoy massive arrays of data, powerful personal computers on our desks, online access to data, and suites of sophisticated analytic packages. Never before has the social scientist been so well armed. Advances in technology can free social scientists from the tyranny of simplification that has often hampered attempts to grasp the complexity of the world.

Political science examines the theory of politics and how it behaves in countries and in international situations. Political science has certain varied aspects, including political history, political philosophy, economics, and international relations. All of these aspects can be used to examine both general and specific political issues today.

For example, a general issue in the United States is the preponderance of the two-party system. American politics is full of political parties, but only the Democrats and Republicans get major funding and large slates of candidates for elections across the country.

- This is due in large part to the political history of the country, which has tended to discourage any other participation. The Reform Party was a major force in America until a few years ago, but it now seems to be fading into irrelevance.
- Political philosophy speaks to this issue in that the ideologies of the Democratic and Republican Parties are generally wide enough to cover the views of most Americans. Extreme left- or right-wing parties have their adherents, but they (the adherents and the parties) are few and far between.
- Economics speaks to this in that it is very difficult for parties other than the two big ones to afford any kind of parity. The two big parties are so much a dichotomous part of American political thinking that any outside forces face an inherently uphill battle just to get dollars and cents to conduct campaigns.
- In international relations, as well, the Democratic and Republican Parties are familiar to leaders of and observers from other countries. Again, we see the ideologies of these parties encompassing a wide range of political beliefs, many of which are common to the leaders of other countries as well.

A specific issue that can be examined in these terms is capital punishment.

- The political history of the United States includes a long history of capital punishment presided over by both the federal and state governments. (Theoretically, local governments have no such power.) This tradition was handed down from the European countries that spawned the settlers who eventually became the forerunners of Americans today. The Supreme Court has, from time to time, found elements of capital punishment unconstitutional because of the Eighth Amendment prohibition of cruel and unusual punishment; but the general practices of lethal injection remain on the legal books of many state governments.

- Political philosophy on this issue generally falls into the two camps of Yes or No. Those in favor of capital punishment usually have their beliefs for a reason, as do those who oppose it. In many cases, those who favor it have been victims of crimes. This is the case for many who oppose it, however, so this issue cannot be classified in just one camp. The U.S. Government doesn't make a habit of executing people. Certain states do, however.

- Economics is definitely a factor in this debate. Those who favor capital punishment point to how much money the state saves by avoiding the expensive legal alternative, life imprisonment. Those who oppose capital punishment, however, rely on the legal system in America, which requires exhaustive appeals and seemingly endless amounts of time, to make sure not only that an innocent person is not executed, but also that that person is not treated inhumanely in the process.

- International relations can be examined as well. The U.S. is one of a handful of First World countries that have laws providing for capital punishment. This subject is sometimes a sore spot for American diplomats when dealing with countries whose people expressly detest executing criminals.

Ideology is a comprehensive set of ideas about, or a way of looking at, something like the world or some political situation. Someone who views the world in conservative terms is likely also to have conservative political views. The opposite of conservatism is usually referred to as liberalism. These two ideologies are generally referred to as "the Right" and "the Left."

In general, conservatives and liberals are on opposite sides of issues. A prime example of this is abortion. Generally speaking, liberals support a woman's right to choose to have an abortion, and conservatives oppose that right. Liberals see that right as a personal issue, one protected by the constitutional right to privacy. This right is guaranteed under a famous Supreme Court case known as *Roe* v. *Wade* (1973). For conservatives, abortion is more a moral or religious issue, with abortion opponents viewing the practice as killing unborn children.

At the center of this divisive issue is the debate over when life begins. Abortion opponents believe that life begins at conception; liberals aren't so sure. If we take a step back, we can see how this issue is a reflection of the overall division in ideologies of the two camps. Conservatives tend to see the world as a dangerous place, one in which religion and morality are extremely influential in society and in their political thinking. These thinkers are reluctant to embrace radical change or other things that go against their way of thinking developed over time and contemplation. Liberals, on the other hand, tend to be more open-minded on issues, being more willing to change their minds or accept ideas or policies that aren't exactly traditional or "safe." The abortion issue represents a deep divide along the lines of religious thinking, with liberals willing to take matters of the body into their own hands and conservatives resisting such rights based on religious reasons.

A global issue that demonstrates ideological differences of liberals and conservatives is environmentalism. In general, conservatives are more willing to desecrate the environment in the name of human progress, whereas liberals are more inclined to curtail any practices that will harm the environment. This is one example of ideological reversal, since conservatives are generally the ones who are averse to change and liberals are the ones who often seek to embrace change and new ideas. Environmentalism is certainly a global issue, especially in the areas of petroleum consumption and global warming. On both of these issues, conservatives are currently the ones pursuing policies that favor more of both, and liberals are working toward curtailing such policies. Extending that thinking further, both liberals and conservatives will look more favorably on people in other countries who embrace the policies that they favor. Such political embraces shape the international debates of many countries.

Skill 8.5 **Infer the economic principle upon which a given explanation is based.**

A **traditional economy** is one based on custom and usually exists in less developed countries. The people do things the way their ancestors did, so they are not too technologically advanced. Technology and equipment are viewed as threats to the old ways of doing things and to tradition. There is very little upward mobility for the same reason. The model of capitalism is based on private ownership of the means of production and operates on the basis of free markets on both the input and output side. The free markets function to coordinate market activity and to achieve an efficient allocation of resources. **Laissez-faire capitalism** is based on the premise of no governmental intervention in the economy. The market will eliminate any unemployment or inflation that occurs. Government needs only to provide the framework for the functioning of the economy and to protect private property. A **command economy** is almost the exact opposite of a market economy. A command economy is based on government ownership of the means of production and the use of planning to take the place of the market. Instead of the market determining the output mix and the allocation of resources, the bureaucracy fulfills this role by determining the output mix and establishing production target for the enterprises, which are publicly owned. The result is inefficiency. A **mixed economy** uses a combination of markets and planning, with the degree of each varying according to country. The real world can be described as mixed economies

The scarcity of resources is the basis for the existence of economics. Economics is defined as a study of how scarce resources are allocated to satisfy unlimited wants. Resources refer to the **four factors of production**: labor, capital, land, and entrepreneurs. Labor refers to anyone who sells his ability to produce goods and services. Capital is anything that is manufactured to be used in the production process. Land refers to the land itself and everything occurring naturally on it, like oil, minerals, and lumber, etc. Entrepreneurship is the ability of an individual to combine the three inputs with his own talents to produce a viable good or service. The entrepreneur takes the risk and experiences the losses or profits.

The fact that the supply of these resources is finite means that society cannot have as much of everything that it wants. There is a constraint on production and consumption and on the kinds of goods and services that can be produced and consumed. **Scarcity** means that choices have to be made. If society decides to produce more of one good, this means that there are fewer resources available for the production of other goods. Assume a society can produce two goods, good X and good Y. The society uses resources in the production of each good. If producing one unit of good X results in an amount of resources used to produce three units of good Y, then producing one more unit of good X results in a decrease in 3 units of good Y. In effect, one unit of good X "costs" three units of good Y. This cost is referred to as **opportunity cost**. Opportunity cost is the value of the sacrificed alternative, the value of what had to be given up in order to have the output of good X.

Opportunity cost does not refer just to production. Your opportunity cost of studying with this guide is the value of what you are not doing because you are studying, whether it is watching TV, spending time with family, working, or whatever. Every **choice** has an opportunity cost.

If wants were limited and/or if resources were unlimited, then the concepts of choice and opportunity cost would not exist and neither would the field of economics. There would be enough resources to satisfy the wants of consumers, businesses, and governments. The allocation of resources wouldn't be a problem. Society could have more of both good X and good Y without having to give up anything. There would be no opportunity cost. But this isn't the situation that societies are faced with.

Because resources are scarce, society doesn't want to waste them. Society wants to obtain the most satisfaction it can from the consumption of the goods and services produced with its scarce resources. The members of the society don't want their scarce resources wasted through inefficiency. This indicates that producers must choose an efficient production process, which is the lowest cost means of production. High costs mean wasted resources, and we then have the situation given above with good X and good Y. Consumers also don't want society's resources wasted by producing goods that they don't want.
How do producers know what goods consumers want? Consumers buy the goods they want and vote with their dollar spending. A desirable good, one that consumers want, earns profits. A good that incurs losses is a good that society doesn't want its resources wasted on. This signals to the producer that society wants its resources used in another way.

Economic systems refer to the arrangements a society has devised to answer what are known as the Three Questions: What goods to produce, how to produce the goods, and for whom are the goods being produced or how is the allocation of the output determined. Different economic systems answer these questions in different ways. These are the different "isms" that exist that define the method of resource and output allocation.

A **market economy** answers these questions in terms of **demand and supply** and the use of markets. Consumers vote for the products they want with their dollar spending. Goods acquiring enough dollar votes are profitable, signaling to the producers that society wants its scarce resources used in this way. This is how the "what" question is answered. The producer then hires inputs in accordance with the goods that consumers want, looking for the most efficient or lowest cost method of production. The lower the firm's costs for any given level of revenue, the higher the firm's profits. This is the way in which the "how" question is answered in a market economy.

The opposite of the market economy is called the **centrally planned economy.** This used to be called Communism, even though the term is not correct in a strict Marxian sense. In a planned economy, the means of production are publicly owned with little, if any, public ownership. Instead of the Three Questions being solved by markets, these economies have a planning authority that makes the decisions in place of markets. The planning authority decides what will be produced and how. Since most planned economies direct resources into the production of capital and military goods, little remains for consumer goods and the result is chronic shortage. Price functions as an accounting measure and does not reflect scarcity. The former Soviet Union and most of the Eastern Bloc countries were planned economies of this sort.

In between the two extremes is **market socialism**. This is a mixed economic system that uses markets and planning. Planning is usually used to direct resources at the upper levels of the economy, with markets being used to determine prices of consumer goods and wages. This kind of economic system answers the three questions with planning and markets. The former Yugoslavia was a market socialist economy.

COMPETENCY 9.0   UNDERSTAND DIFFERENT PERSPECTIVES AND
                  PRIORITIES UNDERLYING HISTORICAL OR
                  CONTEMPORARY ARGUMENTS, INTERPRETATIONS,
                  EXPLANATIONS, OR DEVELOPMENTS.

**Skill 9.1   Identify the values implicit in given political, economic, social,
or religious points of view.**

Social and political movements are group actions in which large informal groups,
persons, and organizations focus on specific social or political issues and work for
either implementing or undoing something. Social movements originated in
England and North America during the first decades of the 19th century. Several
types of social and political movements are often identified and distinguished by
key factors:

1. Distinguished by *Scope*
   (a) reform movements aim to change some norms.
   (b) radical movements seek to change some value systems.

2. Distinguished by *Type of Change*
   (a) innovation movements attempt to introduce new norms or values.
   (b) conservative movements want to preserve existing norms or values.

3. Distinguished by *Target group*
   (a) group-focus movements attempt to affect either society in general or
   specific groups.
   (b) individual-focused movements seek to transform individuals.

4. Distinguished by *Method of action*
   (a) peaceful movements.
   (b) violent movements.

5. Distinguished by *time*
   (a) Old movements – prior to the 20th century.
   (b) New movements – since the second half of the 20th century.

6. Distinguished by *Range*
   (a) global movements.
   (b) local movements.

The role of religion in political movements or as a basis for political action can be
quite varied, depending upon the religion and the exigencies of the time. In
general, one's interpretation of how people should act within the political sphere
will take one of three approaches: (1) withdrawal from politics (and sometimes
from the world), (2) quietism, and (3) activism.

Religion has always been a factor in American life. Many early settlers came to America in search of religious freedom. Religion, particularly Christianity, was an essential element of the value and belief structure shared by the Founding Fathers. Yet, the Constitution prescribes a separation of church and state. Religion is a basis for the actions of believers, no matter which religion is practiced or embraced. Because religion determines values and ethics, it influences individuals and groups to work to change conditions that are perceived to be wrong.

The **First Great Awakening** was a religious movement within American Protestantism in the 1730s and 1740s. This was primarily a movement among Puritans seeking a return to strict interpretation of morality and values and emphasizing the importance and power of personal religious or spiritual experience. Many historians believe the First Great Awakening unified the people of the original colonies and supported the independence of the colonists.

The **Second Great Awakening** (the Great Revival) was a broad movement within American Protestantism that led to several kinds of activities that were distinguished by region and denomination. In general terms, the Second Great Awakening, which began in the 1820s, was a time of recognition that "awakened religion" must weed out sin on both a personal and a social level. It inspired a wave of social activism. In New England, the Congregationalists established missionary societies to evangelize the West. Publication and education societies arose, most notably, the American Bible Society. This social activism gave rise to the temperance movement, prison reform efforts, and help for the handicapped and mentally ill. This period was particularly notable for the abolition movement.

The **Third Great Awakening** (the Missionary Awakening) gave rise to the Social Gospel Movement. This period (1858 to 1908) resulted in a massive growth in membership of all major Protestant denominations through their missionary activities. This movement was partly a response to claims that the Bible was fallible. Many churches attempted to reconcile or change biblical teaching to fit scientific theories and discoveries. Colleges associated with Protestant churches began to appear rapidly throughout the nation. In terms of social and political movements, the Third Great Awakening was the most expansive and profound. Coinciding with many changes in production and labor, it won battles against child labor and stopped the exploitation of women in factories. Compulsory elementary education for children came from this movement, as did the establishment of a set work day. Much was also done to protect and rescue children from abandonment and abuse, to improve the care of the sick, to prohibit the use of alcohol and tobacco, and to address numerous other "social ills."

Skill 9.2   **Recognize the motives, beliefs, and interests that inform differing political, economic, social, or religious points of view.**

Americans had good reason to fear the emergence of political parties. They had witnessed how parties worked in Great Britain. Parties, called "factions" in Britain, thus Washington's warning, were made up of a few people who schemed to win favors from the government. They were more interested in their own personal profit and advantage than in the public good. Thus, the new American leaders were very interested in keeping factions from forming. It was, ironically, disagreements between two of Washington's chief advisors, **Thomas Jefferson** and **Alexander Hamilton,** who spurred the formation of the first political parties in the newly formed United States of America.

By the time Washington retired from office in 1796, the new political parties would come to play an important role in choosing his successor. Each party put up its own candidates for office. The election of 1796 was the first one in which political parties played a role; a role that, for better or worse, has continued to play in various forms since American history began. By the beginning of the 1800s, the Federalist Party, torn by internal divisions, began suffering a decline. The election in 1800 of Thomas Jefferson as President, Hamilton's bitter rival, and the death of its leader, Alexander Hamilton, in an 1804 duel with Aaron Burr marked the beginning of the collapse of the Federalist Party.

By 1816, after losing a string of important elections, (Jefferson was re-elected in 1804, and James Madison, a Democratic-Republican, was elected in 1808), the Federalist Party ceased to be an effective political force and soon passed off the national stage.

By the late 1820s, new political parties had grown up. The **Democratic-Republican** Party, or simply the **Republican** Party, had been the major party for many years, but differences within it about the direction the country was headed in caused a split after 1824. Those who favored strong national growth took the name **Whigs** after a similar party in Great Britain and united around then President John Quincy Adams. Many business people in the Northeast as well as some wealthy planters in the South supported it.

Those who favored slower growth and were more worker and small farmer-oriented, went on to form the new Democratic Party led by Andrew Jackson, who later became President. It is the forerunner of today's party of the same name.

In the mid-1850s, the slavery issue was beginning to heat up, and, in 1854, those opposed to slavery, the Whigs, and some Northern Democrats opposed to slavery united to form the Republican Party. Before the Civil War, the Democratic Party was more heavily represented in the South and was thus pro-slavery for the most part.

Thus, by the time of the Civil War, the present form of the major political parties had been formed. Though there would sometimes be drastic changes in ideology and platforms over the years, no other political parties would manage to gain enough strength to seriously challenge the "Big Two" parties.

The Indian Removal Act of 1830 authorized the government to negotiate treaties with Native Americans to provide land west of the Mississippi River in exchange for lands east of the river. This policy resulted in the relocation of more than 100,000 Native Americans. Theoretically, the treaties were expected to result in voluntary relocation of the native people. In fact, however, many of the native chiefs were forced to sign the treaties.

After the Civil War, the **Emancipation Proclamation** in 1863 and the 13th Amendment in 1865 ended slavery in the United States, but these measures did not erase the centuries of racial prejudices among whites that held blacks to be inferior in intelligence and morality. These prejudices, along with fear of economic competition from newly freed slaves, led to a series of state laws that permitted or required businesses, landlords, school boards, and others to physically segregate blacks and whites in their everyday lives.

Segregation laws were foreshadowed in the **Black Codes**, strict laws proposed by some southern states during the Reconstruction Period that sought, essentially, to recreate the conditions of pre-war servitude. Under these codes, blacks were to remain subservient to their white employers and were subject to fines and beatings if they failed to work. Freedmen, as newly freed slaves were called, were afforded some civil rights protection during the Reconstruction period; however, beginning around 1876, so called Redeemer governments began to take office in southern states after the removal of Federal troops that had supported Reconstruction goals. The Redeemer state legislatures began passing segregation laws which came to be known as Jim Crow laws.

The Jim Crow laws varied from state to state, but the most significant of them required separate school systems and libraries for blacks and whites and separate ticket windows, waiting rooms, and seating areas on trains and, later, other public transportation. Restaurant owners were permitted (or, sometimes, required) to provide separate entrances and tables and counters for blacks and whites in order that the two races would not see one another while dining. Public parks and playgrounds were constructed for each race. Landlords were not allowed to mix black and white tenants in apartment houses in some states. The Jim Crow laws were given credibility in 1896 when the Supreme Court handed down its decision in the case *Plessy vs. Ferguson.* In 1890, Louisiana had passed a law requiring separate train cars for blacks and whites. To challenge this law, in 1892, Homer Plessy, a man who had a black great grandparent and so was considered legally "black" in that state, purchased a ticket in the white section and took his seat. Upon informing the conductor that he was black, he was told to move to the black car. He refused and was arrested. His case was eventually elevated to the Supreme Court.

The Court ruled against Plessy, thereby ensuring that the Jim Crow laws would continue to proliferate and be enforced. The Court held that segregating races was not unconstitutional as long as the facilities for each were identical. This became known as the "separate but equal" principle. In practice, facilities were seldom equal. Black schools were not funded at the same level, for instance. Streets and parks in black neighborhoods were not maintained.

Legal segregation was a part of life for generations of Americans until the separate but equal fallacy was finally challenged in 1954, in another Supreme Court case, *Brown vs. Board of Education.* This case arose when a Topeka, Kansas man attempted to enroll his third-grade daughter in a segregated white elementary school and was refused. In the Court decision, the policy of maintaining separate schools was found to be inherently unequal and unconstitutional.

Even with the new legal interpretation, some states refused to integrate their schools. In Virginia, the state closed some schools rather than integrate them. In Arkansas, Governor Orville Faubus mobilized the National Guard to prevent the integration of Little Rock High School. President Eisenhower sent federal troops to enforce the integration.

Opposition to Jim Crow laws became an important part of the civil rights movement led by **Martin Luther King, Jr**. and others which culminated in the **Civil Rights Act of 1964**. This act ended legal segregation in the United States; however, some forms of de facto segregation continued to exist, particularly in the area of housing.

Paralleling the development of segregation legislation in the mid-nineteenth century was the appearance of organized groups opposed to any integration of blacks into white society. The most notable of these was the Ku Klux Klan.

First organized in the Reconstruction South, the KKK was a loose group made up mainly of former Confederate soldiers who opposed the Reconstruction government and espoused a doctrine of white supremacy. KKK members intimidated and sometimes killed their proclaimed enemies. The first KKK was never completely organized, despite having nominal leadership. In 1871, President Grant took action to use federal troops to halt the activities of the KKK and actively prosecuted them in federal court. Klan activity waned, and the organization disappeared.

In the early years of the American nation, three primary ideas determined American foreign policy:

1. **Isolationism** – The founding fathers and the earliest Americans (after the Revolution) tended to believe that the U.S. had been created and destined for a unique role as what Thomas Jefferson called the "City on the Hill." They understood personal and religious freedom as a unique blessing given by God to the people of the nation. Although many believed that the nation would grow, this expectation did not extend to efforts to plant colonies in other parts of the world.

2. **"No Entangling Alliances"** – George Washington's farewell address had initially espoused the intention of avoiding permanent alliances in any part of the world. This was echoed in Jefferson's inaugural address. In fact, when James Madison led the nation into the war of 1812, he refrained from entering into an alliance with France, which was also at war with England at the time.

3. **Nationalism** – The American experience had created a profound wariness of any encroachment onto the continent by European countries. The Monroe Doctrine was a clear warning: no new colonies in the Americas.

Regionalism can be defined as the political division of an area into partially autonomous regions or as loyalty to the interests of a particular region.

Sectionalism is generally defined as excessive devotion to local interests and customs.

Closely allied to the Second Great Awakening was **the temperance movement**. This movement to end the sale and consumption of alcohol arose from religious beliefs, from the violence many women and children experienced from heavy drinkers, and from the effect of alcohol consumption on the work force. The Society for the Promotion of Temperance was organized in Boston in 1826.

Other social issues were also addressed. It was during this period that efforts were made to transform the prison system and its emphasis on punishment into a penitentiary system that attempted rehabilitation. It was also during this period that Dorothea Dix led a struggle in the North and the South to establish hospitals for the insane. A group of women emerged in the 1840s that was the beginning of the first women's rights movement in the nation's history.

Utopianism is the dream of or the desire to create the perfect society. However by the nineteenth century few believed this was possible. One of the major "causes" of utopianism is the desire for moral clarity. Against the backdrop of the efforts of a young nation to define itself and to ensure the rights and freedoms of its citizens, and within the context of the second great awakening, it becomes quite easy to see how the reform movements, the religious sentiment, and the gathering national storm would lead to the desire to create the perfect society.

The industrial boom produced several very wealthy and powerful "captains of industry" (Andrew Carnegie, John D. Rockefeller, Jay Gould, J.P Morgan, and Philip Armour). While they were envied and respected for their business acumen and success, they were condemned for their exploitation of workers and questionable business practices and were feared because of their power.

While these "captains of industry" were becoming wealthy, the average worker enjoyed some increase in the standard of living. Most workers were required to put in long hours in dangerous conditions doing monotonous work for low wages. Most were not able to afford to participate in the new comforts and forms of entertainment that were becoming available. Farmers believed they were also being exploited by the bankers, suppliers, and the railroads. This produced enough instability to fuel several recessions and two severe depressions.

One result of industrialization was the growth of the **Labor Movement**. There were numerous boycotts and strikes, which often became violent when the police or the militia was called in to stop them. Labor and farmer organizations were became a political force. Industrialization also brought an influx of immigrants from Asia (particularly Chinese and Japanese) and from Europe (particularly European Jews, the Irish, and Russians). High rates of immigration led to the creation of communities in various cities like "little Russia" or "little Italy." Industrialization also led to an overwhelming growth of cities as workers moved closer to their places of work. The economy was booming, but that economy was based on basic needs and luxury goods for which there was to be only limited demand, especially during times of economic recession or depression.

The reforms initiated by these leaders and the spirit of **Progressivism** were far-reaching. Politically, many states enacted the initiative and the referendum. The adoption of the recall occurred in many states. Several states enacted legislation that would undermine the power of political machines. On a national level, the two most significant political changes were (1) the ratification of the 19th Amendment, which required that all U.S. Senators be chosen by popular election, and (2) the ratification of the nineteenth Amendment, which granted women the right to vote.

Until the middle of the nineteenth century, American foreign policy and expansionism were essentially restricted to the North American Continent. America had shown no interest in establishing colonies in other lands. Specifically, the U.S. had stayed out of the rush to claim African territories. The variety of imperialism that found expression under the administrations of McKinley and Theodore Roosevelt was not precisely comparable to the imperialistic goals of European nations. There was a type of idealism in American foreign policy that sought to use military power in territories and other lands only in the interest of human rights and of spreading democratic principles. Much of the concern and involvement in Central and South America and the Caribbean, was to link the two coasts of the nation and to protect the American economy from European encroachment.

Other foreign policy landmarks include the political, economic, and geographic significance of the Panama Canal; the "Open Door" policy with China; Theodore Roosevelt's "Big Stick" Diplomacy; William Howard Taft's "Dollar" Diplomacy; and Woodrow Wilson's Moral Diplomacy.

The **Open Door Policy** refers to maintaining equal commercial and industrial rights for the people of all countries in a particular territory. The Open Door policy generally refers to China, but it has also been used in application to the Congo basin. The policy was first suggested by the U.S., but its basis is the typical nation clause of the treaties made with China after the Opium War (1829-1842). The essential purpose of the policy was to permit equal access to trade for all nations having treaties with China, while protecting the integrity of the Chinese empire. This policy was in effect from about 1900 until the end of WWII. After the war, China was recognized as a sovereign state.

Big Stick Diplomacy was a term adopted from an African proverb, "speak softly and carry a big stick," used to describe President Theodore Roosevelt's policy of the U.S. assuming international police power in the Western Hemisphere. The phrase implied the power to retaliate if necessary. The intention was to safeguard American economic interests in Latin America. The policy led to the expansion of the U.S. Navy and to greater involvement in world affairs. Should any nation in the Western Hemisphere become vulnerable to European control because of political or economic instability, the U.S. had the right and obligation to intervene.

Dollar Diplomacy describes U.S. efforts under President Taft to extend its foreign policy goals in Latin America and East Asia via economic power. The designation derives from Taft's claim that U.S. interests in Latin America had changed from "warlike and political" to "peaceful and economic." Taft justified this policy in terms of protecting the Panama Canal. The practice of dollar diplomacy was from time to time anything but peaceful, particularly in Nicaragua. When revolts or revolutions occurred, the U.S. sent troops to resolve the situation. Immediately upon resolution, bankers were sent in to loan money to the new regimes.

Wilson repudiated the dollar-diplomacy approach to foreign policy within weeks of his inauguration. Wilson's "moral diplomacy" became the model for American foreign policy to this day. Wilson envisioned a federation of democratic nations, believing that democracy and representative government were the foundation stones of world stability. Specifically, he saw Great Britain and the United States as the champions of self-government and the promoters of world peace. Wilson's beliefs and actions set in motion an American foreign policy that was dedicated to the interests of all humanity rather than merely American national interests. Wilson promoted the power of free trade and international commerce as the key to enlarging the national economy into world markets as a means of acquiring a voice in world events. This approach to foreign policy was based on three elements: (1) maintaining a combat-ready military to meet the needs of the nation, (2) promoting democracy abroad, and (3) improving the U.S. economy through international trade. Wilson believed that democratic states would be less inclined to threaten U.S. interests.

Within the context of fear of radicalism, rampant racism, and efforts to repress various groups within the population; it is not surprising that several groups were formed to protect the civil rights and liberties guaranteed to all citizens by the U.S. Constitution. The *American Civil Liberties Union* was formed in 1920. It was originally an outgrowth of the American Union against Militarism, which had opposed American involvement in WWI and provided legal advice and assistance for conscientious objectors and for those who were being prosecuted under the Espionage Act of 1917 and the Sedition Act of 1918. With the name change, there was attention to additional concerns and activities. The agency began to try to protect immigrants threatened with deportation and citizens threatened with prosecution for communist activities and agendas. They also opposed efforts to repress the Industrial Workers of the World and other labor unions.

The National Association for the Advancement of Colored People (NAACP) was founded in 1909 to assist African Americans. In the early years, the work of the organization focused on working through the courts to overturn "Jim Crow" statutes that legalized racial discrimination. The group organized voters to oppose Woodrow Wilson's efforts to weave racial segregation into federal government policy. Between WWI and WWII, much energy was devoted to stopping the lynching of blacks throughout the country.

The Anti-Defamation League was created in 1913 to stop discrimination against the Jewish people. Its charter states, "Its ultimate purpose is to secure justice and fair treatment to all citizens alike and to put an end forever to unjust and unfair discrimination against and ridicule of any sect or body of citizens. The organization has historically opposed all groups considered anti-Semitic and/or racist. This has included the Ku Klux Klan, the Nazis, and a variety of others.

The end of World War I and the decade of the 1920s saw tremendous changes in the United States, signifying the beginning of its development into its modern form. The shift from farm to city life was occurring in tremendous numbers. Social changes and problems were occurring at such a fast pace that it was extremely difficult and perplexing for many Americans to adjust to them. Politically, the 18th Amendment to the Constitution, the so-called Prohibition Amendment, prohibited selling alcoholic beverages throughout the U.S., resulting in problems affecting all aspects of society. The passage of the Nineteenth Amendment gave to women the right to vote in all elections. The decade of the 1920s also showed a marked change in roles and opportunities for women, with more and more of them seeking and finding careers outside the home. They began to think of themselves as the equals of men instead of as simply housewives and mothers.

The influence of the automobile, the entertainment industry, and the rejection of the morals and values of pre-World War I life resulted in the fast-paced "Roaring Twenties". There were significant effects on events leading to the Depression-era 1930s and another world war. Many Americans greatly desired the pre-war life and supported political policies and candidates in favor of the return to what was considered normal. It was desired to end government's strong role and to adopt a policy of isolating the country from world affairs.

Changes in American immigration policy in the 1920s.

Immigration has played a crucial role in the growth and settlement of the United States from the start. With a large interior territory to fill and ample opportunity, the US encouraged immigration throughout most of the nineteenth century, maintaining an almost completely open policy. Famines in Ireland and Germany in the 1840s resulted in over 3.5 million immigrants from these two countries alone between the years of 1830 and 1860.

Following the Civil War, rapid expansion in rail transportation brought the interior states within easy reach of new immigrants who still came primarily from Western Europe and entered the US on the East Coast. As immigration increased, several states adopted individual immigration laws, and, in 1875, the US Supreme Court declared immigration a federal matter. Following a huge surge in European immigration in 1880, the United States began to regulate immigration, first by passing a tax to new immigrants, then by instituting literacy requirements and barring those with mental or physical illness. Even with these new limits in place, immigration remained relatively open in the US for those from European countries and increased steadily until World War I.

With much of Europe left in ruins after WWI, immigration to the US exploded in the years following the war. In 1920 and 1921, some 800,000 new immigrants arrived. The US responded to this sudden shift in the makeup of new immigrants with a quota system, first enacted by Congress in 1921. This system limited immigration in proportion to the ethnic groups that were already settled in the US according to previous census records. This national-origins policy was extended and further defined by Congress in 1924.

This policy remained the official policy of the US for the next 40 years. Occasional challenges to the law from non-white immigrants re-affirmed that the intention of the policy was to limit immigration primarily to white, western Europeans, who the government felt were most likely to assimilate into American culture. Strict limitations on Chinese immigration was extended throughout the period and was not relaxed until 1940. In 1965, Congress overhauled immigration policy, removing the quotas and replacing them with a preference- based system. Now, immigrants reuniting with family members and those with special skills or education were given preference. As a result, immigration from Asian and African countries began to increase. The 40-year legacy of the 1920s immigration restrictions had a direct and dramatic impact on the makeup of modern American society.

The Great Depression and the New Deal

The 1929 Stock Market Crash was the powerful event that is generally interpreted as the beginning of the Great Depression in America. Although the crash of the stock market was unexpected, it was not without identifiable causes. The 1920s had been a decade of social and economic growth and hope. The other factor contributing to the Great Depression was the economic condition of Europe. The U.S. was lending money to European nations to rebuild. Many of these countries used this money to purchase U.S. food and manufactured goods. But they were not able to pay off their debts. While the U.S. was providing money, food, and goods to Europe, however, it was not willing to buy European goods. Trade barriers were enacted to maintain a favorable trade balance.

Several other factors are cited by some scholars as contributing to the Great Depression. First, in 1929, the Federal Reserve increased interest rates. Second, some believe that as interest rates rose and the stock market began to decline, people began to hoard money.

In September 1929, stock prices began to slip somewhat, yet people remained optimistic. On Monday, October 21, prices began to fall quickly. The volume traded was so high that the tickers were unable to keep up. Investors were frightened, and they started selling very quickly. This caused further collapse. For the next two days prices stabilized somewhat. On **Black Thursday**, October 24, prices plummeted again. By this time investors had lost confidence. On Friday and Saturday an attempt to stop the crash was made by some leading bankers. But on Monday the 28th, prices began to fall again, declining by 13% in one day. The next day, **Black Tuesday, October 29**, saw 16.4 million shares traded. Stock prices fell so far, that at many times no one was willing to buy at any price.

Unemployment quickly reached 25% nation-wide. People thrown out of their homes created makeshift domiciles of cardboard, scraps of wood, and tents. With unmasked reference to President Hoover, who was quite obviously overwhelmed by the situation and incompetent to deal with it, these communities were called "**Hoovervilles**." Families stood in bread lines, rural workers left the dust bowl of the plains to search for work in California, and banks failed. More than 100,000 businesses failed between 1929 and 1932. The despair that swept the nation left an indelible scar on all who endured the Depression.

When the stock market crashed, businesses collapsed. Without demand for products, other businesses and industries collapsed. This set in motion a domino effect, bringing down the businesses and industries that provided raw materials or components to these industries. Hundreds of thousands became jobless. Then the jobless often became homeless. Desperation prevailed. Little had been done to assess the toll that hunger, inadequate nutrition, or starvation took on the health of those who were children during this time. Indeed, food was cheap, relatively speaking, but there was little money to buy it.

Hoover's bid for re-election in 1932 failed. The new president, Franklin D. Roosevelt, won the White House on his promise to the American people of a "New Deal." Upon assuming the office, Roosevelt and his advisers immediately launched a massive program of innovation and experimentation to try to bring the Depression to an end and to get the nation back on track. Congress gave the President unprecedented power to act to save the nation. During the next eight years, the most extensive and broadly-based legislation in the nation's history was enacted. The legislation was intended to accomplish three goals: relief, recovery, and reform.

The first step in the "**New Deal**" was to relieve suffering. This was accomplished through a number of job-creation projects. The second step, the recovery aspect, was to stimulate the economy. The third step was to create social and economic change through innovative legislation.

To provide economic stability and prevent another crash, Congress passed the **Glass-Steagall Act**, which separated banking and investing. The Securities and Exchange Commission was created to regulate dangerous speculative practices on Wall Street. The Wagner Act guaranteed a number of rights to workers and unions in an effort to improve worker-employer relations. The **Social Security Act of 1935** established pensions for the aged and infirm and a system of unemployment insurance.

Many of the steps taken by the Roosevelt administration have had far-reaching effects. They alleviated the economic disaster of the Great Depression, they enacted controls that would mitigate the risk of another stock market crash, and they provided greater security for workers. The nation's economy, however, did not fully recover until America entered World War II.

By far the worst natural disaster of the decade came to be known as the **Dust Bowl.** Due to severe and prolonged drought in the Great Plains and to previous reliance on inappropriate farming techniques, a series of devastating dust storms occurred in the 1930s that resulted in destruction, economic ruin for many, and dramatic ecological change.

Crops were ruined, the land was destroyed, and people either lost or abandoned homes and farms. Fifteen percent of Oklahoma's population left. Because so many of the migrants were from Oklahoma, the migrants came to be called "**Okies**" no matter where they came from. Estimates of the number of people displaced by this disaster range from 300,000 or 400,000 to 2.5 million.

There were several major events or actions that are particularly important to the history of **organized labor** during this decade:

- The Davis-Bacon Act provided that employees of contractors and subcontractors on public construction should be paid the prevailing wages (1931).

- The Anti-Injunction Act prohibited Federal injunctions in most labor disputes (1932).

- Wisconsin created the first unemployment insurance act in the country (1932).

- The Wagner-Peyser Act created the United States Employment Service within the Department of Labor (1933).

- The Wagner Act (The National Labor Relations Act) established a legal basis for unions, set collective bargaining as a matter of national policy required by the law, provided for secret ballot elections for choosing unions, and protected union members from employer intimidation and coercion. This law was later amended by the Taft-Hartley Act (1947) and by the Landrum Griffin Act (1959).

- The Social Security Act was approved (1935).

- The Committee for Industrial Organization (CIO) was formed within the AFL to carry unionism to the industrial sector (1935).

- The United Rubber Workers staged the first sit-down strike (1936).

- The United Auto Workers used the sit-down strike against General Motors (1936).

- The Public Contracts Act (the Walsh-Healey Act) of 1936 established labor standards, including minimum wages, overtime pay, child and convict labor provisions, and safety standards on federal contracts.

- The Fair Labor Standards Act created a $0.25 minimum wage, stipulated time-and-a-half pay for hours over 40 per week.

- The CIO becomes the Congress of Industrial Organizations.

Because of **unstable economic** conditions and political unrest, harsh dictatorships arose in several countries, especially where there was no history of experience in democratic government. Countries such as Germany, Japan, and Italy began to **aggressively expand their borders** and acquire additional territory.

In all, 59 nations became embroiled in World War II, which began September 1, 1939 and ended September 2, 1945. These dates include both the European and Pacific Theaters of war. The horrible and tragic results of this second global conflagration were more deaths and more destruction than in any other armed conflict. It completely uprooted and displaced millions of people. The end of the war brought renewed power struggles, especially in Europe and China, with many Eastern European nations as well as China coming under complete control and domination of the Communists, supported and backed by the Soviet Union. With the development and two-time deployment of an atomic bomb against two Japanese cities, the world found itself in the nuclear age. The peace settlement established the United Nations Organization, still existing and operating today.

Harry S. Truman. Truman became president near the end of WWII. He is credited with some of the most important decisions in history. When Japan refused to surrender, Truman authorized the dropping of atomic bombs on Japanese cities dedicated to war support: Hiroshima and Nagasaki. He took to the Congress a 21-point plan that came to be known as the **Fair Deal**. It included expansion of Social Security, a full-employment program, public housing and slum clearance, and a permanent Fair Employment Practices Act. The Truman Doctrine provided support for Greece and Turkey when they were threatened by the Soviet Union. The Marshall Plan (his Secretary of State) stimulated amazing economic recovery for Western Europe. Truman participated in the negotiations that resulted in the formation of the North Atlantic Treaty Organization. He and his administration believed it necessary to support South Korea when it was threatened by the communist government of North Korea. But he contained American involvement in Korea so as not to risk conflict with China or Russia.

Dwight David Eisenhower succeeded Truman. Eisenhower obtained a truce in Korea and worked during his two terms to mitigate the tension of the Cold War. When Stalin died, he was able to negotiate a peace treaty with Russia that neutralized Austria. His domestic policy was a middle road. He continued most of the programs introduced under both the New Deal and the Fair Deal. When desegregation of schools began, he sent troops to Little Rock, Arkansas to enforce desegregation of the schools. He ordered the complete desegregation of the military. During his administration, the Department of Health, Education, and Welfare was established, and the National Aeronautics and Space Administration was formed.

John F. Kennedy is widely remembered for his inaugural address in which the statement was made, "Ask not what your country can do for you – ask what you can do for your country." His campaign pledge was to get America moving again. During his brief presidency, his economic programs created the longest period of continuous expansion in the country since WWII. He wanted the U.S. to again take up the mission as the first country committed to the revolution of human rights. Through the Alliance for Progress and the Peace Corps, the hopes and idealism of the nation reached out to assist developing nations. He was deeply and passionately involved in the cause of equal rights for all Americans, and he drafted new civil rights legislation. He also drafted plans for a broad attack on the systemic problems of privation and poverty. He believed the arts were critical to a society and instituted programs to support the arts. In 1962, Premier Khrushchev and the Soviets decided, as a protective measure for Cuba against an American invasion, to install nuclear missiles on the island. In October, American U-2 spy planes photographed over Cuba what were identified as missile bases under construction. The question facing the White House was how to handle the situation without starting a war. The only recourse was removal of the missile sites and preventing more being set up. Kennedy announced that the U.S. had set up a "quarantine" of Soviet ships heading to Cuba. It was in reality a blockade, but the word itself could not be used publicly because a blockade was actually considered an act of war.

Lyndon B. Johnson assumed the presidency after the assassination of Kennedy. His vision for America was called "A Great Society." He won support in Congress for the largest group of legislative programs in the history of the nation. These included programs Kennedy had been working on at the time of his death, including a new civil rights bill and a tax cut. He defined the "great society" as "a place where the meaning of man's life matches the marvels of man's labor." The legislation enacted during his administration included: an attack on disease, urban renewal, Medicare, aid to education, conservation and beautification, development of economically depressed areas, a war on poverty, voting rights for all, and control of crime and delinquency. Johnson managed an unpopular military action in Vietnam and encouraged the exploration of space. During his administration, the Department of Transportation was formed and the first black, Thurgood Marshall, was nominated and confirmed to the Supreme Court.

Richard Nixon inherited racial unrest and the Vietnam War, from which he extracted the American military. His administration is probably best known for improved relations with both China and the USSR. However, the Watergate scandal divided the country and led to his resignation. His major domestic achievements were the appointment of conservative justices to the Supreme Court, new anti-crime legislation, a broad environmental program, revenue sharing legislation, and ending the draft. Probably the highlight of the foreign policy of President Richard Nixon, after the end of the Vietnam War and withdrawal of troops, was his 1972 trip to China. When the Communists gained control of China in 1949, the policy of the U.S. government was refusal to recognize the Communist government. It regarded as the legitimate government of China to be that of Chiang Kai-shek, exiled on the island of Taiwan.

Gerald Ford was the first Vice President selected under the 25th Amendment. The challenges that faced his administration were a depressed economy, inflation, energy shortages, and the need to champion world peace. Once inflation slowed and recession was the major economic problem, he instituted measures that would stimulate the economy. He tried to reduce the role of the federal government. He reduced business taxes and lessened the controls on business. His international focus was on preventing a major war in the Middle East. He negotiated with Russia limitations on nuclear weapons.

Jimmy Carter strove to make the government "competent and compassionate" in response to the American people and their expectations. The economic situation of the nation was intensely difficult when he took office. Although significant progress was made by his administration in creating jobs and decreasing the budget deficit, inflation and interest rates were nearly at record highs. There were several notable achievements: establishment of a national energy policy to deal with the energy shortage, decontrolling petroleum prices to stimulate production, civil service reform that improved governmental efficiency, deregulation of the trucking and airline industries, the creation of the Department of Education, the framework for peace in the Middle East, the establishment of diplomatic relations with China, and a Strategic Arms Limitation Agreement with the Soviet Union. He expanded the national park system, supported the Social Security system, and appointed a record number of women and minorities to government jobs.

Iran's Ayatollah Khomeini's extreme hatred for the U.S. was the result of the 1953 overthrow of Iran's Mossadegh government, sponsored by the CIA. To make matters worse, the CIA proceeded to train the Shah's ruthless secret police force. So, when the terminally ill exiled Shah was allowed into the U.S. for medical treatment, a fanatical mob, supported and encouraged by Khomeini, stormed into the American embassy, taking the 53 Americans as prisoners,

Ronald Reagan introduced an innovative program that came to be known as the Reagan Revolution. The goal of this program was to reduce the reliance of the American people upon government. The Reagan administration restored the hope and enthusiasm of the nation. His legislative accomplishments include economic growth stimulation, curbing inflation, increasing employment, and strengthening the national defense. He won Congressional support for a complete overhaul of the income tax code in 1986. By the time he left office, there was prosperity in peacetime with no depression or recession. His foreign policy was "peace through strength." Reagan nominated Sandra Day O'Connor as the first female justice on the Supreme Court.

George H. W. Bush was committed to "traditional American values" and to making America a "kinder and gentler nation". During the Reagan administration, Bush held responsibility for anti-drug programs and Federal deregulation. When the Cold War ended and the Soviet Union broke apart, he supported the rise of democracy, but took a position of restraint toward the new nations. Bush also dealt with defense of the Panama Canal and Iraq's invasion of Kuwait, which led to the first Gulf War, known as Desert Storm. Although his international affairs record was strong, he was not able to turn around increased violence in the inner cities and a struggling economy.

William Clinton led the nation in a time of greater peace and economic prosperity than has been experienced at any other time in history. His domestic accomplishments included the lowest inflation in 30 years, the lowest unemployment rate in modern days, the highest home ownership rate in history, lower crime rates in many places, and smaller welfare rolls. He proposed and achieved a balanced budget and a budget surplus.

Since 1941 a number of anti-discrimination laws have been passed by the Congress. These acts have protected the civil rights of several groups of Americans. These laws include:

- Fair Employment Act of 1941
- Civil Rights Act of 1964
- Immigration and Nationality Services Act of 1965
- Voting Rights Act of 1965
- Civil Rights Act of 1968
- Age Discrimination in Employment Act of 1967
- Age Discrimination Act of 1975
- Pregnancy Discrimination Act of 1978
- Americans with Disabilities Act of 1990
- Civil Rights Act of 1991
- Employment Non-Discrimination Act

"Minority rights" encompasses two ideas: the first is the normal individual rights of members of ethnic, racial, class, religious, or sexual minorities; the second is collective rights of minority groups. Various civil rights movements have sought to guarantee that the individual rights of persons are not denied on the basis of being part of a minority group. The effects of these movements may be seen in guarantees of minority representation and affirmative action quotas.

The disability rights movement was a successful effort to guarantee access to public buildings and transportation, equal access to education and employment, and equal protection under the law in terms of access to insurance, and other basic rights of American citizens. As a result of these efforts, public buildings and public transportation must be accessible to persons with disabilities, and discrimination in hiring or housing on the basis of disability is also illegal.

A "prisoners' rights" movement has been working for many years to ensure the basic human rights of persons incarcerated for crimes. Immigrant rights movements have provided for employment and housing rights and have discouraged abuse of immigrants through hate crimes. In some states, immigrant rights movements have led to bi-lingual education and public information access. Another group movement to obtain equal rights is the lesbian, gay, bisexual, and transgender social movement. This movement seeks equal housing, freedom from social and employment discrimination, and equal recognition of relationships under the law.

The women's rights movement is concerned with the freedoms of women as differentiated from broader ideas of human rights. These issues are generally different from those that affect men and boys because of biological conditions or social constructs.

Skill 9.3   Analyze multiple perspectives within U.S. society regarding major historical and contemporary issues.

Analyzing an event or issue from multiple perspectives involves seeking out sources that advocate or express those perspectives and comparing them with one another. Listening to the speeches of Martin Luther King, Jr. provides insight to the perspective of one group of people concerning the issue of civil rights in the U.S. in the 1950s and 1960s. Public statements of George Wallace, an American governor opposed to de-segregation, provides another perspective from the same time period. Looking at the legislation that was proposed at the time and how it came into effect offers a window into the political thinking of the day.

Comparing these perspectives on the matter of civil rights provides information on the key issues that each group was concerned about and gives a fuller picture of the societal changes that were occurring at that time. Analysis of any social event, issue, problem, or phenomenon requires that various perspectives be taken into account in this way.

Humans are social animals who naturally form groups based on familial, cultural, and national lines. Conflicts and differences of opinion are natural between these groups. One source of differing views among groups is ethnocentrism. **Ethnocentrism**, as the word suggests, is the belief that one's own culture is the central and usually superior culture. An ethnocentric view usually considers different practices in other cultures as inferior or even "savage."

Psychologists have suggested that ethnocentrism is a naturally occurring attitude. For the large part, people are most comfortable among other people who share their same upbringing, language, and cultural background and are likely to judge other cultural behaviors as alien or foreign.

Historical developments are likely to affect different groups in different ways, some positively and some negatively. These effects can strengthen the ties that an individual feels to the group he belongs to and solidify differences between groups.

Skill 9.4   Recognize the values or priorities implicit in given public policy positions.

Public policy is the official stance of a government on an issue and is a primary source for studying a society's dominant political beliefs. It can also give insight into a society's cultural values.

The Social Security system of the United States is a program where current workers are required to give a portion of their earnings to the system, which is then paid out to eligible recipients who have reached a certain age and have stopped working. The underlying value behind the system is that society should continue to care for those who can no longer work and that people should be able to retire from working at a certain age.

Skill 9.5   Analyze the perceptions or opinions of observers or participants from different cultures regarding a given world event or development.

Two of the most notable conversions to democracy in the twentieth century were India and Japan. India, one of the most ancient of societies, was most recently a colony of Great Britain. Thanks largely to the efforts of **Mohandas Gandhi** and other activists, India achieved its independence by the mid-twentieth century. The country became a democracy, with a president at the head of a representative government. The change in political theory, however, didn't mean an end to the internal strife that India has seemingly always felt. At the heart of the country's political identity is a religious dichotomy—a struggle between Muslims and Hindus. This religious conflict has continued for many hundreds of years and has certainly not been diminished by the fact that the Indian people can elect their own leaders.

Another huge conflict in the Indian art of the world is with Pakistan over the Kashmir region. The entire area was known as India at various times under various masters, including Great Britain. But the country was partitioned when it was freed, and the result has been a dangerous dispute over political borders that has resulted in much loss of life and the procurement of atomic weapons by both sides. Another main source of internal strife in India is an economic one. India is the world's second most populous country, and a huge number of these people have few or no resources of their own. A half-century of representative government hasn't made much of a difference in the economic prosperity of these people.

Japan, by contrast, has suffered much less religious and political strife since becoming a democracy after its defeat in World War II. The occupying American army instituted a new constitution, which provided for a representative government, and also led efforts to rebuild the country. The result has been, for the most part, an economic powerhouse that is now one of the world's strongest and most wide-ranging economies. Japan has had its periods of economic weakness, of course, but has bounced back each time stronger than ever.

Political divisions on the Korean Peninsula and in Southeast Asia have created intense internal strife of a mostly economic and political nature. North Korea, an authoritarian state, has lived in relative isolation from the rest of the world and has suffered economically from that isolation. South Korea became a democracy after the end of Japanese occupation after World War II and has prospered economically, although the specter of war with North Korea has loomed large for more than 50 years. The two countries did, in fact, go to war in 1950. The resulting three-year conflict involved forces from a handful of other countries, most noticeably China and the United States, and resulted in the status quo geographically. The most notable facet of life in either Korean country is the idea that another war could begin tomorrow. Indeed, an intensely patrolled area known as the Demilitarized Zone (DMZ) serves as the border between the countries. North Korea has become more and more public in its militancy in recent years, perhaps a sign that the country is finally running out of food.

Southeast Asia has also seen its share of strife since the 1950s, most notably in Vietnam, which was once two countries, a mirror image of Korea; the North being Communist and the South being a more representative government. Those two countries began fighting not long after the end of the WWII, and Communist China and the United States again became involved. The war consumed the two countries and most of their neighbors for many years, resulting in horrible economic and social conditions throughout the region for many years afterward. North Vietnam ended up winning the war, absorbing all of South Vietnam into one country, which continues under an authoritarian government, but is a bit of an economic powerhouse these days.

COMPETENCY 10.0 UNDERSTANDING AND APPLYING SKILLS, PRINCIPLES, AND PROCEDURES ASSOCIATED WITH INQUIRY, PROBLEM SOLVING, AND DECISION MAKING IN HISTORY AND THE SOCIAL SCIENCES.

Skill 10.1 Analyze a description of research results to identify additional unanswered questions or to determine potential problems in research methodology.

A clearly presented description of research results will spell out what question the researchers hoped to answer. Analyzing research results includes comparing the information given as it relates to this initial question. One must also consider the methods used to gather the data and whether they truly measure what the researchers claim they do.

A research project that sets out to measure the effect of a change in average temperature on the feeding habits of birds, for instance, should use appropriate measurements, such as weather observations and observations of the birds in question. Measuring rainfall would not be an appropriate method for this research because it is not related to the primary area of research. If, during the experiment, it appeared that rainfall may be affecting the research, a researcher should design another experiment to investigate this additional question.

Skill 10.2 Determine the relevance or sufficiency of given information for supporting or refuting a point of view.

Making a decision based on a set of given information requires a careful interpretation of the information to decide the strength of the evidence supplied and what it means.

A chart showing that the number of people of foreign birth living in the U.S. has increased annually over the last ten years might allow one to make conclusions about population growth and changes in the relative sizes of ethnic groups in the U.S. The chart would not give information about the reason the number of foreign-born citizens increased or address matters of immigration status. Conclusions in these areas would be invalid based on this information.

In the court of **public opinion**, the newspaper or radio offers politicians a fairly easy way to give information for supporting or refuting a point of view. Television changed all that with its visual record of events. The proliferation of cable and satellite television channels has made a variety of venues available to lawmakers and others who wish to share their opinions. The Internet offers a vast, heterogeneous world of opportunities. Internet opportunities include not just news websites, but personal websites and blogs, public opinion pieces that may or may not be true.

The key thing to remember about information on Web pages is that they might not have undergone the sort of scrutiny as comparable efforts released by major media outlets (newspapers, radio, and television) are subjected to. Those media formats have built-in safety officers called editors who will verify information before it is released to the world. In contrast, to blog all you need is access to a Web-enabled computer and time to write a column. Bloggers routinely do not use editors or run their copy by anyone else before publishing it; as such, they have lower standards of professionalism overall and need to be regarded as somewhat suspect.

Public officials will hire one or more people or perhaps a whole department or an entire business to conduct **public relations**, which are efforts intended to make the lawmakers look good in the eyes of their constituents. A public relations person or firm will have an overreaching goal of satisfying the lawmaker who provides compensation and will gladly write press releases, arrange media events (like tours of schools or soup kitchens), and, basically, do everything else to keep promote that person. This includes making the lawmaker's position on important issues known to the public. Gauging what constituents think about the issues of the day is an important consideration for political candidates at re-election time-.

Skill 10.3   Assess the reliability of sources of information cited in historical or contemporary accounts or arguments, and determine whether specific conclusions or generalizations are supported by verifiable evidence.

Primary sources include the following kinds of materials:

Documents that reflect the immediate, everyday concerns of people: memoranda, bills, deeds, charters, newspaper reports, pamphlets, graffiti, popular writings, journals or diaries, records of decision-making bodies, letters, receipts, snapshots, etc.

Theoretical writings reflecting care and consideration in composition and an attempt to convince or persuade. The topic will generally be deeper and more pervasive values than is the case with "immediate" documents. These may include newspaper or magazine editorials, sermons, political speeches, philosophical writings, etc.

Narrative accounts of events, ideas, trends, etc. written with intention by a contemporary of the events described.

Statistical data, although statistics may be misleading.

Literature and nonverbal materials, novels, stories, poetry, and essays from the period; and coins, archaeological artifacts, and art produced during the period.

Guidelines for the use of primary resources:

1. Be certain that you understand how language was used at the time of writing and that you understand the context in which the item was produced.
2. Do not read history blindly; but be certain that you understand both explicit and implicit references in the material.
3. Read the entire text you are reviewing; do not simply extract a few sentences to read.
4. Although anthologies of materials may help you to identify primary source materials, the full, original text should be consulted.

Secondary sources include the following kinds of materials:

- Books written on the basis of primary materials about the period of time.
- Books written on the basis of primary materials about persons who played a major role in the events under consideration.
- Books and articles written on the basis of primary materials about the culture, the social norms, the language, and the values of the period.
- Quotations from primary sources.
- Statistical data on the period.
- The conclusions and inferences of other historians.
- Multiple interpretations of the ethos of the time.

Guidelines for the use of secondary sources:

- Do not rely upon only a single secondary source.
- Check facts and interpretations against primary sources whenever possible.
- Do not accept the conclusions of other historians uncritically.
- Place greatest reliance on secondary sources created by the best and most respected scholars.
- Do not use the inferences of other scholars as if they were facts.
- Ensure that you recognize any bias that writers bring to their interpretation of history.
- Understand the primary point of the book as a basis for evaluating the relevance of the material presented in it to your topic.

Skill 10.4 Evaluate the appropriateness of specific sources to meet given information needs.

For additional information see Skill 11.2 and Skill 11.3.

Libraries of all sorts are valuable when conducting research, and almost all have digitalized search systems to assist in finding information on almost any subject. Even so, the **Internet,** with powerful search engines like Google readily available, can retrieve information that doesn't exist in libraries or, if it does exist, is much more difficult to retrieve.

Encyclopedias are reference materials that appear in book or electronic form. Encyclopedias can be considered general or specific. They are good first sources of information.

Almanacs provide statistical information on various topics. Typically, these references are rather specific. They often cover a specific period of time. One famous example is the *Farmer's Almanac.* This annual publication summarizes, among many other things, weather conditions for the previous year.

Bibliographies contain references for further research. Bibliographies are usually organized topically. They help point people to the in-depth resources they will need for a complete view of a topic.

Conducting a research project once involved the use of punch cards, microfiche, and other manual means of storing the data in a retrievable fashion. No more. With high-powered computers available to anyone who chooses to conduct research, the organizing of the data in a retrievable fashion has been revolutionized. Creating multi-level folders, copying and pasting into the folders, making ongoing additions to the bibliography at the very time that a source is consulted, and using search-and-find functions make this stage of the research process go much faster with less frustration and a decrease in the likelihood that important data might be overlooked.

Serious research requires high-level analytical skills when it comes to processing and interpreting data. A degree in statistics or at least a graduate-level concentration is very useful. However, a team approach to a research project will include a statistician in addition to those members who are knowledgeable in the social sciences.

The world of social science research has never been so open to new possibilities. Where our predecessors were unable to tread for fear of exceeding the limits of the available data, data access and transfer, analytic routines, or computing power; today's social scientists can advance with confidence. Advances in technology can free social scientists from the tyranny of simplification that has often hampered attempts to grasp the complexity of the world.

Skill 10.5   Distinguish between unsupported and informed expressions of opinion.

"The sky is blue" or "the sky looks like rain"; one is a fact, and the other is an opinion. This is because one is **readily provable by objective empirical data**, while the other is a **subjective evaluation based upon personal bias**. This means that facts are things that can be proved by the usual means of study and experimentation. We can look and see the color of the sky. Since the shade we are observing is expressed as the color blue and is an accepted norm, the observation that the sky is blue is therefore a fact. (Of course, this depends on other external factors such as time and weather conditions).

This brings us to our next idea: that it looks like rain. This is a subjective observation in that one individual's perception will differ from another. What looks like rain to one person will not necessarily look like that to another.

This is an important concept to understand since much of what actually is studied in political science is, in reality, simply the opinions of various political theorists and philosophers. The truth of their individual philosophies is demonstrated by how well they (if and when they have been tried) work in the so called "real world."

The question thus remains as to how to differentiate fact from opinion. The best and only way is to ask oneself if what is being stated can be proved from other sources, by other methods, or by the simple process of **reasoning**.

Historians use primary sources from the actual time they are studying whenever possible. Ancient Greek records of interaction with Egypt, letters from an Egyptian ruler to regional governors, and inscriptions from the Fourteenth Egyptian Dynasty are all primary sources created at or near the actual time being studied. Letters from a nineteenth century Egyptologist would not be considered as primary sources because they were created thousands of years after the fact and may not actually be about the subject being studied.

The resources used in the study of history can be divided into two major groups: **primary sources** and **secondary sources**.

Primary sources are works and records that were created during the period being studied or immediately after it. Secondary sources are works written significantly after the period being studied and based upon primary sources. "Primary sources are the basic materials that provide the raw data and information for the historian. Secondary sources are the works that contain the explications of, and judgments on, this primary material." [Source: Norman F Cantor & Richard I. Schneider. "HOW TO STUDY HISTORY," Harlan Davidson, Inc., 1967, pp. 23-24.]

COMPETENCY 11.0   UNDERSTAND AND INTERPRET VISUAL
                   REPRESENTATIONS OF HISTORICAL AND SOCIAL
                   SCIENTIFIC INFORMATION.

Skill 11.1   Translate written or graphic information from one form to the other.

For further information see Skill 11.3.

To apply information obtained from **graphs,** one must understand the two major reasons why graphs are used:

1. To present a model or theory visually in order to show how two or more variables interrelate.

2. To present real world data visually in order to show how two or more variables interrelate.

Most often used are those known as **bar graphs** and **line graphs**. Graphs themselves are most useful when one wishes to demonstrate the sequential increase or decrease of a variable or to show specific correlations between two or more variables in a given circumstance.

Most common is the **bar graph** because it is easy to see and understand a visual showing the difference in a given set of variables. However, it is limited in that it can not really show the actual proportional increase or decrease of each given variable to each other (In order to show a decrease, a bar graph must show the "bar" under the starting line, thus removing the ability to really show how the various different variables would relate to each other).

Thus, in order to accomplish this, one must use a **line graph**. Line graphs can be of two types, a **linear** or a **non-linear** graph. A linear line graph uses a series of straight lines a non-linear line graph uses a curved line. Though the lines can be either straight or curved, all of the lines are called **curves**.

A line graph uses a number line or **axis.** The numbers are generally placed in order, equal distances from one another, and the number line is used to represent a number, degree, or some such other variable at an appropriate point on the line. Two lines are used and intersect at a specific point. They are referred to as the X-axis and the Y-axis. The Y-axis is a vertical line, and the X-axis is a horizontal line. Together they form a **coordinate system**. The difference between a point on the line of the X-axis and the Y-axis is called the **slope** of the line, or the change in the value on the vertical axis divided by the change in the value on the horizontal axis. The Y-axis number is called the rise and the X-axis number is called the **run**, thus the equation for slope is:

SLOPE = RISE - (Change in value on the vertical axis)
RUN - (Change in value on the horizontal axis)

The slope tells the amount of increase or decrease of a given **specific** variable. When using two or more variables one can plot the amount of difference between them in any given situation. This makes presenting information on a line graph more involved. It also makes it more informative and accurate than a simple bar graph. Knowledge of the term slope and what it is and how it is measured helps us to describe verbally the pictures we are seeing visually. For example, if a curve is said to have a slope of "zero", you should picture a flat line. If a curve has a slope of "one", you should picture a rising line that makes a 45-degree angle with the horizontal and vertical axis lines.

The preceding examples are of **linear** (straight line) curves. With **non-linear** curves (the ones that really do curve), the slope of the curve is constantly changing, so we must then understand that the slope of the non-linear curved line will be at a specific point. How is this done? The slope of a non-linear curve is determined by the slope of a straight line that intersects the curve at that specific point. In all graphs, an upward sloping line represents a direct relationship between the two variables. A downward slope represents an inverse relationship between the two variables. In reading any graph, one must always be very careful to understand what is being measured, what can be deduced, and what cannot be deduced from the given graph.

To use **charts** correctly, one should remember the reasons one uses graphs. The general ideas are similar. It is usually a question as to which, a graph or chart, is more capable of adequately portraying the information one wants to illustrate. One can see the difference between them and realize that in many ways graphs and charts are interrelated. One of the most common types, because it is easiest to read and understand, even for the lay person, is the **Pie-chart**.

You see pie-charts used often, especially when one is trying to illustrate the differences in percentages among various items or when one is demonstrating the divisions of a whole.

Skill 11.2 Relate information provided in graphic representations to public policy decisions.

Suppose you are preparing for a presentation on the Civil War and you intend to focus on causes, an issue that has often been debated. If you are examining the matter of slavery as a cause, a graph of the increase in the number of slaves by area of the country for the previous 100 years would be very useful in the discussion. If you are focusing on the economic conditions that were driving the politics of the age, graphs of GDP, distribution of wealth geographically and individually, and relationship of wealth to ownership of slaves would be useful. If you are discussing the war in Iraq, detailed maps with geopolitical elements would help clarify not only the day-to-day happenings, but also the historical features that led up to it. A map showing the number of oil fields and where they are situated with regard to the various political factions and charts and showing the output of those fields historically would be useful.

If you are teaching the history of space travel, photos of the most famous astronauts will add interest to the discussion. Graphs showing the growth of the industry and charts showing discoveries and their relationship to the lives of everyday Americans would be helpful.

Geography and history classes are notoriously labeled by students as dull. With all the visual resources available nowadays, those classes have the potential for being the most exciting courses in the curriculum.

Demography is the branch of statistics most concerned with the social well- being of people. **Demographic tables** may include: (1) Analysis of the population on the basis of age, parentage, physical condition, race, occupation, and civil position; giving the actual size and the density of each separate area.
(2) Changes in the population as a result of birth, marriage, and death. (3) Statistics on population movements and their effects and their relations to given economic, social and political conditions. (4) Statistics of crime, illegitimacy, and suicide. (5) Levels of education and economic and social statistics.

Such information is also similar to **vital statistics** and, as such, is indispensable in studying social trends and making important legislative, economic, and social decisions. Such demographic information is gathered from census, registrar reports, and the like; and, by state laws, such information, especially the vital kind, is kept by physicians, attorneys, funeral directors, member of the clergy, and similar professional people. In the United States, such demographic information is compiled, kept, and published by the Public Health Service of the United States Department of Health, Education, and Welfare.

The most important element of this information is the so-called **rate**, which customarily represents the average of births and deaths for a unit of 1000 population over a given calendar year. These general rates are called **crude rates**, which are then sub-divided into *sex, color, age, occupation, locality, etc.* They are then known as **refined rates**.

In examining **statistics** and the sources of statistical data, one must also be aware of the methods of statistical information gathering. For instance, there are many good sources of raw statistical data. Books such as *The Statistical Abstract of the United States,* published by the United States Chamber of Commerce; *The World Fact Book,* published by the Central Intelligence Agency; or *The Monthly Labor Review* published by the United States Department of Labor are excellent examples that contain much raw data.

Many such yearbooks and the like on various topics are readily available from any library or from the government itself. However, knowing how that data and information was gathered is at least as important as the figures themselves.

In collecting any such statistical information and data, care and adequate precautions must always be taken in order to assure that the knowledge obtained is complete and accurate. It is also important to be aware of just how much data is necessary to collect in order to establish the idea that is attempting to be formulated. One important idea to understand is that statistics usually deal with a specific **model**, **hypothesis**, or **theory** that someone is attempting to support. One should be aware that a theory can never actually be proved correct; it can only really be corroborated. (**Corroboration** meaning that the data presented is more consistent with this theory than with any other theory, so it makes sense to use this theory.) One should also be aware of what is known as **correlation** (the joint movement of various data points) does not infer **causation** (the change in one of those data points caused the other data points to change). It is important that one take these aspects into account in order that one can be in a better position to appreciate what the collected data is really saying

Once collected, data must then be arranged, tabulated, and presented to permit ready and meaningful analysis and interpretation. Often, tables, charts, or graphs will be used to present the information in a concise, easy-to-see manner with the information sometimes presented in raw numerical order as well. **Tests of reliability** are performed by researchers bearing in mind the manner in which the data has been collected and the inherent biases of any artificially created model to be used to explain real world events. Indeed the methods used and the inherent biases and reasons actually for doing the study by the individual(s) involved, must never be discounted.

Skill 11.3   Interpret historical or social scientific information provided in one or more graphs, charts, tables, diagrams, or maps.

We use **illustrations** of various sorts because it is often easier to demonstrate a given idea visually instead of orally. Sometimes it is even easier to do so with an illustration than with a written description. This is especially true in the areas of education and research because humans are visually stimulated. It is a fact that any idea presented visually in some manner is usually easier to understand and to comprehend than simply getting it verbally by hearing it or reading it. Among the more common illustrations used are various types of **maps, graphs, and charts**.

Photographs and globes are useful as well, but they are limited in what kind of information that they can show and are rarely used unless, as in the case of a photograph, the photograph is of a particular political figure or depicts a time that one wishes to visualize.

Although maps have advantages over globes and photographs, they do have a major disadvantage. The major problem of all maps comes about because most maps are flat and Earth is a sphere. It is impossible to reproduce exactly on a flat surface an object shaped like a sphere. In order to put Earth's features onto a map, they must be stretched in some way. This stretching is called **distortion.**

Distortion does not mean that maps are wrong; it simply means that they are not perfect representations of Earth or its parts. **Cartographers,** or mapmakers, understand the problems of distortion. They try to design them so that there is as little distortion as possible in the maps.

The process of putting the features of Earth onto a flat surface is called **projection**. All maps are really map projections. There are many different types. Each one deals in a different way with the problem of distortion. Map projections are made in a number of ways. Some are done using complicated mathematics. However, the basic ideas behind map projections can be understood by looking at the three most common types:

(1) **Cylindrical Projections** - These are done by taking a cylinder of paper and wrapping it around a globe. A light is used to project the globe's features onto the paper. Distortion is least where the paper touches the globe. For example, suppose that the paper was wrapped so that it touched the globe at the equator; the map from this projection would have just a little distortion near the equator. However, in moving north or south of the equator, the distortion would increase as you moved further away from the equator. The best known and most widely used cylindrical projection is the **Mercator Projection.** It was first developed in 1569 by Gerardus Mercator, a Flemish mapmaker.

(2) **Conical Projections** - The name for these maps comes from the fact that the projection is made onto a cone of paper. The cone is made so that it touches a globe at the base of the cone only. It can also be made so that it cuts through part of the globe in two different places. Again, there is the least distortion where the paper touches the globe. If the cone touches at two different points, there is some distortion at both of them. Conical projections are most often used to map areas in the **middle latitudes**. Maps of the United States are most often conical projections. This is because most of the country lies within these latitudes.

(3) **Flat-Plane Projections** - These are made with a flat piece of paper. It touches the globe at one point only. Areas near this point show little distortion. Flat-plane projections are often used to show the areas of the North and South Poles. One such flat projection is called a **Gnomonic Projection**. On this kind of map, all meridians appear as straight lines, Gnomonic projections are useful because any straight line drawn between points on them form a **Great-Circle Route**. Great-Circle Routes can best be described by thinking of a globe and understanding that, when using the globe, the shortest route between two points on it can be found by simply stretching a string from one point to the other.

To properly analyze a given map, one must be familiar with the various parts and symbols that most modern maps use. For the most part, this is standardized, with different maps using similar parts and symbols. These can include:

The Title - All maps should have a title, just like all books should. The title tells you what information is to be found on the map.

The Legend - Most maps have a legend. A legend explains the various symbols that are used on that particular map and what the symbols represent, (also called a *map key*).

The Grid - A grid is a series of lines that are used to find exact places and locations on the map. There are several different kinds of grid systems in use; however, most maps do use the longitude and latitude system, known as the **Geographic Grid System**.

Directions - Most maps have some directional system to show which way the map is being presented. Often on a map, a small compass will be present, with arrows showing the four basic directions--north, south, east, and west.

The Scale - This is used to show the relationship between a unit of measurement on the map versus the real world measure on Earth. Maps are drawn to many different scales. Some maps show a lot of detail for a small area. Others show a greater span of distance. Whichever is being used, one should always be aware of just what scale is being used. For instance, the scale might be something like 1 inch = 10 miles for a small area, or, for a map showing the whole world, it might have a scale in which 1 inch = 1,000 miles. The point is that one must look at the map key in order to see what units of measurements the map is using.

Maps have four main properties. They are (1) the size of the areas shown on the map. (2) The shapes of the areas, (3) Consistent scales, and (4) Straight-line directions. A map can be drawn so that it is correct in one or more of these properties. No map can be correct in all of them.

Equal areas - One property which maps can have is that of equal areas. In an equal-area map, the meridians and parallels are drawn so that the areas shown have the same proportions as they do on Earth. For example, Greenland is about one-eighteenth the size of South America, thus it will be show as one-eighteenth the size on an equal area map. The **Mercator projection** is an example of a map that does not have equal areas. In it, Greenland appears to be about the same size as South America. This is because the distortion is very bad at the poles and Greenland lies near the North Pole.

Conformal - A second map property is conformal, or correct, shapes. There are no maps which can show very large areas of the earth in their exact shapes. Only globes can really do that, however Conformal Maps are as close as possible to true shapes. The United States is often shown by a Lambert Conformal Conic Projection Map.

Consistent Scales - Many maps attempt to use the same scale on all parts of the map. Generally, this is easier when maps show a relatively small part of Earth's surface. For example, a map of Florida might be a Consistent Scale Map. Generally, maps showing large areas are not consistent-scale maps. This is so because of distortion. Often, such maps will have two scales noted in the key. One scale, for example, might be accurate to measure distances between points along the Equator. Another might be then used to measure distances between the North Pole and the South Pole.

Maps showing physical features often try to show information about the elevation or **relief** of the land. **Elevation** is the distance above or below the sea level. The elevation is usually shown with colors, for instance, all areas on a map which are at a certain level will be shown in the same color.

Relief Maps - Show the shape of the land surface; flat, rugged, or steep. Relief maps usually give more detail than simply showing the overall elevation of the land's surface. Relief is also sometimes shown with colors, but another way to show relief is by using **contour lines**. These lines connect all points of a land surface which are the same height surrounding the particular area of land.

Thematic Maps - These are used to show more specific information, often on a single **theme**, or topic. Thematic maps show the distribution or amount of something over a given area; such as population density, climate, economic information, cultural and political information, etc.

Information can be gained looking at a map that might take hundreds of words to explain otherwise. Maps reflect the great variety of knowledge covered by political science. To show such a variety of information, maps are made in many different ways. Because of this variety, maps must be studied carefully.

Spatial organization is a description of how things are grouped in a given space. In geographical terms, this can describe people, places, and environments anywhere and everywhere on Earth.

The most basic form of spatial organization for people is where they live. The vast majority of people live near other people in villages, towns, cities, and settlements. These people live near others in order to take advantage of the goods and services that naturally arise from cooperation. These villages, towns, cities, and settlements are, to varying degrees, near bodies of water. Water is a staple of survival for every person on the planet, a good source of energy for factories and other industries, and a form of transportation for people and goods.

Another way to describe where people live is by the **geography** and **topography** around them. The vast majority of people on the planet live in areas that are very hospitable. Yes, people live in the Himalayas and in the Sahara, but the populations in those areas are small indeed when compared to the plains of China, India, Europe, and the United States. People naturally want to live where they won't have to work really hard just to survive, and world population patterns reflect this.

We can examine the spatial organization of the places where people live. For example, in a city, where are the factories and heavy industry buildings? Are they near airports or train stations? Are they on the edge of town, near major roads? What about housing developments? Are they near these industries, or are they far away? Where are the other industry buildings? Where are the schools, hospitals, and parks? What about the police and fire stations? How close are homes to each of these things? Towns, and especially cities, are routinely organized into neighborhoods in order that each house or home is near to most things that its residents might need on a regular basis. This means that large cities have multiple schools, hospitals, grocery stores, fire stations, etc.

Related to this is the distance between cities, towns, villages, or settlements. In certain parts of the United States, and definitely in many countries in Europe, the population settlement patterns achieve megalopolis standards, with no clear boundaries from one town to the next. Other, more sparsely populated areas have towns that are few and far between and have relatively few people in them. Some exceptions to this exist, of course, like oases in the deserts; for the most part, however, population centers tend to be relatively near one another or, at least,near smaller towns.

Most places in the world are in some manner close to agricultural land as well. Food makes the world go round, and some cities are more agriculturally inclined than others. Rare is the city, however, that grows absolutely no crops. The kind of food grown is almost entirely dependent on the kind of land available and the climate surrounding that land. Rice doesn't grow well in the desert, for instance, nor do bananas grow well in snowy lands. Certain crops are easier to transport than others, and the ones that aren't are usually grown near ports or other areas of export.

Settlements begin in areas that offer the natural resources to support life – food and water. With the ability to manage the environment, one finds a concentration of populations. With the ability to transport raw materials and finished products comes mobility. With increasing technology and the rise of industrial centers comes a migration of the workforce.

Cities are the major hubs of human settlement. Almost half of the population of the world now lives in cities. These percentages are much higher in developed regions. Established cities continue to grow. The fastest growth, however, is occurring in developing areas. In some regions, there are "metropolitan areas" made up of urban and sub-urban areas. In some places, cities and urban areas have become interconnected into "megalopoli" (e.g., Tokyo-Kawasaki-Yokohama).

The concentrations of populations and the divisions of these areas among various groups that constitute the cities can differ significantly. North American cities are different from European cities in terms of shape, size, population density, and modes of transportation. While in North America, the wealthiest economic groups tend to live outside the cities, the opposite is true in Latin American cities.

There are significant differences among the cities of the world in terms of connectedness to other cities. While European and North American cities tend to be well-linked both by transportation and communication connections, there are other places in the world in which communication between the cities of the country may be inferior to communication with the rest of the world.

Skill 11.4   Infer significant information about a historical or contemporary society based on examination of a photograph, painting, drawing, cartoon, or other visual representation.

Posters. The power of the political poster in the twenty-first century seems trivial considering the barrage of electronic campaigning, mudslinging, and reporting that seems to have taken over the video and audio media in election season. Even so, the political poster has been a powerful propaganda tool, and it has been around for a long time. For example, in the first century AD, a poster that calls for the election of a Satrius as quinquennial has survived to this day. Nowhere have political posters been used more powerfully or effectively than in Russia in the 1920s in the campaign to promote communism. Many of the greatest Russian writers of that era were the poster writers. Those posters would not be understood at all except in the light of what was going on in the country at the time.

However, today we see them primarily at rallies and protests, where they are usually hand-lettered and hand-drawn. The message is rarely subtle. Understanding the messages of posters requires little thought as a rule. However, they are usually meaningless unless the context is clearly understood. For example, a poster reading "Camp Democracy" can only be understood in the context of the protests of the Iraq War near President George W. Bush's home near Crawford, Texas. "Impeach" posters are understood in 2006 to be directed at President Bush, not a local mayor or representative.

Cartoons. The political cartoon (aka editorial) presents a message or point of view concerning people, events, or situations using caricature and symbolism to convey the cartoonist's ideas, sometimes subtly, sometimes brashly, but always quickly. A good political cartoon will have wit and humor, which is usually obtained by exaggeration that is slick and not used merely for comic effect. It will also have a foundation in truth; that is, the characters must be recognizable to the viewer, and the point of the drawing must have some basis in fact even if it has a philosophical bias. The third requirement is a moral purpose.

Using political cartoons as a teaching tool enlivens lectures, prompts classroom discussion, promotes critical thinking, develops multiple talents and learning styles, and helps prepare students for standardized tests. It also provides humor. However, it may be the most difficult form of literature to teach. Many teachers who choose to include them in their social studies curricula caution that, while students may enjoy them, it's doubtful whether they are actually getting the cartoonists' messages.

The best strategy for teaching such units is through a sub-skills' approach that leads students step-by-step to higher orders of critical thinking. For example, the teacher can introduce caricature and use cartoons to illustrate the principles. Students are able to identify and interpret symbols if they are given the principles for doing so and get plenty of practice, and cartoons are excellent for this. It can cut down the time it takes for students to develop these skills, and many of the students who might lose the struggle to learn to identify symbols may overcome the roadblocks through the analysis of political cartoons. Many political cartoons exist for the teacher to use in the classroom, and they are more readily available than ever before.

A popular example of an editorial cartoon that provides a way to analyze current events in politics is the popular comic strip "Doonesbury" by Gary Trudeau. For example, in the time period prior to the 2004 presidential election, Alex, the media-savvy teenager, does her best for political participation. In January, she rallies her middle-school classmates to the phones for a Deanathon, and, by August, she is luring Ralph Nader supporters into discussions on Internet chat rooms. Knowledgeable about government, active in the political process, and willing to enlist others, Alex has many traits sought by the proponents of civics education.

Sample Test: Historical and Social Scientific Awareness

Directions: Read each item and select the best response.

1. **Which of the following best describes current thinking on the major purpose of social science?**

   A. Social science is designed primarily for students to acquire facts

   B. Social science should not be taught earlier than the middle school years

   C. A primary purpose of social sciences is the development of good citizens

   D. Social science should be taught as an elective

2. **Economics is best described as:**

   A. The study of how money is used in different societies

   B. The study of how different political systems produce goods and services

   C. The study of how human beings use limited resources to supply their necessities and wants

   D. The study of how human beings have developed trading practices through the years

3. **For the historian studying ancient Egypt, which of the following would be least useful?**

   A. The record of an ancient Greek historian on Greek-Egyptian interaction

   B. Letters from an Egyptian ruler to his/her regional governors

   C. Inscriptions on stele of the Fourteenth Egyptian Dynasty

   D. Letters from a nineteenth century Egyptologist to his wife

4. **A political scientist might use all of the following except:**

   A. An investigation of government documents

   B. A geological time-line

   C. Voting patterns

   D. Polling data

5. A geographer wishes to study the effects of a flood on subsequent settlement patterns. Which might he or she find most useful?

    A. A film clip of the floodwaters

    B. An aerial photograph of the river's source

    C. Census data taken after the flood

    D. A soil map of the A and B horizons beneath the flood area

6. A social scientist observes how individual persons react to the presence or absence of noise. This scientist is most likely a:

    A. Geographer

    B. Political Scientist

    C. Economist

    D. Psychologist

7. As a sociologist, you would be most likely to observe:

    A. The effects of an earthquake on farmland

    B. The behavior of rats in sensory-deprivation experiments

    C. The change over time in Babylonian obelisk styles

    D. The behavior of human beings in television focus groups

8. An economist investigates the spending patterns of low-income individuals. Which of the following would yield the most pertinent information?

    A. Prime lending rates of neighborhood banks

    B. The federal discount rate

    C. City-wide wholesale distribution figures

    D. Census data and retail sales figures

9. A teacher and a group of students take a field trip to an Indian mound to examine artifacts. This activity most closely fits under which branch of the social sciences?

    A. Anthropology

    B. Sociology

    C. Psychology

    D. Political Science

10. We can credit modern geography with which of the following?

A. Building construction practices designed to withstand earthquakes

B. Advances in computer cartography

C. Better methods of linguistic analysis

D. Making it easier to memorize countries and their capitals

11. Adam Smith is most closely identified with which of the following?

A. The law of diminishing returns

B. The law of supply and demand

C. The principle of motor primacy

D. The territorial imperative

12. Margaret Mead may be credited with major advances in the study of:

A. The marginal propensity to consume

B. The thinking of the Anti - Federalists

C. The anxiety levels of non-human primates

D. Interpersonal relationships in non-technical societies

13. A physical geographer would be concerned with which of the following groups of terms?

A. Landform, biome, precipitation

B. Scarcity, goods, services

C. Nation, state, administrative subdivision

D. Cause and effect, innovation, exploration

14. An economist might engage in which of the following activities?

A. An observation of the historical effects of a nation's banking practices

B. The application of a statistical test to a series of data

C. Introduction of an experimental factor into a specified population to measure the effect of the factor

D. An economist might engage in all of these

15. If geography is the study of how human beings live in relationship to Earth, why do geographers include physical geography within the discipline?

A. The physical environment serves as the location for the activities of human beings

B. No other branch of the natural or social sciences studies the same topics

C. The physical environment is more important than the activities carried out by human beings

D. It is important to be able to subdue natural processes for the advancement of humankind

16. Capitalism and communism are alike in that they are both:

A. Organic systems

B. Political systems

C. Centrally planned systems

D. Economic systems

17. A social scientist studies the behavior of four persons in a carpool. This is an example of:

A. Developmental psychology

B. Experimental psychology

C. Social psychology

D. Macro-economics

18. Indo-European languages are native languages to each of the following EXCEPT:

A. Germany

B. India

C. Italy

D. Finland

19. A cultural geographer is investigating the implications of <u>The Return of the Native</u> by Thomas Hardy. He or she is most likely concentrating on:

A. The reactions of British city-dwellers to the in-migration of French professionals

B. The activities of persons in relation to poorly-drained, coarse-soiled land with low-lying vegetation

C. The capacity of riverine lands to sustain a population of edible amphibians

D. The propagation of new crops introduced by settlers from North America

20. As your income rises, you tend to spend more money on entertainment. This is an expression of the:

A. Marginal propensity to consume

B. Allocative efficiency

C. Compensating differential

D. Marginal propensity to save

Answer Key: Historical and Social Scientific Awareness

1. C
2. C
3 D
4. B
5. C
6. D
7. D
8. D
9. A
10. B
11. B
12. D
13. A
14. D
15. A
16. D
17. C
18. D
19. B
20. A

Rationales with Sample Questions: Historical and Social Scientific Awareness

1. **Which of the following best describes current thinking on the major purpose of social science?**

   A. Social science is designed primarily for students to acquire facts

   B. Social science should not be taught earlier than the middle school years

   C. A primary purpose of social sciences is the development of good citizens

   D. Social science should be taught as an elective

Answer: C

C. A primary purpose of social sciences is the development of good citizens.

By making students aware of the importance of their place in society, how their society and others are governed, how societies develop and advance, and how cultural behaviors arise, the social sciences are currently thought to be of primary importance in (C) developing good citizens.

2. **Economics is best described as:**

   A. The study of how money is used in different societies

   B. The study of how different political systems produce goods and services

   C. The study of how human beings use limited resources to supply their necessities and wants

   D. The study of how human beings have developed trading practices through the years

Answer: C

C. The study of how human beings use limited resources to supply their necessities and wants

(A) How money is used in different societies might be of interest to a sociologist or anthropologist. (B) The study of how different political systems produce goods and services is a topic of study that could be included under the field of political science. (D) The study of historical trading practices could fall under the study of history. Only (C) is the best general description of the social science of economics as a whole.

3. For the historian studying ancient Egypt, which of the following would be least useful?

A. The record of an ancient Greek historian on Greek-Egyptian interaction

B. Letters from an Egyptian ruler to his/her regional governors

C. Inscriptions on stele of the Fourteenth Egyptian Dynasty

D. Letters from a nineteenth century Egyptologist to his wife

Answer: D

D. Letters from a nineteenth century Egyptologist to his wife

Historians use primary sources from the actual time they are studying whenever possible. (A) Ancient Greek records of interaction with Egypt, (B) letters from an Egyptian ruler to regional governors, and (C) inscriptions from the Fourteenth Egyptian Dynasty are all primary sources created at or near the actual time being studied. (D) Letters from a nineteenth century Egyptologist would not be considered primary sources, as they were created thousands of years after the fact and may not actually be about the subject being studied.

4. A political scientist might use all of the following except:

A. An investigation of government documents

B. A geological time-line

C. Voting patterns

D. Polling data

Answer: B

B. A geological time-line

Political science is primarily concerned with the political and governmental activities of societies. (A) Government documents can provide information about the organization and activities of a government. (C) Voting patterns reveal the political behavior of individuals and groups. (D) Polling data can provide insight into the predominant political views of a group of people. (B) A geological timeline describes the changes in the physical features of the earth over time and would not be useful to a political scientist.

5. A geographer wishes to study the effects of a flood on subsequent settlement patterns. Which might he or she find most useful?

A. A film clip of the floodwaters

B. An aerial photograph of the river's source

C. Census data taken after the flood

D. A soil map of the A and B horizons beneath the flood area

Answer: C

C. Census data taken after the flood

(A) A film clip of the flood waters may be of most interest to a historian, (B) an aerial photograph of the river's source, and (D) soil maps tell little about the behavior of the individuals affected by the flood. (C) Census surveys record the population for certain areas on a regular basis, allowing a geographer to tell if more or fewer people are living in an area over time. These would be of most use to a geographer undertaking this study.

6. A social scientist observes how individual persons react to the presence or absence of noise. This scientist is most likely a:

A. Geographer

B. Political Scientist

C. Economist

D. Psychologist

Answer: D

D. Psychologist

(D) Psychologists scientifically study the behavior and mental processes of individuals. Studying how individuals react to changes in their environment falls under this social science. (A) Geographers, (B) political scientists and (C) economists are more likely to study the reactions of groups rather than individual reactions.

7. As a sociologist, you would be most likely to observe:

A. The effects of an earthquake on farmland

B. The behavior of rats in sensory-deprivation experiments

C. The change over time in Babylonian obelisk styles

D. The behavior of human beings in television focus groups

Answer: D

D. The behavior of human beings in television focus groups.

Predominant beliefs and attitudes within human society are studied in the field of sociology. (A) The effects of an earthquake on farmland might be studied by a geographer. (B) The behavior of rats in an experiment falls under the field of behavioral psychology. (C) Changes in Babylonian obelisk styles might interest a historian. None of these answers fit easily within the definition of sociology. (D) A focus group, where people are asked to discuss their reactions to a certain product or topic, would be the most likely method for a sociologist of observing and discovering attitudes among a selected group.

8. **An economist investigates the spending patterns of low-income individuals. Which of the following would yield the most pertinent information?**

   A. Prime lending rates of neighborhood banks

   B. The federal discount rate

   C. City-wide wholesale distribution figures

   D. Census data and retail sales figures

Answer: D

D. Census data and retail sales figures

(A) Local lending rates and (B) the federal discount rate might provide information on borrowing habits, but not necessarily spending habits and give no information on income levels. (C) Citywide wholesale distribution figures would provide information on the business activity of a city, but tell nothing about consumer activities. (D) Census data records the income levels of households within a certain area and retail sales figures for that area would give an economist data on spending, which can be compared to income levels, making this the most pertinent source.

9. **A teacher and a group of students take a field trip to an Indian mound to examine artifacts. This activity most closely fits under which branch of the social sciences?**

   A. Anthropology

   B. Sociology

   C. Psychology

   D. Political Science

Answer: A

A. Anthropology

(A) Anthropology is the study of human culture and of the way in which people of different cultures live. The artifacts created by people of a certain culture can provide information about the behaviors and beliefs of that culture, making anthropology the best fitting field of study for this field trip. (B) Sociology, (C) psychology and (D) political science are more likely to study behaviors and institutions directly than through individual artifacts created by a specific culture.

10. We can credit modern geography with which of the following?

    A. Building construction practices designed to withstand earthquakes

    B. Advances in computer cartography

    C. Better methods of linguistic analysis

    D. Making it easier to memorize countries and their capitals

Answer: B

B. Advances in computer cartography.

(B) Cartography is concerned with the study and creation of maps and geographical information, and falls under the social science of geography.

11. Adam Smith is most closely identified with which of the following?

    A. The law of diminishing returns

    B. The law of supply and demand

    C. The principle of motor primacy

    D. The territorial imperative

Answer: B

B. The law of supply and demand

Adam Smith was an economist who developed the theory that value was linked to the supply of a good or service compared to the demand for it. Something in low supply but high demand will have a high value. Something in great supply but low demand is worth less. This has become known as (B) the law of supply and demand. (A) The law of diminishing returns is an economic principle described by Thomas Malthus in 1798. (C) The principle of motor primacy refers to a stage in developmental psychology. (D) The territorial imperative is a theory of the origin of property outlined by anthropologist Robert Ardrey in 1966.

12. Margaret Mead may be credited with major advances in the study of:

A. The marginal propensity to consume

B. The thinking of the Anti -Federalists

C. The anxiety levels of non-human primates

D. Interpersonal relationships in non-technical societies

Answer: D

D. Interpersonal relationships in non-technical societies

Margaret Mead (1901-1978) was a pioneer in the field of anthropology, living among the people of Samoa observing and writing about their culture in the book Coming of Age in Samoa in 1928. (A) The marginal propensity to consume is an economic subject. (B) The thinking of the Anti-Federalists is a topic in American history. (C) The anxiety levels of non-human primates are a subject studied in behavioral psychology.

13. A physical geographer would be concerned with which of the following groups of terms?

A. Landform, biome, precipitation

B. Scarcity, goods, services

C. Nation, state, administrative subdivision

D. Cause and effect, innovation, exploration

Answer: A

A. Landform, biome, precipitation.

(A) Landform, biome, and precipitation are all terms used in the study of geography. A landform is a physical feature of the earth, such as a hill or valley. A biome is a large community of plants or animals, such as a forest. Precipitation is the moisture that falls to earth as rain or snow. (B) Scarcity, goods and services are terms encountered in economics. (C) Nation, state, and administrative subdivision are terms used in political science. (D) Cause and effect, innovation, and exploration are terms in developmental psychology.

14. An economist might engage in which of the following activities?

A. An observation of the historical effects of a nation's banking practices

B. The application of a statistical test to a series of data

C. Introduction of an experimental factor into a specified population to measure the effect of the factor

D. An economist might engage in all of these

Answer: D

D.   An economist might engage in all of these

Economists use statistical analysis of economic data, controlled experimentation as well as historical research in their field of social science.

15. If geography is the study of how human beings live in relationship to Earth, why do geographers include physical geography within the discipline?

A. The physical environment serves as the location for the activities of human beings

B. No other branch of the natural or social sciences studies the same topics

C. The physical environment is more important than the activities carried out by human beings

D. It is important to be able to subdue natural processes for the advancement of humankind

Answer: A

A. The physical environment serves as the location for the activities of human beings.

Cultures will develop different practices depending on the predominant geographical features of the area in which they live. Cultures that live along a river will have a different kind of relationship to the surrounding land than those living in the mountains, for instance. Answer (A) best describes why physical geography is included in the social science of geography. Answer (B) is false, as physical geography is also studied under other natural sciences (such as geology.) Answers (C) and (D) are matters of opinion and do not pertain to the definition of geography as a social science.

16. Capitalism and communism are alike in that they are both:

A. Organic systems

B. Political systems

C. Centrally planned systems

D. Economic systems

Answer: D

D. Economic systems

While economic and (B) political systems are often closely connected, capitalism and communism are primarily (D) economic systems. Capitalism is a system of economics that allows the open market to determine the relative value of goods and services. Communism is an economic system where the market is planned by a central state. While communism is a (C) centrally planned system, this is not true of capitalism. (A) Organic systems are studied in biology, a natural science.

17. A social scientist studies the behavior of four persons in a carpool. This is an example of:

A. Developmental psychology

B. Experimental psychology

C. Social psychology

D. Macroeconomics

Answer: C

C. Social psychology

(A) Developmental psychology studies the mental development of humans as they mature. (B) Experimental psychology uses formal experimentation with control groups to examine human behavior. (C) Social psychology is a branch of the field that investigates people's behavior as they interact within society, and is the type of project described in the question. (D) Macroeconomics is a field within economics and would not apply to this project.

18. **Indo-European languages are native languages to each of the following EXCEPT:**

    A. Germany

    B. India

    C. Italy

    D. Finland

Answer: D

D. Finland

German, the native language of (A) Germany, Hindi, the official language of (B) India, and Italian, spoken in (C) Italy are three of the hundreds of languages that are part of the Indo-European family which also includes French, Greek. and Russian. Finnish, the language of (D) Finland, is part of the Uralic family of languages, which also includes Estonian. It developed independently of the Indo-European family.

19. A cultural geographer is investigating the implications of <u>The Return of the Native</u> by Thomas Hardy. He or she is most likely concentrating on:

A. The reactions of British city-dwellers to the in-migration of French professionals

B. The activities of persons in relation to poorly-drained, coarse-soiled land with low-lying vegetation

C. The capacity of riverine lands to sustain a population of edible amphibians

D. The propagation of new crops introduced by settlers from North America

Answer: B

B. The activities of persons in relation to poorly-drained, coarse-soiled land with low-lying vegetation

Thomas Hardy's novel <u>The Return of the Native</u> takes place in England, in a fictional region based on Hardy's home area, Dorset. Hardy describes the people and landscape of this area, which is primarily heath. A heath is a poorly drained, coarse-soiled land with low-lying vegetation, as described in answer (B). This is the most likely concentration for a cultural geographer studying Hardy's novel.

20. As your income rises, you tend to spend more money on entertainment. This is an expression of the:

A. Marginal propensity to consume

B. Allocative efficiency

C. Compensating differential

D. Marginal propensity to save

Answer: A

A. Marginal propensity to consume

The (A) marginal propensity to consume is a measurement of how much consumption changes compared to how much disposable income changes. Entertainment expenses are an example of disposable income. Dividing your change in entertainment spending by your total change in disposable income will give you your marginal propensity to consume.

SUBAREA III. ARTISTIC EXPRESSION AND THE HUMANITIES

COMPETENCY 12.0 **UNDERSTAND AND ANALYZE ELEMENTS OF FORM AND CONTENT IN WORKS FROM THE VISUAL AND PERFORMING ARTS FROM DIFFERENT PERIODS AND CULTURES**

Skill 12.1 **Recognize important elements in a given work of the visual or performing arts (e.g., focal point, symmetry, repetition of shapes, perspective, motif, rhythm)**

Visual art
Students should have an early introduction to the principles of visual art and should become familiar with the basic level of the following terms:

Abstract - An image that reduces a subject to its essential visual elements; such as lines, shapes, and colors.

Background - Those portions or areas of composition that are set back from the primary or dominant subject matter or design areas.

Balance - A principle of art and design concerned with the arrangement of one or more elements in a work of art so that they appear symmetrical or asymmetrical in design and proportion.

Contrast - A principle of art and design concerned with juxtaposing one or more elements in opposition, so as to emphasize their differences.

Emphasis - A principle of art and design concerned with making one or more elements in a work of art stand out in such a way as to appear important or significant.

Sketch - An image-development strategy; a preliminary drawing.

Texture - An element of art and design that pertains to the way something feels by representation of the tactile character of surfaces.

Unity - A principle of art and design concerned with the arrangement of one or more of the elements used to create a coherence of parts and a feeling of completeness or wholeness.

Basic Music Techniques

Some of the most basic music techniques include learning about rhythm, tempo, melody, and harmony. **Rhythm** refers to the pattern of regular or irregular pulses in music that result from the melodic beats of the music. When rhythm is measured and divided into parts of equal time value, it is called **meter**. Simple techniques to teach and practice rhythm include clapping hands and tapping feet to the beat of the music. Teachers can also incorporate the use of percussion instruments to examine rhythmic patters, which also increases students' awareness of rhythm. As a result of exercises such as these, students learn the basics of conducting music, and, through conducting, students learn to appreciate and develop musical awareness. Understanding rhythm also introduces students to the concept of **tempo**, or the speed of a given musical piece. Practicing with well-known songs with a strong musical beat, such as "Happy Birthday," helps students become aware of patterns and speed.

The **melody** of a musical piece refers to the pattern of single tones in a composition that does more that simply reinforce rhythm or provide harmony. The melody of a musical piece is often considered the "horizontal" aspect of the piece that flows from start to finish. **Harmony** refers to the combination of single tones at one time in a musical piece or to the full sound of different notes sounded at the same time. To practice these concepts, students can compose their own ascending and descending melodies on staff paper. Students should be able to sing the melodies by reading the notation.

Other Musical Components and Terms

mood, expression, dynamics, nocturne, orchestra, tenor, clef, baritone, sonata, soprano, measure, cantata, march, alto, concerto, octave, staccato and legato

Skill 12.2	**Determine how a sense of unity or balance is achieved in a given work from the visual or performing arts**

See Skill 12.2

Skill 12.3	**Characterizing the theme, mood, or tone of a given work from the visual or performing arts**

The field of the humanities is overflowing with examples of works of art that hold in common various themes, motifs, and symbols. Themes, motifs and symbols effortlessly cross the lines between the visual arts, literature, music, theater, and dance. Listed below are a few examples culled from the immense heritage of the arts.

Examples of Works that Share Thematic and Symbolic Motifs

A popular symbol or motif of the fifteenth, sixteenth, and seventeenth centuries was David, the heroic second king of the Hebrews. The richness of the stories pertaining to David and the opportunities for visual interpretation made him a favorite among artists, all of whom cast him in different lights. Donatello's bronze statue of *David* is a classically proportioned nude portrayed with Goliath's head between his feet. This David is not gloating over his kill, but instead seems to be viewing his own, sensuous body with a Renaissance air of self-awareness. Verrocchio's bronze sculpture of *David*, also with the severed head of Goliath, represents a confident young man proud of his accomplishment and seemingly basking in praise. Michelangelo, always original, gives us a universal interpretation of the David theme. Weapon in hand, Michelangelo's marble *David* tenses muscles as he summons up the power to deal with his colossal enemy, symbolizing as he does so every person or community having had to battle against overwhelming odds. Bernini's marble *David*, created as it was during the Baroque era, explodes with energy as it captures forever the most dramatic moment of David's action, the throwing of the stone that kills Goliath. Caravaggio's painting titled *David and Goliath* treats the theme in yet another way. Here, David is shown as if in the glare of a spotlight, looking with revulsion at the bloodied, grotesque head of Goliath, leaving the viewer to speculate about the reason for disgust. Is David revolted at the ungodliness of Goliath, or is he sickened at his own murderous action?

Symbols related to the David theme include David, Goliath's head, and the stone and slingshot.

Another popular religious motif, especially during the medieval and renaissance periods, was the Annunciation. This event was the announcement by the archangel Gabriel to the Virgin Mary that she would bear a son and name him Jesus. It is also believed that this signified the moment of Incarnation. Anonymous medieval artists treated this theme in altarpieces, murals, and illuminated manuscripts. During the thirteenth century, both Nicola and his son, Giovanni, Pisano carved reliefs of the Annunciation theme. Both men included the Annunciation and the Nativity theme into a single panel. Martini's painted rendition of *the Annunciation* owes something to the court etiquette of the day in the use of the heraldic devises of the symbolic colorings and stilted manner of the Virgin. Della Francesca's fresco of the Annunciation borders on the abstract with it's simplified gestures and lack of emotion and the ionic column providing a barrier between Gabriel and Mary. Fra Angelico's *Annunciation* is a lyrical painting combining soft, harmonious coloring with simplicity of form and gesture.

Symbols related to the Annunciation theme are Gabriel, Mary, the dove of the Holy Spirit, the lily, an olive branch, a garden, a basket of wool, a closed book, and various inscriptions.

During the 1800's, a new viewpoint surfaced in Europe. Intellectuals from several countries became painfully aware of the consequences of social conditions and abuses of the day and set out to expose them. The English social satirist Hogarth created a series of paintings entitled *Marriage a-la-Mode*, which honed in on the absurdity of arranged marriages. Other works by Hogarth explored conditions which led to prostitution and the poor-house.

In France, Voltaire was working on the play *Candide*, which recounted the misfortunes of a young man while providing biting commentary on the social abuses of the period.

In the field of music, Mozart's *Marriage of Figaro*, based on a play by Beaumarchais, explores the emotion of love as experienced by people from all ages and walks of life. At the same time, it portrays the follies of convention in society.

Attitudes toward universal themes are reflected in the humanities.

Each artist and author brings to his/her work a personal view of the world. Those of us who view the works and read the books also bring our own biases to the experience. Therefore, the universal themes that are reflected in artistic works are colored both by the hands that create the works and the eyes that perceive them. Is it any wonder, then, that every work in the arts and humanities is open to so many varied interpretations?

Universal themes are themes that reflect the human experience regardless of time period, location, social standing, economic considerations, or religious or cultural beliefs. However, individuals or societies may condone or object to the particular manner in which a theme is approached.

For example, during the Renaissance, Michelangelo painted the ceiling of the Sistine Chapel with glowing frescoes depicting the creation of the universe and man. Although the frescoes are based on stories from the Old Testament, the theme is universal in that mankind has always sought to understand his origins. During Michelangelo's own time, controversy surrounded the ceiling frescoes, due in large measure to the manner in which Michelangelo portrayed the theme. Church scholars were divided over whether Michelangelo had departed too far from the classical notions of beauty advocated by the ancient Greeks or whether he had followed the Greek conventions (including nudity) too closely! Michelangelo contended that his style was a personal one, derived in part from observation of classical sculpture and in part from his observations from life. He expressed a desire to paint differently from the Greeks because the society he was painting for was dramatically different from the Greek society.

The most obvious way in which attitudes toward universal themes are reflected in the humanities is the ability of the artist to express his opinions through his work. For example, the English satirist William Hogarth addressed the universal themes of social cruelty through his paintings. Because of his dramatic portrayals and biting satire, Hogarth's works reflect his own humanitarian viewpoints regarding his 18th century English society. The fact that his paintings aroused similar emotions among the general public is evidenced by the fact that his series of paintings was made into engravings in order that it would be more affordable to the masses of people who sought to buy prints from it. The wide distribution of these prints indicates the extent to which the public sought social change.

COMPETENCY 13.0 **ANALYZE AND INTERPRET WORKS FROM THE VISUAL AND PERFORMING ARTS REPRESENTING DIFFERENT PERIODS AND CULTURES, AND UNDERSTAND THE RELATIONSHIP OF WORKS OF ART TO THEIR SOCIAL AND HISTORICAL CONTEXTS**

Skill 13.1 **Identify similarities and differences in forms and styles of art from different movements or periods of time**

Theatre

Greek History
The history of theatre can be dated back to early sixth century B.C. in Greece. The Greek theatre was the earliest known theater experience. Drama was expressed in many Greek spiritual ceremonies. There are two main forms of drama that have both evolved in their own time.

Tragedy- typically involving conflict between characters

Comedy- typically involving paradoxical relationships between humans and the gods written by Sophocles and Euripides

The same playwrights seldom composed both comedies and tragedies. Plays such as these were designed to entertain and contained little violence and were based on knowledge and the teachings of Aristotle.

Roman History
The history of theatre in Roman times began with theater shows in the third century. These theatre shows were based on religious aspects of the lives of Roman gods and goddesses. Drama wasn't able to withstand the fall of the Roman empire in 476 A.D. By the end of the sixth century, drama was nearly dead in Rome.

Medieval Drama
Medieval theatre was a new revelation of drama that appeared in around the tenth century. New phases of religion were introduced in many holiday services such as Christmas and Easter. In the church itself, many troupes that toured churches presented religious narratives and life stories meant to encourage morality. Over time, these presentations of small traveling groups evolved into full-sized plays, presentations, and elaborate passions. Performances became spectacles at outdoor theaters, marketplaces, and any place large audiences could gather. The main focuses of these presentations of drama were to glorify God and humanity and to celebrate local artisan trades.

Puritan Commonwealth
The Puritan Commonwealth ruled by Oliver Cromwell outlawed dramatic performances, and that ban lasted for nearly twenty years. Following the Puritan era was the restoration of the English monarchy, and new, more well-rounded plays became the focus of art. For the first time in history, women were allowed to participate.

Melodrama
Melodrama, in which good always triumphed over evil, eventually took over the stage. This form of drama was usually pleasing to the audience, yet ,sometimes, unrealistic.

Serious Drama
Serious Drama emerged late in the nineteenth and twentieth centuries. It came following the movement of realism. Realism attempted to combine the dealings of nature with realistic and ordinary situations on stage.

Realism
Today, realism is the most common form of stage presentation. The techniques used today to stage drama combine many of the past histories and cultures of drama.

Visual art

The greatest works in art, literature, music, theater, and dance all mirror universal themes. Universal themes are themes which reflect the human experience, regardless of time period, location, or socio-economic standing. Universal themes tend to fall into broad categories, such as Man vs. Society, Man vs. Himself, Man vs. God, Man vs. Nature, and Good vs. Evil. The general themes listed below all fall into one of these broad categories.

Prehistoric Arts, (circa 1,000,000-circa 8,000 B.C)

> Major themes of this vast period appear to center around religious fertility rites and sympathetic magic and consists of imagery of pregnant animals and faceless, pregnant women.

Mesopotamian Arts, (circa 8,000-400 B.C.)

> The prayer statues and cult deities of the period point to the theme of polytheism in religious worship.

Egyptian Arts, (circa 3,000-100 B.C.)

> The predominance of funerary art from ancient Egypt illustrates the theme of preparation for the afterlife and polytheistic worship. Another dominant theme, reflected by artistic convention, is the divinity of the pharaohs. In architecture, the themes were monumentality and adherence to ritual.

Greek Arts, (800-100 B.C.)

The sculpture of ancient Greece is replete with human figures, most nude and some draped. Most of these sculptures represent athletes and various gods and goddesses. The predominant theme is that of the ideal human, in both mind and body. In architecture, the theme was scale based on the ideal human proportions.

Roman Arts, (circa 480 B.C.-476 A.D.)

Judging from Roman arts, the predominant themes of the period deal with the realistic depiction of human beings and how they related to Greek classical ideals. The emphasis is on practical realism. Another major theme is the glory in serving the Roman state. In architecture, the theme was rugged practicality mixed with Greek proportions and elements.

Middle Ages Arts, (300-1400 A.D.)

Although the time span is expansive, the major themes remain relatively constant. Since the Roman Catholic Church was the primary patron of the arts, most work was religious in nature. The purpose of much of the art was to educate. Specific themes varied from the illustration of Bible stories to interpretations of theological allegory, to lives of the saints, and to consequences of good and evil. Depictions of the Holy Family were popular. Themes found in secular art and literature centered around chivalric love and warfare. In architecture, the themes were glorification of God and the education of congregations about religious principles.

Renaissance Arts, (circa 1400-1630 A.D.)

Renaissance themes include Christian religious depictions (see Middle Ages), but tend to reflect a renewed interest in all things classical. Specific themes include Greek and Roman mythological and philosophic figures and ancient battles and legends. Dominant themes mirror the philosophic beliefs of Humanism, emphasizing individuality and human reason, such as those of the High Renaissance which center around the psychological attributes of individuals. In architecture, the theme was scale based on human proportions.

Baroque Arts, (1630-1700 A.D.)

The predominant themes found in the arts of the Baroque period include the dramatic climaxes of well-known stories, legends and battles, and the grand spectacle of mythology. Religious themes are found frequently, but it is drama and insight that are emphasized and not the medieval "salvation factor". Baroque artists and authors incorporated various types of characters into their works, taking care to include minute details. Portraiture focused on psychology. In architecture, the theme was large-scale grandeur and splendor.

Eighteenth Century Arts, (1700-1800 A.D.)

Rococo themes of this century focused on religion, light mythology, portraiture of aristocrats, pleasure and escapism, and, occasionally, satire. In architecture, the theme was artifice and gaiety, combined with an organic quality of form. Neo-classic themes centered around examples of virtue and heroism, usually in classical settings, and historical stories. In architecture, classical simplicity and utility of design was regained.

Nineteenth Century Arts, (1800-1900 A.D.)

Romantic themes include human freedom, equality, and civil rights, a love for nature, and a tendency toward the melancholic and mystic. The underlying theme is that the most important discoveries are made within the self, and not in the exterior world. In architecture, the theme was fantasy and whimsy, known as "picturesque". Realistic themes included social awareness and a focus on society victimizing individuals. The themes behind Impressionism were the constant flux of the universe and the immediacy of the moment. In architecture, the themes were strength, simplicity, and upward thrust as skyscrapers entered the scene.

Twentieth Century Arts, (1900-2000 A.D.)

Diverse artistic themes of the century reflect a parting with traditional religious values and a painful awareness of man's inhumanity to man. Themes also illustrate a growing reliance on science while simultaneously expressing disillusionment with man's failure to adequately control science. A constant theme is the quest for originality and self-expression while seeking to express the universal in human experience. In architecture, "form follows function".

Genres By Historical Periods

Ancient Greek Art, (circa 800-323 B.C.)

Dominant genres from this period were vase paintings, both black-figure and red-figure, and classical sculpture.

Roman Art, (circa 480 B.C.-476 A.D.)

Major genres from the Romans include frescoes (murals done in fresh plaster to affix the paint), classical sculpture, funerary art, state propaganda art, and relief work on cameos.

Middle Ages Art, (circa 300-1400 A.D.)

Significant genres during the Middle Ages include Byzantine mosaics, illuminated manuscripts, ivory relief, altarpieces, cathedral sculpture, and fresco paintings in various styles.

Renaissance Art, (1400-1630 A.D.)

Important genres from the Renaissance included Florentine fresco painting (mostly religious), High Renaissance painting and sculpture, Northern oil painting, Flemish miniature painting, and Northern printmaking.

Baroque Art, (1630-1700 A.D.)

Pivotal genres during the Baroque era include Mannerism, Italian Baroque painting and sculpture, Spanish Baroque, Flemish Baroque, and Dutch portraiture. Genre paintings in still-life and landscape appear prominently in this period.

Eighteenth Century Art, (1700-1800 A.D.)

Predominant genres of the century include Rococo painting, portraiture, social satire, Romantic painting, and Neoclassic painting and sculpture.

Nineteenth Century Art, (1800-1900 A.D.)

Important genres include Romantic painting, academic painting and sculpture, landscape painting of many varieties, realistic painting of many varieties, impressionism, and many varieties of post-impressionism.

Twentieth Century Art, (1900-2000 A.D.)

Major genres of the twentieth century include symbolism, art nouveau, fauvism, expressionism, cubism (both analytical and synthetic), futurism, non-objective art, abstract art, surrealism, social realism, constructivism in sculpture, Pop and Op art, and conceptual art.

Skill 13.2   Analyze ways in which the content of a given work from the visual or performing arts reflects a specific cultural or historical context

Although the elements of design have remained consistent throughout history, the emphasis on specific aesthetic principles has periodically shifted. Aesthetic standards or principles vary from time period to time period and from society to society.

An obvious difference in aesthetic principles occurs between works created by Eastern and Western cultures. Eastern works of art are more often based on spiritual considerations; while much western art is secular in nature. In attempting to convey reality, Eastern artists generally prefer to use line, local color, and a simplistic view. Western artists tend toward a literal use of line, shape, color, and texture to convey a concise, detailed, complicated view. Eastern artists portray the human figure with symbolic meanings and little regard for muscle structure, resulting in a mystical view of the human experience. Western artists use the "principle of ponderation", which requires the knowledge of both human anatomy and an expression of the human spirit.

In attempts to convey the illusion of depth or visual space in a work of art, Eastern and Western artists use different techniques. Eastern artists prefer a diagonal projection of eye movement into the picture plane and often leave large areas of the surface untouched by detail. The result is the illusion of vast space, an infinite view that coincides with the spiritual philosophies of the Orient. Western artists rely on several techniques; such as overlapping planes, variation of object size, object position on the picture plane, linear and aerial perspective, color change, and various points of perspective to convey the illusion of depth. The result is space that is limited and closed.

In the application of color, Eastern artists use arbitrary choices of color. Western artists generally rely on literal color usage or emotional choices of color. The end result is that Eastern art tends to be more universal in nature, while Western art is more individualized.

An interesting change in aesthetic principles occurred between the Renaissance period (1400-1630 A.D.) and the Baroque period (1630-1700 A.D.) in Europe. The shift is easy to understand when viewed in the light of Wolfflin's categories of stylistic development (see 5.3).

The Renaissance period was concerned with the rediscovery of the works of classical Greece and Rome. The art, literature, and architecture was inspired by classical orders, which tended to be formal, simple, and concerned with the ideal human proportions. This means that the painting, sculpture, and architecture was of a Teutonic, or closed nature, composed of forms that were restrained and compact. For example, consider the visual masterpieces of the period: Raphael's painting *The School of Athens*, with its highly precise use of space;

Michelangelo's sculpture *David*, with its compact mass; and the facade of the *Palazzo Strozzi*, with its defined use of the rectangle, arches, and rustication of the masonry.

Compare the Renaissance characteristics to those of the Baroque period. The word "baroque" means "grotesque", which was the contemporary criticism of the new style. In comparison to the styles of the Renaissance, the Baroque was concerned with the imaginative flights of human fancy. The painting, sculpture, and architecture were of an a-Teutonic, or open nature, composed of forms that were whimsical and free-flowing. Consider again the masterpieces of the period: Ruben's painting *The Elevation of the Cross*, with it's turbulent forms of light and dark tumbling diagonally through space; Puget's sculpture *Milo of Crotona*, with it's use of open space and twisted forms; and Borromini's *Chapel of St.Ivo*, with a facade that plays convex forms against concave ones.

In the 1920's and 30's, the German art historian, Professor Wolfflin outlined these shifts in aesthetic principles in his influential book, Principles of Art History. He arranged these changes into five categories of "visual analysis", sometimes referred to as the "categories of stylistic development." Wolfflin was careful to point out that no style is inherently superior to any other. They are simply indicators of the phase of development of that particular time or society.

However, Wolfflin goes on to state, correctly or not, that once the evolution occurs, it is impossible to regress. These modes of perception apply to drawing, painting, sculpture, and architecture. They are as follows:

1. From a linear mode to a painterly mode.
This shift refers to stylistic changes that occur when perception or expression evolves from a linear form that is concerned with the contours and boundaries of objects to perception or expression that stresses the masses and volumes of objects. From viewing objects in isolation to seeing the relationships between objects is an important change in perception. Linear mode implies that objects are stationary and unchanging, while the painterly mode implies that objects and their relationships to other objects are always in a state of flux.

2. From plane to recession.
This shift refers to perception or expression that evolves from a planar style, when the artist views movement in the work in an "up and down" and "side to side" manner to a recessional style, when the artist views the balance of a work in an "in and out" manner. The illusion of depth may be achieved through either style, but only the recessional style uses an angular movement forward and backward through the visual plane.

3. From closed to open form.
This shift refers to perception or expression that evolves from a sense of enclosure or limited space, "closed form", to a sense of freedom in "open form". The concept is obvious in architecture, as it is easy to differentiate between the buildings with obvious "outside" and "inside" space and those that open up the space to allow the outside to interact with the inside.

4. From multiplicity to unity.
This shift refers to an evolution from expressing unity through the use of balancing many individual parts to expressing unity by subordinating some individual parts to others. Multiplicity stresses the balance between existing elements; whereas unity stresses emphasis, domination, and accent of some elements over other elements.

5. From absolute to relative clarity.
This shift refers to an evolution from works which clearly and thoroughly express everything there is to know about the object to works that express only part of what there is to know and leave the viewer to fill in the rest from his own experiences. Relative clarity, then, is a sophisticated mode because it requires the viewer to actively participate in the "artistic dialogue." Each of the previous four categories is reflected in this, as linearity is considered to be concise while painterliness is more subject to interpretation. Planarity is more factual, while recessional movement is an illusion, and so on.

COMPETENCY 14.0   UNDERSTAND FORMS AND THEMES USED IN LITERATURE FROM DIFFERENT PERIODS AND CULTURES

Skill 14.1   Identify characteristic features of various genres of fiction and nonfiction (e.g., novels, plays, essays, autobiographies)

The major literary genres include allegory, ballad, drama, epic, epistle, essay, fable, novel, poem, romance, and the short story.

Allegory: A story in verse or prose with characters representing virtues and vices. There are two meanings, symbolic and literal. John Bunyan's *The Pilgrim's Progress* is the most renowned of this genre.

Autobiography: A form of biography, but it is written by the subject himself or herself. Autobiographies can range from the very formal to intimate writings made during a subject's life that were not intended for publication. These include letters, diaries, journals, memoirs, and reminiscences. Autobiography, generally speaking, began in the 15th century; one of the first examples is one written in England by Margery Kempe. There are four kinds of autobiography: thematic, religious, intellectual, and fictionalized. Some "novels" may be thinly disguised autobiography, such as the novels of Thomas Wolfe.

Ballad: An *in medias res* story told or sung, usually in verse and accompanied by music. Literary devices found in ballads include the refrain, or repeated section, and incremental repetition, or anaphora, for effect. Earliest forms were anonymous folk ballads. Later forms include Coleridge's Romantic masterpiece, "The Rime of the Ancient Mariner."

Biography: A form of nonfiction, the subject of which is the life of an individual. The earliest biographical writings were probably funeral speeches and inscriptions (usually) praising the life and example of the deceased. Early biographies evolved from this and were almost invariably uncritical, even distorted, and always laudatory.

Beginning in the 18th century, this form of literature saw major development; an eminent example is James Boswell's *Life of Johnson*, which is very detailed and even records conversations. Eventually, the antithesis of the grossly exaggerated tomes praising an individual, usually a person of circumstance, developed. This form is denunciatory, debunking, and often inflammatory. A famous modern example is Lytton Strachey's *Eminent Victorians* (1918).

Drama: Plays – comedy, modern, or tragedy - typically in five acts. Traditionalists and neoclassicists adhere to Aristotle's unities of time, place, and action. Plot development is advanced via dialogue. Literary devices include asides, soliloquies, and the chorus representing public opinion. Greatest of all dramatists/playwrights is William Shakespeare. Other dramaturges include Ibsen, Williams, Miller, Shaw, Stoppard, Racine, Moliére, Sophocles, Aeschylus, Euripides, and Aristophanes.

Epic: Long poem usually of book length reflecting values inherent in the generative society. Epic devices include an invocation to a Muse for inspiration, a purpose for writing, a universal setting, a protagonist and antagonist who possess supernatural strength and acumen, and interventions of a God or the gods. Understandably, there are very few epics: Homer's *Iliad* and *Odyssey*, Virgil's *Aeneid*, Milton's *Paradise Lost*, Spenser's *The Fairie Queene*, Barrett Browning's *Aurora Leigh*, and Pope's mock-epic, *The Rape of the Lock*.

Epistle: A letter that is not always originally intended for public distribution, but due to the fame of the sender and/or recipient, becomes public domain. Paul wrote epistles that were later placed in the Bible.

Essay: Typically, a limited length prose work focusing on a topic and propounding a definite point of view and authoritative tone. Great essayists include Carlyle, Lamb, DeQuincy, Emerson, and Montaigne, who is credited with defining this genre.

Fable: Terse tale offering up a moral or exemplum. Chaucer's "The Nun's Priest's Tale" is a fine example of a *bete fabliau,* or beast fable, in which animals speak and act in characteristically human ways, illustrating human foibles.

Informational books and articles: Make up much of the reading of modern Americans. Magazines began to be popular in the 19th century in this country, and, while many of the contributors to those publications intended to influence the political/social/religious convictions of their readers, many also simply intended to pass on information. A book or article whose purpose is simply to be informative (that is, not to persuade) is called exposition (adjectival form: expository). An example of an expository book is the *MLA Style Manual.* The writers do not intend to persuade their readers to use the recommended stylistic features in their writing; they are simply making them available in case a reader needs such a guide.

Articles in magazines such as *Time* may be persuasive in purpose, such as Joe Klein's regular column, but for the most part they are expository, giving information that television coverage of a news story might not have time to include.

Legend: A traditional narrative or collection of related narratives, popularly regarded as historically factual, but actually a mixture of fact and fiction.

Myth: Stories that are more or less universally shared within a culture to explain its history and traditions.

Newspaper accounts of events: Expository in nature, of course, a reporting of a happening. That happening might be a school board meeting, an automobile accident that sent several people to a hospital and accounted for the death of a passenger, or the election of the mayor. They are not intended to be persuasive; although the bias of a reporter or of an editor must be factored in. A newspapers' editorial stance is often openly declared, and it may be reflected in such things as news reports. Reporters are expected to be unbiased in their coverage, and most of them will defend their disinterest fiercely, but what writers *see* in an event is inevitably shaped to some extent by their beliefs and experiences.

Novel: The longest form of fictional prose, containing a variety of characterizations, settings, local color and regionalism. Most have complex plots, expanded description, and attention to detail. Some of the great novelists include Austin, the Brontes, Twain, Tolstoy, Hugo, Hardy, Dickens, Hawthorne, Forster, and Flaubert.

Poem: The only requirement is rhythm. Sub-genres include fixed types of literature such as the sonnet, elegy, ode, pastoral, and villanelle. Unfixed types of poetic literature include blank verse and dramatic monologue.

Romance: A highly imaginative tale set in a fantastical realm dealing with the conflicts between heroes, villains, and/or monsters. "The Knight's Tale" from Chaucer's *Canterbury Tales*, *Sir Gawain and the Green Knight,* and Keats' "The Eve of St. Agnes" are prime representatives.

Short Story: Typically a terse narrative, with less developmental background about characters. May include description, author's point of view, and tone. Poe emphasized that a successful short story should create one focused impact. Considered to be great short story writers are Hemingway, Faulkner, Twain, Joyce, Shirley Jackson, Flannery O'Connor, de Maupasssant, Saki, Edgar Allen Poe, and Pushkin.

Dramatic Texts

Comedy: The comedic form of dramatic literature is meant to amuse and often ends happily. It uses techniques such as satire or parody, and can take many forms, from farce to burlesque.

Examples include Dante Alighieri's *The Divine Comedy,* Noel Coward's play *Private Lives,* some of Geoffrey Chaucer's *Canterbury Tales,* and William Shakespeare's plays.

Tragedy: Tragedy is comedy's other half. It is defined as a work of drama written in either prose or poetry telling the story of a brave, noble hero who, because of some tragic character flaw, brings ruin upon himself. It is characterized by serious, poetic language that evokes pity and fear. In modern times, dramatists have tried to update its image by drawing its main characters from the middle class and showing their nobility through their natures instead of their social standing. The classic example of tragedy is Sophocles' *Oedipus Rex*; while Henrik Ibsen and Arthur Miller epitomize modern writers of tragedy.

Drama: In its most general sense, a drama is any work that is designed to be performed by actors on stage. It can also refer to the broad literary genre that includes comedy and tragedy. Contemporary usage, however, denotes drama as a work that treats serious subjects and themes, but does not aim for the same grandeur as tragedy. Drama usually deals with characters of a less stately nature than tragedy. A classical example is Sophocles' tragedy *Oedipus Rex,* while Eugene O'Neill's *The Iceman Cometh* represents modern drama.

Dramatic Monologue: A dramatic monologue is a speech given by actors as if to themselves, but actually for the benefit of audience. It reveals key aspects of the character's psyche and sheds insight on the situation at hand. The audience takes the part of the silent listener, passing judgment and giving sympathy at the same time. This form was invented and used predominantly by Victorian poet Robert Browning.

Skill 14.2   Distinguish the dominant theme in a literary passage

Theme in a work of fiction is similar to a thesis in an essay. It's the *point* the story makes. In a story, it may possibly be spoken by one of the characters; but, more often, it is left to the writer to determine. This requires careful reading and should take into account the other aspects of the story before a firm decision is made. Different analysts will come to different conclusions about what a story means. Very often, the thesis of an analytical essay will be expressed as a well-reasoned opinion.

Skill 14.3 **Recognize common literary elements and techniques (e.g., imagery, metaphor, symbolism, allegory, foreshadowing, irony), and use those elements to interpret a literary passage**

1. Simile: Indirect comparison of two things. "My love is like a red-red rose."

2. Metaphor: Direct comparison of two things. The use of a word or phrase denoting one kind of object or action in place of another to suggest a comparison between them. While poets use them extensively, they are also integral to everyday speech. For example, chairs are said to have "legs" and "arms" although we know that it's humans and other animals who have these appendages.

3. Parallelism: The arrangement of ideas in phrases, sentences, and paragraphs that balance one element with another of equal importance and similar wording. An example from Francis Bacon's *Of Studies:* "Reading maketh a full man, conference a ready man, and writing an exact man."

4. Personification: Human characteristics are attributed to an inanimate object, an abstract quality, or animal. Examples: John Bunyan wrote characters named Death, Knowledge, Giant Despair, Sloth, and Piety in his *Pilgrim's Progress.* The metaphor of an arm of a chair is a form of personification.

5. Euphemism: The substitution of an agreeable or inoffensive term for one that might offend or suggest something unpleasant. Many euphemisms are used to refer to death to avoid using the real word; such as "passed away," "crossed over," or nowadays "passed."

6. Hyperbole: Deliberate exaggeration for effect or comic effect. An example from Shakespeare's *The Merchant of Venice*:
   > Why, if two gods should play some heavenly match
   > And on the wager lay two earthly women,
   > And Portia one, there must be something else
   > Pawned with the other, for the poor rude world
   > Hath not her fellow.

7. Climax: A number of phrases or sentences are arranged in ascending order of rhetorical forcefulness. Example from Melville's *Moby Dick*:

> All that most maddens and torments; all that stirs up the lees of things; all truth with malice in it; all that cracks the sinews and cakes the brain; all the subtle demonisms of life and thought; all evil, to crazy Ahab, were visibly personified and made practically assailable in Moby Dick.

8. Bathos: A ludicrous attempt to portray pathos—that is, to evoke pity, sympathy, or sorrow. It may result from inappropriately dignifying the commonplace, elevated language to describe something trivial, or greatly exaggerated pathos.

9. Oxymoron: A contradiction in terms deliberately employed for effect. It is usually seen in a qualifying adjective whose meaning is contrary to that of the noun it modifies, such as 'wise folly.'

10. Irony: Expressing something other than (particularly, opposite of) the literal meaning, such as words of praise when blame is intended. In poetry, it is often used as a sophisticated or resigned awareness of contrast between what is and what ought to be and expresses a controlled pathos without sentimentality. It is a form of indirection that avoids overt praise or censure. An early example: the Greek comic character Eiron, a clever underdog who by his wit repeatedly triumphs over the boastful character Alazon.

11. Alliteration: The repetition of consonant sounds in two or more neighboring words or syllables.

12. In its simplest form, it reinforces one or two consonant sounds. Example: Shakespeare's Sonnet #12:
    When I do **c**ount the **c**lock that **t**ells the **t**ime.
    Some poets have used more complex patterns of alliteration by creating consonants both at the beginning of words and at the beginning of stressed syllables within words. Example: Shelley's "Stanzas Written in Dejection Near Naples"

> The **C**ity's voice it**s**elf is **s**oft like **So**litude's

13. Onomatopoeia: The naming of a thing or action by a vocal imitation of the sound associated with it; such as buzz, hiss, or any other words whose sounds suggests what the word is intended to communicate. A good example: from "The Brook" by Tennyson:

> I chatter over stony ways,
> In little sharps and trebles,
> I bubble into eddying bays,
> I babble on the pebbles.

14. Malapropism: A verbal blunder in which one word is replaced by another similar in sound but different in meaning. Comes from Sheridan's Mrs. Malaprop in *The Rivals* (1775). Thinking of the geography of contiguous countries, she spoke of the "geometry" of "contagious countries."

Skill 14.4   Determine the meaning of figurative language used in a literary passage

Imagery can be described as a word or sequence of words that refers to any sensory experience—that is, anything that can be seen, tasted, smelled, heard, or felt on the skin or fingers. While writers of prose may also use these devices, it is most distinctive of poetry. PoetS intend to make an experience available to readers. In order to do that, they must appeal to one of the senses. The most-often-used one, of course, is the visual imagery. Poets will deliberately paint a scene in such a way that readers can see it. However, the purpose is not simply to stir the visceral feeling, but also to stir the emotions. A good example is "The Piercing Chill" by Taniguchi Buson (1715-1783):

> The piercing chill I feel:
>   My dead wife's comb, in our bedroom,
>   Under my heel . . .

In only a few short words, the reader can feel many things: the shock that might come from touching the comb, a literal sense of death, the contrast between her death and the memories he has of her when she was alive. Imagery might be defined as speaking of the abstract in concrete terms--a powerful device in the hands of a skillful poet.

A **symbol** is an object or action that can be observed with the senses in addition to its suggesting many other things. The lion is a symbol of courage; the cross a symbol of Christianity; the color green a symbol of envy. These can almost be defined as metaphors because society pretty much agrees on the one-to-one meaning of them. Symbols used in literature are usually of a different sort. They tend to be private and personal; their significance is only evident in the context of the work where they are used. A good example is the huge pair of spectacles on a sign board in Fitzgerald's *The Great Gatsby*. They are interesting as a part of the landscape, but they also symbolize divine myopia.

A symbol can certainly have more than one meaning, and the meaning may be as personal as the memories and experiences of the particular reader. In analyzing a poem or a story, it's important to identify the symbols and their possible meanings.

Looking for symbols is often challenging, especially for novice poetry readers. However, these suggestions may be useful. First, pick out all the references to concrete objects; such as a newspaper or black cats. Note any that the poet emphasizes by describing in detail, by repeating, or by placing at the very beginning or ending of a poem. Ask yourself what the poem is about. What does it add up to? Paraphrase the poem, and determine whether or not the meaning depends upon certain concrete objects. Then ponder what the concrete object symbolizes. Look for a character with the name of a prophet who does little but utter prophecy or for a trio of women who resemble the Three Fates. A symbol may be a part of a person's body; such as the eye of the murder victim in Poe's story *The Tell-Tale Heart,* a look, a voice, or a mannerism.

Some things a symbol is not--an abstraction such as truth, death, and love; in narrative, a well-developed character who is not at all mysterious.

An **allusion** is very much like a symbol, and the two sometimes tend to run together. An allusion is defined by Merriam Webster's *Encyclopedia of Literature* as "an implied reference to a person, event, thing, or a part of another text." Allusions are based on the assumption that there is a common body of knowledge shared by poets and readers and that a reference to that body of knowledge will be immediately understood. Allusions to the Bible and to classical mythology are common in Western literature on the assumption that they will be immediately understood. This is not always the case, of course. T. S. Eliot's *The Wasteland* requires research and annotation for understanding. He assumed more background on the part of average readers than actually exists. However, when Michael Moore on his web page headlines an article on the war in Iraq: "Déjà Fallouja: Ramadi surrounded, thousands of families trapped, no electricity or water, onslaught impending," we understand immediately that he is referring first of all to a repeat of the human disaster in New Orleans although the "onslaught" is not a storm but an invasion by American and Iraqi troops.

COMPETENCY 15.0   **ANALYZE AND INTERPRET LITERATURE FROM DIFFERENT PERIODS AND CULTURES, AND UNDERSTAND THE RELATIONSHIP OF WORKS OF LITERATURE TO THEIR SOCIAL AND HISTORICAL CONTEXTS**

Skill 15.1   **Analyze how the parts of a literary passage contribute to the whole, and compare and contrast the tone or mood of two or more literary passages**

A piece of writing is an integrated whole. It's not enough to just look at the various parts; the total entity must be examined. It should be considered in two ways:

- As an emotional expression of the author
- As an artistic embodiment of a meaning or set of meanings.

This is what is sometimes called "**tone**" in literary criticism.

It's important to remember that writers are human beings with their own individual bents, prejudices, and emotions. Writers are telling readers about the world as they see it and will give voice to certain phases of their own personalities. By reading their works, we can know something of their personal qualities and emotions. However, it's important to remember that not all their characteristics will be revealed in a single work. People change and may have very different attitudes at different times in their lives. Sometimes, they will be influenced by a desire to have a piece of work accepted, to appear to be current, or simply to satisfy the interests and desires of potential readers. It can destroy a work or make it less than it might be. Sometimes the best works are not commercial successes in the generation when they were written but are discovered at a later time and by another generation.

There are three places to look for tone:

- Choice of form: tragedy or comedy; melodrama or farce; parody or sober lyric.

- Choice of materials: characters who have attractive human qualities; others who are repugnant. What authors show in a setting will often indicate what their interests are.

- Writers' interpretations: they may be explicit—telling us how they feel.

- Writers' implicit interpretations: their feelings for a character come through in the description. For example, the use of "smirked" instead of "laughed"; "minced," "stalked," "marched," instead of "walked."

Readers are asked to join writers in the feelings expressed about the world and the things that happen in it. The tone of a piece of writing is important in a critical review of it.

Style, in literature, means a distinctive manner of expression and applies to all levels of language, beginning at the phonemic level—word choices, alliteration, assonance, etc.; the syntactic level—length of sentences, choice of structure and phraseology, patterns, etc.; and extends even beyond the sentence to paragraphs and chapters. What

In Steinbeck's *Grapes of Wrath*, for instance, the style is quite simple in the narrative sections, and the dialogue employs dialect. Because the emphasis is on the story—the narrative—his style is straightforward, for the most part. He just tells the story.

However, there are inter chapters where he varies his style. He uses symbols and combines them with description that is realistic. He sometimes shifts to a crisp, repetitive pattern to underscore the beeping and speeding of cars. By contrast, some of those inter chapters are lyrical, almost poetic.

These shifts in style reflect the attitude of authors toward their subject matter. They intend to make a statements, and they use a variety of styles to strengthen their points.

Skill 15.2 Analyze aspects of cultural or historical context implied in a literary passage

Prior to twentieth century research on child development and child/adolescent literature's relationship to that development, books for adolescents were primarily didactic. They were designed to be instructive concerning history, manners, and morals.

Middle Ages

As early as the eleventh century, Anselm, the Archbishop of Canterbury, wrote an encyclopedia designed to instill in children the beliefs and principles of conduct acceptable to adults in medieval society. Early monastic translations of the *Bible* and other religious writings were written in Latin for the edification of the upper class. Fifteenth-century hornbooks were designed to teach reading and religious lessons. William Caxton printed English versions of *Aesop's Fables*, Malory's *Le Morte d'Arthur,* and stories from Greek and Roman mythology. Though printed for adults, tales of adventures of Odysseus and the Arthurian knights were also popular with literate adolescents.

Renaissance

The Renaissance saw the introduction of the inexpensive chapbooks, small in size and 16-64 pages in length. Chapbooks were condensed versions of mythology and fairy tales. Designed for the common people, chapbooks were imperfect grammatically, but were immensely popular because of their adventurous contents. Though most of the serious, educated adults frowned on the sometimes-vulgar little books, they received praise from Richard Steele of *Tatler* fame for inspiring his grandson's interest in reading and pursuing his other studies.

Meanwhile, the Puritans' three most popular reads were the *Bible*, John Foxe's *Book of Martyrs*, and John Bunyan's *Pilgrim's Progress*. Though venerating religious martyrs and preaching the moral propriety which was to lead to eternal happiness, the stories of the *Book of Martyrs* were often lurid in their descriptions of the fate of the damned. Not written for children and difficult reading even for adults, *Pilgrim's Progress* was as attractive to adolescents for its adventurous plot as for its moral import. In Puritan America, the *New England Primer* set forth the prayers, catechisms, *Bible* verses, and illustrations meant to instruct children in the Puritan ethic. The seventeenth-century French used fables and fairy tales to entertain adults, but children found them enjoyable as well.

Seventeenth century

The late seventeenth century brought the first concern with providing literature that specifically targeted the young. Pierre Perrault's *Fairy Tales*, Jean de la Fontaine's retellings of famous fables, Mme. d'Aulnoy's novels based on old folktales, and Mme. de Beaumont's "Beauty and the Beast" were written to delight as well as instruct young people. In England, publisher John Newbury was the first to publish a line for children. It includes a translation of Perrault's *Tales of Mother Goose; A Little Pretty Pocket-Book*, "intended for instruction and amusement," but decidedly moralistic and bland in comparison to the previous century's chapbooks; and *The Renowned History of Little Goody Two Shoes*, allegedly written by Oliver Goldsmith for a juvenile audience.

Eighteenth century

By and large, however, into the eighteenth century, adolescents were finding their reading pleasure in adult books: Daniel Defoe's *Robinson Crusoe*, Jonathan Swift's *Gulliver's Travels*, and Johann Wyss's *Swiss Family Robinson*. More books were being written for children, but the moral didacticism, though less religious, was nevertheless ever present. The short stories of Maria Edgeworth, the four-volume *The History of Sandford and Merton* by Thomas Day, and Martha Farquharson's twenty-six volume *Elsie Dinsmore* series dealt with pious protagonists who learned restraint, repentance, and rehabilitation from sin.

Two bright spots in this period of didacticism were Jean Jacques Rousseau's *Emile* and *The Tales of Shakespeare*, Charles and Mary Lamb's simplified versions of Shakespeare's plays. Rousseau believed that a child's abilities were enhanced by a free, happy life, and the Lambs subscribed to the notion that children were entitled to more entertaining literature written in language comprehensible to them.

Nineteenth century

Child/adolescent literature truly began its modern rise in nineteenth century Europe. Hans Christian Andersen's *Fairy Tales* were fanciful adaptations of the somber revisions of the Grimm brothers in the previous century. Andrew Lang's series of colorful fairy books contain the folklores of many nations and are still part of the collections of many modern libraries. Clement Moore's "A Visit from St. Nicholas" is a cheery, non-threatening child's view of the "night before Christmas." The humor of Lewis Carroll's books about Alice's adventures, Edward Lear's poems with caricatures, Lucretia Nole's stories of the Philadelphia Peterkin family were full of fancy and not a smidgen of morality. Other popular Victorian novels introduced the modern fantasy and science fiction genres: William Makepeace Thackeray's *The Rose and the Ring*, Charles Dickens' *The Magic Fishbone*, and Jules Verne's *Twenty Thousand Leagues Under the Sea*. Adventure to exotic places became a popular topic: Rudyard Kipling's *Jungle Books*, Verne's *Around the World in Eighty Days*, and Robert Louis Stevenson's *Treasure Island* and *Kidnapped*. In 1884, the first English translation of Johanna Spyre's *Heidi* appeared.

North America was also finding its voices for adolescent readers. American Louisa May Alcott's *Little Women* and Canadian L.M. Montgomery's *Anne of Green Gables* ushered in the modern age of realistic fiction. American youth were enjoying the misadventures of Tom Sawyer and Huckleberry Finn. For the first time children were able to read books about real people just like themselves.

Twentieth century

The literature of the twentieth century is extensive and diverse and, as in previous centuries, much influenced by the adults who write, edit, and select books for consumption by youngsters. In the first third of the century, suitable adolescent literature dealt with children from good homes and large families. These books projected an image of a peaceful, rural existence. Though the characters and plots were more realistic, the stories maintained focus on topics that were considered emotionally and intellectually proper. Popular at this time were Laura Ingalls Wilder's Little House on the Prairie Series and Carl Sandburg's biography *Abe Lincoln Grows Up*. English author J.R.R. Tolkein's fantasy, *The Hobbit,* prefaced modern adolescent readers' fascination with the works of Piers Antony, Madelaine L'Engle, and Anne McCaffery.

Fiction and Nonfiction

Fiction is the opposite of fact, and, simple as that may seem, it's the major distinction between fiction works and nonfiction works. The earliest nonfiction came in the form of cave-paintings, the record of what prehistoric man procured on hunting trips. On the other hand, we don't know that some of it might be fiction—that is, what they would like to catch on future hunting trips. Cuneiform inscriptions, which hold the earliest writings, are probably nonfiction about conveying goods such as oxen and barley and dealing with the buying and selling of these items. It's easy to assume that nonfiction, then, is pretty boring; since it simply serves the purpose of recording everyday facts. Fiction, on the other hand, is the result of imagination and is recorded for the purpose of entertainment. If a work of nonfiction endures beyond its original time, then it tends to be viewed as either exceptionally well made or perfectly embodying the ideas, manners, and attitudes of the time when it was produced.

Some (not all) types of nonfiction:
- Almanac
- Autobiography
- Biography
- Blueprint
- Book report
- Diary
- Dictionary
- Documentary film
- Encyclopedia
- Essay
- History
- Journal
- Letter
- Philosophy
- Science book
- Textbook
- User manual

These can also be called genres of nonfiction—divisions of a particular art according to criteria particular to that form. How these divisions are formed is vague. There are actually no fixed boundaries for either fiction or nonfiction. They are formed by sets of conventions, and many works cross into multiple genres by way of borrowing and recombining these conventions.

Some genres of fiction (not all):
- Action-adventure
- Crime
- Detective
- Erotica
- Fantasy
- Horror
- Mystery
- Romance
- Science fiction
- Thriller
- Western

A *bildungsroman* (from the German) means "novel of education" or "novel of formation" and is a novel that traces the spiritual, moral, psychological, or social development and growth of the main character from childhood to maturity. Dickens' *David Copperfield* (1850) represents this genre, as does Thomas Wolfe's *Look Homeward Angel* (1929).

A work of fiction typically has a central character, called the protagonist, and a character that stands in opposition, called the antagonist. The antagonist might be something other than a person. In Stephen Crane's short story, *The Open Boat*, for example, the antagonist is a hostile environment, a stormy sea. Conflicts between protagonist and antagonist are typical of a work of fiction, and climax is the point at which those conflicts are resolved. The plot has to do with the form or shape that the conflicts take as they move toward resolution. A fiction writer artistically uses devices labeled characterization to reveal character. Characterization can depend on dialogue, description, and/or the attitude or attitudes of one or more characters toward one another.

Enjoying fiction depends upon the ability of readers to suspend disbelief, to some extent. Readers makes a deal with writers that for the time it takes to read the story, their own belief will be put aside and be replaced by the convictions and reality that the writers has presented in the story. This is not true in nonfiction. Writers of nonfiction declare in the choice of that genre that their work is reliably based upon reality. The *MLA Style Manual*, for instance, can be relied upon because it is not the result of someone's imagination.

Skill 15.3 **Make inferences about character, setting, author's point of view, etc., based on the content of a literary passage**

It's no accident that **plot** is sometimes called action. If the plot does not *move*, the story quickly dies. Therefore, successful writers of stories use a wide variety of active verbs in creative and unusual ways. If readers are kept on their toes by the movement of the story, then the experience of reading it will be pleasurable. Those readers will probably want to read more of the writers' work. Careful, unique, and unusual choices of active verbs will bring about that effect. William Faulkner is a good example of a successful writer whose stories are lively and memorable because of his use of unusual active verbs. In analyzing the development of plot, it's wise to look at the verbs. However, the development of believable conflicts is also vital. If there is no conflict, there is no story. What devices do writers use to develop the conflicts, and are those conflicts real and believable?

Character is portrayed in many ways: description of physical characteristics, dialogue, interior monologue, the thoughts of the character, the attitudes of other characters toward this one, etc. Descriptive language depends on the ability to recreate a sensory experience for readers. If the description of the character's appearance is a visual one, then readers must be able to *see* the character. What's the shape of the nose? What color are the eyes? How tall or how short is this character? Thin or chubby? How does the character move? How does the character walk? Terms must be chosen that will create a picture for readers. It's not enough to say the eyes are blue, for example. What blue? Often the color of eyes is compared to something else to enhance readers' ability to visualize the character. A good test of characterization is the level of emotional involvement of readers in the character. If readers are to become involved, the description must provide an actual experience—seeing, smelling, hearing, tasting, or feeling.

Dialogue will reflect characteristics. Is it clipped? Does it employ significant dialect? Does a character use a lot of colloquialisms? The ability to portray the speech of a character can make or break a story. The kind of person the character is in the mind of readers is dependent on impressions created by description and dialogue. How do other characters feel about a particular character as revealed by their interactions with that character, their discussions with each other about that character, or their overt descriptions of that character. For example, "John, of course, can't be trusted with another person's possessions." In analyzing a story, it's useful to discuss the devices used to produce character.

Setting may be visual, temporal, psychological, or social. Descriptive words are often used here, also. In Edgar Allan Poe's description of the house in "The Fall of the House of Usher," as the protagonist/narrator approaches it, the air of dread and gloom that pervades the story is caught in the setting and sets the stage. A setting may also be symbolic (it is in Poe's story): the house is a symbol of the family that lives in it. As the house disintegrates, so does the family.

The language used in all of these aspects of a story—plot, character, and setting—work together to create the **mood** of a story. Poe's first sentence establishes the mood of the story: "During the whole of a dull, dark, and soundless day in the autumn of the year, when the clouds hung oppressively low in the heavens, I had been passing alone, on horseback, through a singularly dreary tract of country; and at length found myself, as the shades of the evening drew on, within view of the melancholy House of Usher."

COMPETENCY 16.0   ANALYZE AND INTERPRET EXAMPLES OF RELIGIOUS OR PHILOSOPHICAL IDEAS FROM VARIOUS PERIODS OF TIME, AND UNDERSTAND THEIR SIGNIFICANCE IN SHAPING SOCIETIES AND CULTURES

Skill 16.1   Distinguish the religious and philosophical traditions associated with given cultures and world regions

Eight common religions are practiced today. Interestingly, all of these religions have divisions or smaller sects within them. Not one of them is completely unified.

Judaism: the oldest of the eight and the first to teach and practice the belief in one God, Yahweh.

Christianity: came from Judaism, grew and spread in the First Century throughout the Roman Empire, despite persecution. A later schism resulted in the Western (Roman Catholic) and Eastern (Orthodox) parts. Protestant sects developed as part of the Protestant Revolution. The name "Christian" means one who is a follower of Jesus Christ, who started Christianity. Christians follow his teachings and examples, living by the laws and principles of the Bible.

Islam: founded in Arabia by Mohammed, who preached about God, Allah. Islam spread through trade, travel, and conquest; and followers of it fought in the Crusades. In addition, Islam figures in other wars against Christians and, today, against the Jewish nation of Israel. Followers of Islam, called Muslims, live by the teachings of the Koran, their holy book, and of their prophets.

Hinduism: a complex religion, centering around the belief that, through many reincarnations of the soul, man will eventually be united with the universal soul, which assumes the three forms of Brahma (the creator), Vishnu (the preserver) and Siva (the destroyer). Hinduism was begun by people called Aryans around 1500 BC and spread into India. The Aryans blended their culture with the culture of the Dravidians, natives they conquered. Today it has many sects and promotes the worship of hundreds of gods and goddesses and the belief in reincarnation. Though forbidden today by law, a prominent feature of Hinduism in the past was a rigid adherence to, and practice of, the infamous caste system.

Buddhism: a religion similar to Hinduism, but which rejects the caste system in favor of all men following the "eightfold path" toward spiritual living. Nirvana (spiritual peace), may be reached even in one lifetime by righteous living. Buddhism was developed in India from the teachings of Prince Gautama and spread to most of Asia. Its beliefs opposed the worship of numerous deities, the Hindu caste system, and preoccupation with the supernatural. Worshippers must be free of attachment to all things worldly and devote themselves to finding release from life's suffering.

Confucianism is a Chinese religion based on the teachings of the 5th century Chinese philosopher Confucius; noted for his teachings that reflect faith in mankind, he advocated living an active life of learning, participating in government, and devotion to family. There is no clergy, no organization, and no belief in a deity or in life after death. It emphasizes political and moral ideas with respect for authority and ancestors. Rulers were expected to govern according to high moral standards.

Taoism: 6th century B.C. philosopher Lao-tse, taught that since laws cannot improve man's lot, government should be a minimal force in man's life. Man should live passively in harmony with Tao (nature). Lao-tse wrote a book known as *The Tao The Ching.* .

Shinto: ancient religious beliefs, known as the "Way of the Gods", incorporate nature and ancestor worship with shamanistic practices, such as belief in magic to control nature, heal sickness, and predict the future. The native religion of Japan developed from native folk beliefs worshipping spirits and demons in animals, trees, and mountains. According to its mythology, deities created Japan and its people, which resulted in worshipping the emperor as a god. Shinto was strongly influenced by Buddhism and Confucianism, but never had strong doctrines on salvation or life after death.

Skill 16.2 Recognize assumptions and beliefs underlying ideas presented in religious or philosophical writing

Preliterate societies probably passed religious and historical information on from one generation to the next by using mnemonic exercises as part of initiation rites and religious rituals. Group memories of important tribal events were the domain of the community storytellers and were transmitted from one generation to the next through the use of long poems and chants set to music. It is likely that dance was also enlisted to communicate tribal history and to insure it's continuity in the tribe's traditions Ancient cultures relied on oral epic poems and mythologies from the past on which to base their traditions. Often the historical information was couched in religious terms, as in the Sumerian mythologies in which warring gods and goddesses actually portrayed feuding city-states. Eventually, these orally transmitted stories were written down, forming the basis for the mythologies and legends we know today.

"To the victors go the spoils", and so, apparently, do the publishing rights. The winners in any war gain the privilege of having history viewed through their eyes, and, usually, through their eyes alone. The Romans were masters at propaganda and enlisted the aid of many historians and other writers to create history books favorable to the Roman perspective. They also wrote Roman mythologies that "altered" the past in order to help the new Roman conquerors gain respectability with their new subjects.

During the Medieval period, the Roman Catholic Church served as both religious institution and government. Since there was no real separation of church and state, portrayals of religious events and historical events tended to mesh together, as evidenced by the many church paintings depicting both historical characters and contemporary people in religious settings. Religious law became state law, and religious truths were assumed to be the truths that all people, regardless of personal beliefs, must adhere to. Because the Church collected taxes, it had money to construct buildings which served both church and municipal functions. The churches were filled with religious art, depicting stories which were accepted as historically accurate fact.

Social, Political and Religious Forces and the Humanities

It is often said that the arts are a mirror of society, reflecting the morals, attitudes, and concerns of people in any given culture. Because the humanities deal with the expression of the human experience, it stands to reason that society's views of what is appropriate to reveal about that experience plays a major role in what artists express. At any time in history, political, social, and religious powers have influenced what artists feel comfortable expressing.

(In contrast to this is the view of "art for art's sake", a slogan touted by Oscar Wilde and Samuel Coleridge, among others. This opinion holds that the arts, out of necessity, are outside the realm of these forces, and that art can and should exist solely for its own benefit and because of its intrinsic beauty.)

Political influence can be seen in the monumental sculpture of the Roman Empire, constructed to glorify the state. An example is the 6'8" sculpture of *Augustus in Armor*, depicting the emperor as a consul confidently striding forward to deliver an inspiring speech to his legions. The bare feet denote courage; while the staff symbolizes the power of the emperor over the Roman Senate. The bronze *Equestrian Statue of Marcus Aurelius* serves as a second example, illustrating the "philosopher-king" concept of the emperor as a man of learning ruling over Rome with wisdom and justice instead of brute force.

A recent example of how governmental powers affect the humanities can be seen in the context of the early twentieth-century in the Soviet Union. The communist regime feared that artists might encourage the onset of capitalism and democracy and, accordingly, took actions to repress freedom of expression in favor of rhetoric favorable to the cause of communism, including persecution of artists and authors. The result was an outpouring of state-produced, stilted graphic art and literature; while meaningful expressions in the arts had to be smuggled out of the country to receive acclaim. Aleksandr Solzhenitsyn, author of *One Day in the Life of Ivan Denisovich* and *The Gulag Archipelago*, was forced to live in exile for several years.

C) The influence of religion on art can most clearly be viewed in the works of the medieval European period. During this era, the Roman Catholic Church ruled as a state government and, as such, was the major patron of the arts. As a result, much of the art from this period was religious in nature. Examples are Duccio's *Christ Entering Jerusalem* and Master Honore's *David and Goliath*.

Sample Test: Artistic Expression and the Humanities

1. **The world religion associated with the caste system, is**:

   A. Buddhism
   B. Hinduism
   C. Sikhism
   D. Jainism

2. **A combination of three or more tones sounded at the same time is called a**

   A. Harmony
   B. Consonance
   C. A chord
   D. Dissonance

3. **A series of single tones which add up to a recognizable pattern is called a:**

   A. Cadence
   B. Rhythm
   C. Melody
   D. Sequence

4. **The following is not a good activity to encourage fifth graders' artistic creativity:**

   A. Ask them to make a decorative card for a family member.
   B. Have them work as a team to decorate a large wall display.
   C. Ask them to copy a drawing from a book, with the higher grades being awarded to those students who come closest to the model.
   D. Have each student try to create an outdoor scene with crayons, giving them a choice of scenery.

5. **The history of theatre is important to describe how theatre has evolved over time. Which of the following is not a vital part of the many time periods of theatre history?**

   A. Roman theatre
   B. American theatre
   C. Medieval drama
   D. Renaissance theatre

6. **Creating movements in response to music helps students to connect music and dance in which of the following ways?**

   A. rhythm
   B. costuming
   C. speed
   D. vocabulary skills

7. Often, local elected officials and artists are brought into the classroom to:

   A. explain their jobs or trades
   B. observe teaching skills
   C. enrich and extend arts curriculum
   D. entertain students and teachers

8. In the visual arts, a genre may refer to

   A. scenes of everyday life
   B. a type of tempra paint
   C. the choice of medium
   D. opera

9. Classicism in music and literature

   A. was designed to appeal to the masse
   B. originated in the medieval period in Europe
   C. was based on linear perspective
   D. was formal, quiet and restrained.

10. The guiding principle of the Italian Renaissance was

   A. Humanis
   B. Manneris
   C. Neoclassicis
   D. Sfumato

11. Impressionism in art and music was an attempt to

   A. capture the transitory aspects of the world
   B. impress the audience with a photographic view of the world
   C. express heart-felt emotions about nature
   D. portray the common people in a heroic light

12. In the religion of Hinduism, the three aspects of the God-head are

   A. Brahma, Vishnu, and Shiva
   B. Nirvana, Vishnu, and Buddha
   C. Veda, Ramayana, and Buddha
   D. Rig-Veda, Rama, and Shiva

13. The Japanese religion of Zen Buddhism emphasizes

   A. belief in reincarnation
   B. adherence to the caste system
   C. ancestor worship
   D. spirituality through meditation

14. The contribution to Western Civilization not associated with Judaism is the

   A. belief in ethical treatment of others
   B. belief in polytheism
   C. belief in monotheism
   D. belief in the supremacy of law

15. The main contribution of Christianity to Western Civilization is the

A. advocating of ethical treatment of others
B. belief in saints
C. spirituality found in church art and architecture
D. transmission of Hebraic history

16. Universal themes are those which

A. explain how the universe was created
B. explain the nature of the universe
C. can be experienced by all people
D. belong to specific groups of people

17. Twentieth century themes are marked by

A. practicality
B. idealism
C. realism
D. diversity

18. "Aesthetics" deals with

A. subject matter
B. theme
C. quality of materials
D. the nature of beauty

19. The philosophy best associated with Lao-tse is

A. government should be a strong force in society
B. mankind should live in fear of the gods
C. mankind should live in harmony with nature
D. mankind should strive toward intellectual perfection

Answer Key: Artistic Expression and the Humanities

1. B.
2. C.
3. C.
4. C.
5. B.
6. A.
7. C.
8. A.
9. D.
10. A.
11. A.
12. A.
13. D.
14. B.
15. A.
16. C.
17. D.
18. D.
19. C.

COMPETENCY 17.0   DERIVE INFORMATION FROM A VARIETY OF SOURCES (E.G., MAGAZINES, ARTICLES, ESSAYS, WEBSITES)

Skill 17.1   Identify the stated or implied main idea of a paragraph or passage

Main Idea

The **main idea** of a passage or paragraph is the basic message, idea, point concept, or meaning that the author wants to convey to you, the reader. Understanding the main idea of a passage or paragraph is the key to understanding the more subtle components of the author's message. The main idea is what is being said about a topic or subject. Once you have identified the basic message, you will have an easier time answering other questions that test critical skills.

Main ideas are either *stated* or *implied*. A *stated main idea* is explicit: it is directly expressed in a sentence or two in the paragraph or passage. An *implied main idea* is suggested by the overall reading selection. In the first case, you need not pull information from various points in the paragraph or passage in order to form the main idea because it is already stated by the author. If a main idea is implied, however, you must formulate, in your own words, a main idea statement by condensing the overall message contained in the material itself.

Skill 17.2   Select an accurate summary or outline of a passage

Sample Passage

Sometimes too much of a good thing can become a very bad thing indeed. In an earnest attempt to consume a healthy diet, dietary supplement enthusiasts have been known to overdose. Vitamin C, for example, long thought to help people ward off cold viruses, is currently being studied for its possible role in warding off cancer and other disease that cases tissue degeneration. Unfortunately, an overdose of vitamin C – more than 10,000 mg – on a daily basis can cause nausea and diarrhea. Calcium supplements, commonly taken by women, are helpful in warding off osteoporosis. More than just a few grams a day, however, can lead to stomach upset and even to kidney and bladder stones. Niacin, proven useful in reducing cholesterol levels, can be dangerous in large doses for those who suffer from heart problems, asthma or ulcers.

The main idea expressed in this paragraph is:

    A.   supplements taken in excess can be a bad thing indeed
    B.   dietary supplement enthusiasts have been known to overdose
    C.   vitamins can cause nausea, diarrhea, and kidney or bladder stones.
    D.   people who take supplements are preoccupied with their health.

Answer A is a paraphrase of the first sentence and provides a general framework for the rest of the paragraph: excess supplement intake is bad. The rest of the paragraph discusses the consequences of taking too many vitamins. Options B and C refer to major details, and Option D introduces the idea of preoccupation, which is not included in this paragraph.

Skill 17.3   Comprehend stated or implied relationships in an excerpt (e.g., cause-and effect, sequence of events)

The **organization** of a written work includes two factors: the order in which writers have chosen to present the different parts of the discussion or argument, and the relationships they construct between these parts.

Written ideas need to be presented in a **logical order** so that readers can follow the information easily and quickly. There are many different ways in which to order a series of ideas, but they all share two related foundation: to lead readers along a desired path to the main idea and to avoid backtracking and skipping around . *Some* of the ways in which a paragraph might be organized:

Sequence of events – In this type of organization, the details are presented in the order in which they have occurred. Paragraphs that describe a process or procedure, give directions, or outline a given period of time (such as a day or a month) are often arranged chronologically.

Statement support – In this type of organization, the main idea is stated, and the rest of the paragraph explains or proves it. This is also referred to as relative importance. There are four ways in which this type of order is organized: most to least, least to most, most-least-most, and least-most-least.

Comparison-Contrast – In this type of organization, the compare-contrast pattern is used in paragraphs describes the differences or similarities of two or more ideas, actions, events, or things. Usually, the topic sentence describes the basic relationship between the ideas or items, and the rest of the paragraph explains this relationship.

Classification – in this type of organization, the paragraph presents grouped information about a topic. The topic sentence usually states the general category, and the rest of the sentences show how various elements of the category have a common base and/or how they differ from the common base.

Cause and Effect – This pattern describes how two or more events are connected. The main sentence usually states the primary cause(s), the primary effect(s), and how they are basically connected. The rest of the sentences explain the connection – how one event caused the next.

Spatial/Place – In this type of organization, certain descriptions are organized according to the location of items in relation to each other and to a larger context. The orderly arrangement guides readers' eyes as they mentally envision the scene or place being described.

Many times, all of these organizations follow the basic P.I.E sequence:
P – The point, or main idea, of the paragraph
I – The information (data, details, facts) that supports the main idea
E – The explanation or analysis of the information and how it proves, is related to or connected to the main idea.

Even if the sentences that make up a given paragraph or passage are arranged in logical order, the document as a whole can still seem choppy and the various ideas disconnected. **Transitions**, words that signal relationships between ideas, can help improve the flow of a document. Transitions can help achieve clear and effective presentation of information by establishing connections between sentences, paragraphs, and whole sections of a document. With transitions, each sentence builds on the ideas in the last, and each paragraph has clear links to the preceding one. As a result, readers receive clear directions on how to piece together the writers' ideas in a logically coherent argument. By signaling how to organize, interpret, and react to information; transitions allow a writer to effectively and elegantly explain their ideas

Logical Relationship	Transitional Expression
Similarity	also, in the same way, just as ... so too, likewise, similarly
Exception/Contrast	but, however, in spite of, on the one hand ... on the other hand, nevertheless, nonetheless, notwithstanding, in contrast, on the contrary, still, yet
Sequence/Order	first, second, third, ... next, then, finally
Time	after, afterward, at last, before, currently, during, earlier, immediately, later, meanwhile, now, recently, simultaneously, subsequently, then
Example	for example, for instance, namely, specifically, to illustrate
Emphasis	even, indeed, in fact, of course, truly
Place/Position	above, adjacent, below, beyond, here, in front, in back, nearby, there
Cause and Effect	accordingly, consequently, hence, so, therefore, thus
Additional Support or Evidence	additionally, again, also, and, as well, besides, equally important, further, furthermore, in addition, moreover, then
Conclusion/Summary	finally, in a word, in brief, in conclusion, in the end, in the final analysis, on the whole, thus, to conclude, to summarize, in sum, in summary

The following example shows good logical order and transitions

No one really knows how Valentine's Day started. There are several legends, however, which are often told. The first attributes Valentine's Day to a Christian priest who lived in Rome during the third century under the rule of Emperor Claudius. Rome was at war, and, apparently Claudius felt that married men didn't fight as well as bachelors. Consequently, Claudius banned marriage for the duration of the war. But Valentinus, the priest, risked his life to secretly marry couples in violation of Claudius' law. The second legend is even more romantic. In this story, Valentinus is a prisoner having been condemned to die for refusing to worship pagan deities. While in jail, he fell in love with his jailer's daughter, who happened to be blind. Daily, he prayed for her sight to return, and, miraculously, it did. On February 14, the day that he was scheduled to die, he was allowed to write the young woman a note. In this farewell letter, he promised eternal love and signed at the bottom of the page the now famous words, "Your Valentine."

Skill 17.4 **Recognize information that supports, illustrates, or elaborates the main idea of a passage**

Supporting Details

Paragraphs should contain concrete, interesting information and supporting details to support the main idea or point of view. Fact statements add weight to opinions, especially when writers are trying to convince readers of their viewpoints Because every good thesis has an assertion, a well-written passage offers specifics, facts, data, anecdotes, expert opinions and other details to *show* or *prove* that assertion. While *the authors* know what they want to convey, the *readers* do not.

In the following paragraph, the sentences in **bold print** provide a skeleton of a paragraph on the benefits of recycling. The sentences in bold are generalizations that by themselves do not explain the need to recycle. The sentences in *italics* add details to SHOW the general points in bold. Notice how the supporting details help you to understand the necessity for recycling.

While, one day, recycling may become mandatory in all states; right now, it is voluntary in many communities. *Those of us who participate in recycling are amazed by how much material is recycled.* **For many communities, the blue-box recycling program has had an immediate effect.** *By just recycling glass, aluminum cans, and plastic bottles, we have reduced the volume of disposable trash by one third, thus extending the useful life of local landfills by over a decade. Imagine the difference if those dramatic results were achieved nationwide.* **The amount of reusable items we thoughtlessly dispose of is staggering.** *For example, Americans dispose of enough steel everyday to supply Detroit car manufacturers for three months. Additionally, we dispose of enough aluminum annually to rebuild the nation's air fleet. These statistics, available from the Environmental Protection Agency (EPA), should encourage all of us to watch what we throw away.* **Clearly, recycling in our homes and in our communities directly improves the environment.**

COMPETENCY 18.0   ANALYZE AND INTERPRET WRITTEN MATERIALS FROM A VARIETY OF SOURCES

Skill 18.1   Recognize a writer's purpose for writing (e.g., to persuade, to describe)

An essay is an extended discussion of a writer's point of view about a particular topic. This point of view may be supported by using such writing modes as examples, argument and persuasion, analysis, or comparison/contrast. In any case, a good essay is clear, coherent, well-organized, and fully developed.

When authors set out to write a passage, they usually have a purpose for doing so. That purpose may be to simply give information that might be interesting or useful to some readers or other; it may be to persuade the reader to a point of view or to move the reader to act in a particular way; it may be to tell a story; or it may be to describe something in such a way that an experience becomes available to the reader through one of the five senses. Following are the primary devices for expressing a particular purpose in a piece of writing:

- **Basic expository writing** simply gives information not previously known about a topic or is used to explain or define one. Facts, examples, statistics, cause and effect, direct tone, objective rather than subjective delivery, and non-emotional information are presented in a formal manner.

- **Descriptive writing** centers on person, place, or object using concrete and sensory words to create a mood or impression and arranges details in a chronological or spatial sequence.

- **Narrative writing** is developed using an incident, anecdote, or related series of events. Chronology, the 5 W's, topic sentence, and conclusion are essential ingredients.

- **Persuasive writing** implies ability to select vocabulary and arrange facts and opinions in such a way as to influence readers. Persuasive writing may incorporate elements of exposition and narration.

- **Journalistic writing** is theoretically free of author bias. It is essential when relaying information about an event, person, or thing that writing be factual and objective. Provide students with opportunities to examine newspapers and to create their own. Many newspapers have educational programs that offer free papers to schools.

Tailoring language for a particular **audience** is an important skill. Writing to be read by a business associate will surely sound different from writing to be read by a younger sibling. Not only are the vocabularies different, but the formality/informality of the discourse will need to be adjusted.

The things to be aware of in determining what the language should be for a particular audience, then, hinges on two things: **word choice** and formality/informality. The most formal language does not use contractions or slang. The most informal language will probably feature a more casual use of common sayings and anecdotes. Formal language will use longer sentences and will not sound like a conversation. The most informal language will use shorter sentences (not necessarily simple sentences) and may sound like a conversation.

In both formal and informal writing, there exists **tone** conveying writers' attitudes toward material and/or readers. Tone may be playful, formal, intimate, angry, serious, ironic, outraged, baffled, tender, serene, depressed, etc. The overall tone of a piece of writing is dictated by both the subject matter and the audience. Tone is also related to the actual words which make up the document because we attach affective meanings to words; these are called **connotations**. Gaining this conscious control over language makes it possible to use language appropriately in various situations and to evaluate its uses in literature and other forms of communication. By evoking the proper responses from readers/listeners, we can prompt them to take action.

The following questions are an excellent way to assess the audience and tone of a given piece of writing.

1. Who is your audience? (friend, teacher, business person, someone else)
2. How much does this person know about you and/or your topic?
3. What is your purpose? (to prove an argument, to persuade, to amuse, to register a complaint, to ask for a raise, etc)
4. What emotions do you have about the topic? (nervous, happy, confident, angry, sad, no feelings at all)
5. What emotions do you want to register with your audience? (anger, nervousness, happiness, boredom, interest)
6. What persona do you need to create in order to achieve your purpose?
7. What choice of language is best suited to achieving your purpose with your particular subject? (slang, friendly but respectful, formal)
8. What emotional quality do you want to transmit to achieve your purpose (matter of fact, informative, authoritative, inquisitive, sympathetic, angry), and to what degree do you want to express this tone?

If a writer's attitude toward snakes involves active dislike and fear, then the tone would also reflect that attitude by being negative:

> *Countless species of snakes, some more dangerous than others, still lurk on the urban fringes of Florida's towns and cities. They will often invade domestic spaces, terrorizing people and their pets.*

Here, obviously, the snakes are the villains. They *lurk*, they *invade*, and they *terrorize.* The tone of this paragraph might be said to be distressed about snakes.

In the same manner, a writer can use language to portray characters as good or bad. A writer uses positive and negative adjectives, as seen above, to convey an impression of a character.

Skill 18.2   Draw conclusions, or make generalizations, based on information presented in an excerpt

An **inference** is sometimes called an "educated guess" because it requires that you go beyond the strictly obvious to create additional meaning by taking the text one logical step further. Inferences and conclusions are based on the content of the passage – that is, on what the passage says or how the writer says it – and are derived by reasoning.

Inference is an essential and automatic component of most reading; for example, in making educated guesses about the meaning of unknown words, the author's main idea, or whether he or she is writing with a bias. Such is the essence of inference: you use your own ability to reason in order to figure out what writers imply. As a reader, then, you must often logically apprehend meaning that is only implied.

Consider the following example. Assume that you are an employer and that you are reading over the letters of reference submitted by a prospective employee for the position of clerk/typist in your real estate office. The position requires the applicant to be neat, careful, trustworthy, and punctual. You come across this letter of reference submitted by an applicant:

> *To whom it may concern,*
>
> *Todd Finley has asked me to write a letter of reference for him. I am well qualified to do so because he worked for me for three months last year. His duties included answering the phone, greeting the public, and producing some simple memos and notices on the computer. Although Todd initially had few computer skills and little knowledge of telephone etiquette, he did acquire some during his stay with us. Todd's manner of speaking, both on the telephone and with the clients who came to my establishment, could be described as casual. He was particularly effective when communicating with peers. Please contact me by telephone if you wish to have further information about my experience.*

Here the writer implies, rather than openly states, the main idea. This letter calls attention to itself because there's a problem with its tone. A truly positive letter would say something like "I have distinct honor to recommend Todd Finley." Here, however, the letter simply verifies that Todd worked in the office. Second, the praise is obviously lukewarm. For example, the writer says that Todd "was particularly effective when communicating with peers." And educated guess translates that statement into a nice way of saying Todd was not serious about his communication with clients.

In order to draw **inferences** and make **conclusions**, readers must use prior knowledge and apply it to the current situation. A conclusion or inference is never stated. You must rely on your common sense.

Practice question

Read the following passages and select an answer.

1. Tim Sullivan had just turned 15. As a birthday present, his parents had given him a guitar and a certificate for 10 guitar lessons. He had always shown a love of music and a desire to learn an instrument. Tim began his lessons and before long, he was making up his own songs. At the music studio, Tim met Josh, who played the piano, and Roger, whose instrument was the saxophone. They all shared the same dream, to start a band, and each was identified by his teacher as possessing real talent.

   From this passage one can infer that
   (A) Tim, Roger & Josh are going to start their own band.
   (B) Tim is going to give up his guitar lessons.
   (C) Tim, Josh & Roger will no longer be friends.
   (D) Josh & Roger are going to start their own band.

2. The Smith family waited patiently around Carousel Number 7 for their luggage to arrive. They were exhausted after their five-hour trip and were anxious to get to their hotel. After about an hour, they realized that they no longer recognized any of the other passengers' faces. Mrs. Smith asked the person who appeared to be in charge if they were at the right carousel. The man replied, "Yes, this is it, but we finished unloading that baggage almost half an hour ago."

From the man's response, we can infer that:
   (A) The Smiths were ready to go to their hotel.
   (B) The Smith's luggage was lost.
   (C) The man had their luggage.
   (D) They were at the wrong carousel.

1. (A) is the correct choice. Given the facts that Tim wanted to be a musician and start his own band, we can infer that they joined together in an attempt to make their dreams become a reality after meeting others who shared the same dreams.

2. Since the Smiths were still waiting for their luggage, we know that they were not yet ready to go to their hotel. From the man's response, we know that they were not at the wrong carousel and that he did not have their luggage. Therefore, though not directly stated, it appears that their luggage was lost. Choice (B) is the correct answer.

Skill 18.3   **Interpret figurative language in an excerpt**

15. Simile: Indirect comparison between two things. "My love is like a red-red rose."

16. Metaphor: Direct comparison between two things. The use of a word or phrase denoting one kind of object or action in place of another to suggest a comparison between them. While poets use them extensively, they are also integral to everyday speech. For example, chairs are said to have "legs" and "arms"; although we know that it's humans who have these appendages.

17. Parallelism: The arrangement of ideas in phrases, sentences, and paragraphs that balance one element with another of equal importance and similar wording. An example from Francis Bacon's *Of Studies:* "Reading maketh a full man, conference a ready man, and writing an exact man."

18. Personification: Human characteristics are attributed to an inanimate object, an abstract quality, or animal. Examples: John Bunyan wrote characters named Death, Knowledge, Giant Despair, Sloth, and Piety in his *Pilgrim's Progress.* The metaphor of an arm of a chair is a form of personification.

19. Euphemism: The substitution of an agreeable or inoffensive term for one that might offend or suggest something unpleasant. Many euphemisms are used to refer to death to avoid using the real word such as "passed away," "crossed over," or nowadays "passed."

20. Hyperbole: Deliberate exaggeration for effect or comic effect. An example from Shakespeare's *The Merchant of Venice*:

> Why, if two gods should play some heavenly match
> And on the wager lay two earthly women,
> And Portia one, there must be something else
> Pawned with the other, for the poor rude world
> Hath not her fellow.

21. Climax: A number of phrases or sentences are arranged in ascending order of rhetorical forcefulness. Example from Melville's *Moby Dick*:

> All that most maddens and torments; all that stirs up the lees of things; all truth with malice in it; all that cracks the sinews and cakes the brain; all the subtle demonisms of life and thought; all evil, to crazy Ahab, were visibly personified and made practically assailable in Moby Dick.

22. Bathos: A ludicrous attempt to portray pathos—that is, to evoke pity, sympathy, or sorrow. It may result from inappropriately dignifying the commonplace, from using elevated language to describe something trivial, or simply from greatly exaggerating pathos.

23. Oxymoron: A contradiction in terms deliberately employed for effect. It is usually seen in a qualifying adjective whose meaning is contrary to that of the noun it modifies, such as "wise folly."

24. Irony: Expressing something other than (particularly, opposite) the literal meaning, such as words of praise when blame is intended. In poetry, it is often used to express sophisticated or resigned awareness of some contrast between what is and what ought to be and expresses a controlled pathos without sentimentality. It is a form of indirection that avoids overt praise or censure. An early example: the Greek comic character Eiron, a clever underdog who by his wit repeatedly triumphs over the boastful character Alazon.

25. Alliteration: The repetition of consonant sounds in two or more neighboring words or syllables.

26. In its simplest form, it reinforces one or two consonant sounds. Example: Shakespeare's Sonnet #12:

> When I do count the clock that tells the time.

Some poets have used more complex patterns of alliteration by creating consonants both at the beginning of words and at the beginning of stressed syllables within words. Example: Shelley's "Stanzas Written in Dejection Near Naples"

> The City's voice itself is soft like Solitude's

27. Onomatopoeia: The naming of a thing or action by a vocal imitation of the sound associated with it, such as buzz, hiss, or any other words whose sounds suggests what they mean. A good example: from "The Brook" by Tennyson:

> I chatter over stony ways,
> In little sharps and trebles,
> I bubble into eddying bays,
> I babble on the pebbles.

28. Malapropism: A verbal blunder in which one word is replaced by another similar in sound, but different in meaning. Comes from Sheridan's Mrs. Malaprop in *The Rivals* (1775). Thinking of the geography of contiguous countries, she spoke of the "geometry" of "contagious countries."

Imagery can be described as a word or sequence of words that refers to any sensory experience—that is, anything that can be seen, tasted, smelled, heard, or felt on the skin or fingers. While writers of prose may also use these devices, it is most distinctive of poetry. Poets intend to make an experience available to readers. In order to do that, they must appeal to one of the senses. The most-often used one, of course, is visual imagery. Poets will deliberately paint a scene in such a way that readers can see it. However, the purpose is not simply to stir the visceral feeling, but also to stir the emotions. A good example is "The Piercing Chill" by Taniguchi Buson (1715-1783):

> The piercing chill I feel:
>   My dead wife's comb, in our bedroom,
>   Under my heel . . .

In only a few short words, the reader can feel many things: the shock that might come from touching the comb, a literal sense of death, the contrast between her death, and the memories he has of her when she was alive. Imagery might be defined as speaking of the abstract in concrete terms--a powerful device in the hands of a skillful poet.

A **symbol** is an object or action that can be observed with the senses in addition to its suggesting many other things. The lion is a symbol of courage; the cross is a symbol of Christianity; the color green is a symbol of envy. These can almost be defined as metaphors because society pretty much agrees on the one-to-one meaning of them. Symbols used in literature are usually of a different sort. They tend to be private and personal; their significance is only evident in the context of the work where they are used. A good example is the huge pair of spectacles on a sign board in Fitzgerald's *The Great Gatsby*. They are interesting as a part of the landscape, but they also symbolize divine myopia.

A symbol can certainly have more than one meaning, and the meaning may be as personal as the memories and experiences of the particular reader. In analyzing a poem or a story, it's important to identify the symbols and their possible meanings.

Looking for symbols is often challenging, especially for novice poetry readers. However, these suggestions may be useful: First, pick out all the references to concrete objects such as a newspaper or black cats. Note any that the poet emphasizes by describing in detail, by repeating, or by placing at the very beginning or ending of a poem. Ask yourself what the poem is about. What does it add up to? Paraphrase the poem, and determine whether or not the meaning depends upon certain concrete objects. Then ponder what the concrete object symbolizes in this particular poem. Look for a character with the name of a prophet who does little but utter prophecy or for a trio of women who resemble the Three Fates. A symbol may be a part of a person's body, such as the eye of the murder victim in Poe's story *The Tell-Tale Heart*, a look, a voice, or a mannerism.

Some things that are not symbols include an abstraction such as truth, death, or love; in narrative, a well-developed character who is not at all mysterious; or the second term in a metaphor.

An **allusion** is very much like a symbol, and the two sometimes tend to run together. An allusion is defined by Merriam Webster's *Encyclopedia of Literature* as "an implied reference to a person, event, thing, or a part of another text." Allusions are based on the assumption that there is a common body of knowledge shared by poets and readers and that a reference to that body of knowledge will be immediately understood. Allusions to the Bible and to classical mythology are common in Western literature on the assumption that they will be immediately understood. This is not always the case, of course. T. S. Eliot's *The Wasteland* requires research and annotation for understanding. He assumed more background on the part of average readers than actually exists. However, when Michael Moore on his web page headlines an article on the war in Iraq: "Déjà Fallouja: Ramadi surrounded, thousands of families trapped, no electricity or water, onslaught impending," we understand immediately that he is referring first of all to a repeat of the human disaster in New Orleans; although the "onslaught" is not a storm, but an invasion by American and Iraqi troops.

Skill 18.4 Compare and contrast views or arguments presented in two or more excerpts

Comparison and contrast, two skills that seem quite complementary, require different sets of skills. Simply put, when we compare two or more views or arguments, we find the similarities between them. When we contrast, we find the differences.

Teachers who are not careful in their selections of materials for which students will compare and contrast will find great difficulty. While there are differences and similarities in just about everything conceivable, the best compare/contrast exercise is one in which there is a good balance between similarities and differences. When looking at arguments, this is fairly easy. We can simply compare and contrast two views on the same subject. Often, when considering arguments, we are drawn toward arguments that are completely opposite each other. The similarity is the topic; the difference is the attitude or opinion about the topic. In younger grades, this is a very easy way to teach the concepts of compare and contrast. But note that in terms of balance, distinctly opposite perspectives yield similarities only in topic and differences only in viewpoint.

A more important skill involves teaching students how to compare and contrast arguments or viewpoints that share common ground, but differ more subtly. Generally, in the real world, most people can find some agreement on most topics. For example, consider arguments about environmental regulation. Two completely opposite viewpoints might look like this: One side believes that all regulation hurts the economy; the other side believes that no considerations for the economy should be given when developing regulations. Most of us can quickly see that very few people fall into either of these camps. Instead, most people compromise a bit. This is the type of compare and contrast that is most important for students. They need to be able to understand the similarities in belief (or the areas of compromise), as well as the areas that each side will not compromise on.

So, to make this more specific to extracting viewpoints from excerpts, students can first identify the topic that is up for discussion and argument. Immediately, that is known to be a similarity. Next, students can identify differences. It is better to start with the distinct differences than the specific similarities, as it will help students to put an identity on each argument. Finally, students can look for similarities or areas of compromise.

In an excerpt, students should not only look at the message; they should also look for tone. Often, in argumentation, irony and exaggeration are used; when students pick up on these traits, the task of comparison and contrast is much easier.

COMPETENCY 19.0   USE CRITICAL REASONING SKILLS TO ASSESS AN AUTHOR'S TREATMENT OF CONTENT IN WRITTEN MATERIAL FROM A VARIETY OF SOURCES

Skill 19.1   Analyze the logical structure of an argument in an excerpt, and identify possible instances of faulty reasoning

On the test, the terms **valid** and invalid have special meaning. If an argument is valid, it is reasonable. It is objective (not biased) and can be supported by evidence. If an argument is invalid, it is not reasonable. It is not objective. In other words, one can find evidence of bias.

Read the following passage.

> Most dentists agree that Bright Smile Toothpaste is the best for fighting cavities. It tastes good and leaves your mouth minty fresh.

Is this a valid or invalid argument?

(A) valid
(B) invalid

It is invalid (B). It mentions that "most" dentists agree. What about those who do not agree? The author is clearly exhibiting bias in leaving those who disagree out.

Practice question

Read the following passage.

It is difficult to decide who will make the best presidential candidate, Senator Johnson or Senator Keeley. They have both been involved in scandals and have both gone through messy divorces while in office.

Is this argument valid or invalid?

(A) valid
(B) invalid

The answer can be found at the end of the reading section.

Skill 19.2   Distinguish between fact and opinion in written material

Facts are statements that are verifiable. Opinions are statements that must be supported in order to be accepted such as beliefs, values, judgments or feelings. Facts are objective statements used to support subjective opinions. For example, "Jane is a bad girl" is an opinion. However, "Jane hit her sister with a baseball bat" is a *fact* upon which the opinion is based. Judgments are opinions— decisions or declarations based on observation or reasoning that express approval or disapproval. Facts report what has happened or exists and come from observation, measurement, or calculation. Facts can be tested and verified; whereas opinions and judgments cannot. They can only be supported with facts.

Most statements cannot be so clearly distinguished. "I believe that Jane is a bad girl" is a fact. Speakers do know what they believe. However, the statement obviously includes a judgment that could be disputed by another person. Judgments are not usually firm. They are, rather, plausible opinions that provoke thought or lead to factual development.

Joe DiMaggio, a Yankees' center-fielder, was replaced by Mickey Mantle in 1952.

This is a fact. If necessary, evidence can be produced to support this.

First year players are more ambitious than seasoned players.

This is an opinion. There is no proof to support that everyone feels this way.

Practice questions

1. The Inca were a group of Indians who ruled an empire in South America.

   (A) fact
   (B) opinion

2. The Inca were clever.

   (A) fact
   (B) opinion

3. The Inca built very complex systems of bridges.

   (A) fact
   (B) opinion

Skill 19.3   Determine the relevance of specific facts, examples, or data to a writer's argument

The main idea of a passage may contain a wide variety of supporting information, but it is important that each sentence be related to the main idea. When a sentence contains information that bears little or no connection to the main idea, then it is said to be **irrelevant**. It is important to continually assess whether or not a sentence contributes to the overall task of supporting the main idea. When a sentence is deemed irrelevant, then it is best to either omit it from the passage or to make it relevant by one of the following strategies:

1. Adding detail – Sometimes a sentence can seem out of place if it does not contain enough information to link it to the topic. Adding specific information can show how the sentence is related to the main idea.

2. Adding an example – This is especially important in passages in which information is being argued, compared, or contrasted. Examples can support the main idea and give the document overall credibility.

3. Using diction effectively – It is important to understand connotation, avoid ambiguity, and steer clear of too much repetition.

4. Adding transitions – Transitions are extremely helpful for making sentences relevant because they are specifically designed to connect one idea to another. They can also reduce paragraph choppiness.

The following passage has several irrelevant sentences highlighted in bold

The New City Planning Committee is proposing a new capitol building to represent the multicultural face of New City. **The current mayor is a Democrat.** The new capitol building will be on 10th street across from the grocery store and next to the Recreational Center. It will be within walking distance of the subway and bus depot because the designers want to emphasize the importance of public transportation. Aesthetically, the building will have a contemporary design featuring a brushed-steel exterior and large, floor-to-ceiling windows. **It is important for employees to have a connection with the outside world even when they are in their offices.** Inside the building, the walls will be moveable. This not only will facilitate a multitude of creative floor plans, but it will also create a focus on open communication and flow of information. **It sounds a bit gimmicky to me.** Finally, the capitol will feature a large outdoor courtyard full of lush greenery and serene fountains. **Work will now seem like Club Med to those who work at the New City capitol!**

Skill 19.4 Interpret the content, word choice, and phrasing of a passage to determine a writer's opinions, point of view, or position on an issue

Authors' tone is their attitude as reflected in the statement or passage. Their choice of words will help readers to determine the overall tone of a statement or passage.

Read the following paragraph.

> I was shocked by your article, which said that sitting down to breakfast was a thing of the past. Many families consider breakfast time to be family time. Children need to realize the importance of having a good breakfast. It is imperative that they be taught this at a young age. I cannot believe that a writer with your reputation has difficulty comprehending this.

The person who wrote the paragraph felt

(A) concern
(B) anger
(C) excitement
(D) disbelief

Since the person directly states that he or she "cannot believe" that the writer feels this way, the answer is (D) disbelief.

Practice question

Read the following paragraph.

I remember when I first started teaching, twenty years ago. I was apprehensive at first, but, within a short time, I felt like an old pro. If I had my life to live over again, I would still choose to be a teacher.

The author's tone can be best described as:

(A) joyous
(B) nostalgic
(C) bitter
(D) optimistic

(B) is the correct answer. The author appears to be "taking a trip down memory lane".

See also Skill 18.1

Skill 19.5   Evaluate the credibility, objectivity, or bias of an author's argument or sources

Bias is defined as an opinion, feeling, or influence that strongly favors one side in an argument. A statement or passage is biased if an author attempts to convince a reader of something.

Read the following statement.

Using a calculator cannot help a student understand the process of graphing, so its use is a waste of time.

Is there evidence of bias in the above statement?

(A) yes
(B) no

Since the author makes it perfectly clear that he does not favor the use of the calculator in graphing problem, the answer is (A). He has included his opinion in this statement.

Practice question

Read the following paragraph.

There are teachers who feel that computer programs are quite helpful in helping students grasp certain math concepts. There are also those who disagree with this feeling. It is up to individual math teachers to decide if computer programs benefit their particular group of students.

Is there evidence of bias in this paragraph?

(A) yes
(B) no

(B) is the correct answer. The author seems to state both sides of the argument without favoring a particular side.

See also Skill 21.7.

COMPETENCY 20.0   ANALYZE AND EVALUATE THE EFFECTIVENESS OF EXPRESSION IN A WRITTEN PARAGRAPH OR PASSAGE ACCORDING TO THE CONVENTIONS OF EDITED AMERICAN ENGLISH

Skill 20.1   Revise text to correct problems relating to grammar (e.g., syntax, pronoun-antecedent agreement)

Identify inappropriate shifts in verb tense

Verb tenses must refer to the same time period consistently, unless a change in time is required.

Error: Despite the increased number of students in the school this year, overall attendance is higher last year at the sporting events.

Problem: The verb *is* represents an inconsistent shift to the present tense when the action refers to a past occurrence.

Correction: *Despite the increased number of students in the school this year, overall attendance <u>was</u> higher last year at sporting events.*

Error: My friend Lou, who just competed in the marathon, ran since he was twelve years old.

Problem: Because Lou continues to run, the present perfect tense is needed.

Correction: *My friend Lou, who just competed in the marathon, <u>has run</u> since he was twelve years old.*

Error: The Mayor congratulated Wallace Mangham, who renovates the city hall last year.

Problem: Although the speaker is talking in the present, the action of renovating the city hall was in the past.

Correction: *The Mayor congratulated Wallace Mangham, who <u>renovated</u> the city hall last year.*

PRACTICE EXERCISE
SHIFTS IN TENSE

Choose the option that corrects an error in the underlined portion(s).
If no error exists, choose "No change is necessary".

1)   After we <u>washed</u> the fruit that had <u>growing</u> in the garden, we knew
        there <u>was</u> a store that would buy them.

        A) washing
        B) grown
        C) is
        D) No change is necessary.

2)   The tourists <u>used</u> to visit the Atlantic City boardwalk whenever they
        <u>vacationed</u> during the summer. Unfortunately, their numbers have
        <u>diminished</u> every year.

        A) use
        B) vacation
        C) diminish
        D) No change is necessary.

3)   When the temperature <u>drops</u> to below thirty-two degrees Fahrenheit,
        the water on the lake <u>freezes</u>, which <u>allowed</u> children to skate across it.

        A) dropped
        B) froze
        C) allows
        D) No change is necessary.

4)   The artists were <u>hired</u> to <u>create</u> a monument that would pay tribute to
        the men who were <u>killed</u> in World War Two.

        A) hiring
        B) created
        C) killing
        D) No change is necessary.

5)   Emergency medical personnel rushed to the scene of the shooting,
        where many injured people <u>waiting</u> for treatment.

        A) wait
        B) waited
        C) waits
        D) No change is necessary.

ANSWER KEY : PRACTICE EXERCISE FOR SHIFTS IN TENSE

1) B   The past participle *grown* is needed instead of *growing,* which is the progressive tense. Option A is incorrect because the past participle *washed* takes the *ed.* Option C incorrectly replaces the past participle *was* with the present tense *is.*

2) D   Option A is incorrect because *use* is the present tense. Option B incorrectly uses the noun *vacation.* Option C incorrectly uses the present tense *diminish* instead of the past tense *diminished.*

3) C   The present tense *allows* is necessary in the context of the sentence. Option A is incorrect because *dropped* is a past participle. Option B is incorrect because *froze* is past tense.

4) D   In Option A is incorrect because *hiring* is the present tense. In Option B is incorrect because *created* is a past participle. In Option C, *killing,* doesn't fit into the context of the sentence.

5) B   In Option B, *waited,* corresponds with the past tense *rushed.* In Option A, *wait,* is incorrect because it is present tense. In Option C, *waits,* is incorrect because the noun *people* is plural and requires the singular form of the verb.

A verb must correspond in the singular or plural form with the simple subject; it is not affected by any interfering elements. Note: A simple subject is never found in a prepositional phrase (a phrase beginning with a word such as of, by, over, through, until).

Present Tense Verb Form

	Singular	Plural
1st person (talking about oneself)	I do	We do
2nd person (talking to another)	You do	You do
3rd person (talking about someone or something)	He She does It	They do

Error: Sally, as well as her sister, plan to go into nursing.

Problem: The subject in the sentence is *Sally* alone, not the word *sister*. Therefore, the verb must be singular.

Correction: *Sally, as well as her sister, <u>plans</u> to go into nursing.*

Error: There has been many car accidents lately on that street.

Problem: The subject accidents in this sentence is plural; the verb must be plural also --even though it comes before the subject.

Correction: *There <u>have</u> been many car accidents lately on that street.*

Error: Everyone of us have a reason to attend the school musical.

Problem: The simple subject is the word *everyone*, not the *us* in the prepositional phrase. Therefore, the verb must be singular also.

Correction: *Everyone of us <u>has</u> a reason to attend the school musical.*

Error: Either the police captain or his officers is going to the convention.

Problem: In either/or and neither/nor constructions, the verb agrees with the subject closer to it.

Correction: *Either the police captain or his officers <u>are</u> going to the convention.*

PRACTICE EXERCISE
SUBJECT-VERB AGREEMENT

Choose the option that corrects an error in the underlined portion(s).
If no error exists, choose "No change is necessary."

1)   Every year, the store <u>stays</u> open late when shoppers, as they <u>prepare</u> for the holiday, desperately <u>try</u> to purchase Christmas presents.

   A. stay
   B. tries
   C. prepared
   D. No change is necessary.

2)   Paul McCartney, together with George Harrison and Ringo Starr, <u>sing</u> classic Beatles songs on a special greatest-hits CD.

   A. singing
   B. sings
   C. sung
   D. No change is necessary.

3)   My friend's cocker spaniel, while <u>chasing</u> cats across the street, always <u>manages</u> to <u>knock</u> over the trash cans.

   A. chased
   B. manage
   C. knocks
   D. No change is necessary.

4)   Some of the ice on the driveway <u>have melted.</u>

   A. having melted
   B. has melted
   C. has melt.
   D. No change is necessary.

5)   Neither the criminal forensics expert nor the DNA blood evidence <u>provided</u> enough support for that verdict.

   A. provides
   B. were providing
   C. are providing
   D. No change is necessary.

ANSWER KEY: PRACTICE EXERCISE FOR SUBJECT-VERB AGREEMENT

1) D   Option D is correct because *store* is third person singular and requires the third person singular verbs *stays*. Option B is incorrect because the plural noun *shoppers* requires a plural verb *try*. In Option C, there is no reason to shift to the past tense *prepared*.

2) B   Option B is correct because the subject, *Paul McCartney,* is singular and requires the singular verb *sings*. Option A is incorrect because the present participle *singing* does not stand alone as a verb. Option C is incorrect because the past participle *sung* alone cannot function as the verb in this sentence.

3) D   Option D is the correct answer because the subject *cocker spaniel* is singular and requires the singular verb *manages*. Options A,B, and C do not work structurally with the sentence.

4) B   The subject of the sentence is *some*, which requires a third person singular verb, *has melted*. Option A incorrectly uses the present participle *having*, which does not act as a helping verb. Option C does not work structurally with the sentence.

5) A   In Option A, the singular subject *evidence* is closer to the verb and thus requires the singular in the neither/nor construction. Both Options B and C are plural forms with the helping verb and the present participle.

A pronoun must correspond to its antecedent in number (singular or plural), person (first, second, or third person) and gender (male, female, or neuter). A pronoun must refer clearly to a single word, not to a complete idea.

A **pronoun shift** is a grammatical error in which the author starts a sentence, paragraph, or section of a paper using one particular type of pronoun and then suddenly shifts to another. This often confuses the reader.

Error: A teacher should treat all their students fairly.

Problem: Since *A teacher* is singular, the pronoun referring to it must also be singular. Otherwise, the noun has to be made plural.

Correction: *Teachers should treat all their students fairly.*

Error: When an actor is rehearsing for a play, it often helps if you can memorize the lines in advance.

Problem: *Actor* is a third-person word; that is, the writer is talking about the subject. The pronoun *you* is in the second person, which means the writer is talking to the subject.

Correction: *When actors are rehearsing for plays, it helps if they can memorize the lines in advance.*

Error: The workers in the factory were upset when his or her paychecks didn't arrive on time.

Problem: *Workers* is a plural form, while *his or her* refers to one person.

Correction: *The workers in the factory were upset when their paychecks didn't arrive on time.*

Error: The charity auction was highly successful, which pleased everyone.

Problem: In this sentence the pronoun *which* refers to the idea of the auction's success. In fact, *which* has no antecedent in the sentence; the word success is not stated.

Correction: *Everyone was pleased at the success of the auction.*

Error: Lana told Melanie that she would like aerobics.

Problem: The person that she refers to is unclear; it could be either Lana or Melanie.

Correction: *Lana said that Melanie would like aerobics.*

OR

Lana told Melanie that she, Melanie, would like aerobics.

Error: I dislike accounting, even though my brother is one.

Problem: A person's occupation is not the same as a field, and the pronoun *one* is thus incorrect. Note that the word *accountant* is not used in the sentence, so *one* has no antecedent.

Correction: *I dislike accounting, even though my brother is in <u>it.</u>*

PRACTICE EXERCISE
PRONOUN/ANTECEDENT AGREEMENT

Choose the option that corrects an error in the underlined portion(s).
If no error exists, choose "No change is necessary."

1) <u>You</u> can get to Martha's Vineyard by driving from Boston to Woods Hole. Once there, you can travel over on a ship, but <u>you</u> may find traveling by <u>airplane</u> to be an exciting experience.

    A. They
    B. visitors
    C. it
    D. No change is necessary.

2) Both the city leader and the <u>journalist</u> are worried about the new interstate; <u>she fears</u> <u>the new roadway</u> will destroy precious farmland.

    A. journalist herself
    B. they fear
    C. it
    D. No change is necessary.

3) When <u>hunters</u> are looking for deer in <u>the woods, you</u> must remain quiet for long periods of time.

    A. they
    B. it
    C. we
    D. No change is necessary.

4) Florida's strong economy is based on the importance of the citrus industry. <u>Producing</u> orange juice for most of the country.

    A. They produce
    B. Who produce
    C. Farmers there produce
    D. No change is necessary.

5) Dr. Kennedy told Paul Elliot, <u>his</u> assistant, that <u>he</u> would have to finish grading the tests before going home, no matter how long <u>it</u> took.

    A. their
    B. he, Paul
    C. they
    D. No change is necessary.

ANSWER KEY: PRACTICE EXERCISE FOR PRONOUN AGREEMENT

1) D   Pronouns must be consistent. As *you* is used throughout the sentence, the shift to *visitors* is incorrect. Option A, *They*, is vague and unclear. Option C, *it*, is also unclear.

2) B   The plural pronoun *they* is necessary to agree with the two nouns *leader* and *journalist*. There is no need for the reflexive pronoun *herself* in Option A. Option C, *it*, is vague.

3) A   The shift to *you* is unnecessary. The plural pronoun *they* is necessary to agree with the noun *hunters*. The word *we* in Option C is vague; the reader does not know who the word *we* might refer to. Option B, *it*, has no antecedent.

4) C   The noun *farmers* is needed for clarification because *producing* is vague. Option A is incorrect because *they produce* is vague. Option B is incorrect because *who* has no antecedent and creates a fragment.

5) B   The repetition of the name *Paul* is necessary to clarify who the pronoun *he* is referring to. (It could be Dr. Kennedy.) Option A is incorrect because the singular pronoun *his* is needed, not the plural pronoun *their*. Option C is incorrect because the pronoun *it* refers to the plural noun *tests*.

Rules for clearly identifying pronoun reference

Make sure that the antecedent reference is clear and cannot refer to something else

A "distant relative" is a relative pronoun or a relative clause that has been placed too far away from the antecedent to which it refers. it is a common error to place a verb between the relative pronoun and its antecedent.

Error: Return the books to the library that are overdue.
Problem: The relative clause "that are overdue" refers to the "books" and should be placed immediately after the antecedent.
Correction: Return the books that are overdue to the library.
          or
          Return the overdue books to the library.

A pronoun should not refer to adjectives or possessive nouns

Adjectives, nouns, or possessive pronouns should not be used as antecedents. This will create ambiguity in sentences.

Error: In Todd's letter he told his mom he'd broken the priceless vase.
Problem: In this sentence the pronoun "he" seems to refer to the noun phrase "Todd's letter" though it was probably meant to refer to the possessive noun "Todd's."
Correction: In his letter, Todd told his mom that he had broken the priceless vase.

A pronoun should not refer to an implied idea

A pronoun must refer to a specific antecedent rather than an implied antecedent. When an antecedent is not stated specifically, the reader has to guess or assume the meaning of a sentence. Pronouns that do not have antecedents are called expletives. "It" and "there" are the most common expletives, though other pronouns can also become expletives as well. In informal conversation, expletives allow for casual presentation of ideas without supporting evidence. However, in more formal writing, it is best to be more precise.

Error: She said that it is important to floss every day.
Problem: The pronoun "it" refers to an implied idea.
Correction: She said that flossing every day is important.

Error: They returned the book because there were missing pages.
Problem: The pronouns "they" and "there" do not refer to the antecedent.
Correction: The customer returned the book with missing pages.

Using Who, That, and Which

Who, whom, and **whose** refer to human beings and can either introduce essential or nonessential clauses. **That** refers to things other than humans and is used to introduce essential clauses. **Which** refers to things other than humans and is used to introduce nonessential clauses.

Error: The doctor that performed the surgery said the man would fully recover.
Problem: Since the relative pronoun is referring to a human, *who* should be used.
Correction: The doctor <u>who</u> performed the surgery said the man would fully recover.

Error: That ice cream cone that you just ate looked really delicious.
Problem: That has already been used, so you must use *which* to introduce the next clause, whether it is essential or nonessential.
Correction: That ice cream cone, which you just ate, looked really delicious.

Pronouns

Pronouns, unlike nouns, change case forms. Pronouns must be in the nominative, objective, or possessive form according to their function in the sentence.

Personal Pronouns

Subject (Nominative)			Possessive		Objective	
	Singular	Plural	Singular	Plural	Singular	Plural
1st person	I	We	My	Our	Me	Us
2nd person	You	You	Your	Your	You	You
3rd person	He She It	They	His Her Its	Their	Him Her It	them

Relative Pronouns

Who	Subject/Nominative
Whom	Objective
Whose	Possessive

Error: Tom and me have reserved seats for next week's baseball game.

Problem: The pronoun *me* is the subject of the verb *have reserved* and should be in the subject, or nominative, form.

Correction: *Tom and I have reserved seats for next week's baseball game.*

Error: Mr. Green showed all of we students how to make paper hats.

Problem: The pronoun *we* is the object of the preposition *of*. It should be in the objective form, us.

Correction: *Mr. Green showed all of <u>us</u> students how to make paper hats.*

Error: Who's coat is this?

Problem: The interrogative possessive pronoun is whose; *who's* is the contraction for who is.

Correction: <u>*Whose*</u> *coat is this?*

Error: The voters will choose the candidate whom has the best qualifications for the job.

Problem: The case of the relative pronoun who or whom is determined by the pronoun's function in the clause in which it appears. The word who is in the subjective case, and whom is in the objective. Analyze how the pronoun is being used within the sentence.

Correction: *The voters will choose the candidate <u>who</u> has the best qualifications for the job.*

TEACHER CERTIFICATION STUDY GUIDE

PRACTICE EXERCISE
PRONOUN CASE

Choose the option that corrects an error in the underlined portion(s).
If no error exists, choose "No change is necessary".

1) Even though Sheila and <u>he</u> had planned to be alone at the diner,
    <u>they</u> were joined by three friends of <u>their's</u> instead.

    A) him
    B) him and her
    C) theirs
    D) No change is necessary.

2) Uncle Walter promised to give his car to <u>whomever</u> will guarantee
    to drive it safely.

    A) whom
    B) whoever
    C) them
    D) No change is necessary.

3) Eddie and <u>him</u> gently laid <u>the body</u> on the ground next to <u>the sign</u>.

    A) he
    B) them
    C) it
    D) No change is necessary.

4) Mary, <u>who</u> is competing in the chess tournament, is a better player
    than <u>me</u>.

    A) whose
    B) whom
    C) I
    D) No change is necessary.

5) <u>We, ourselves,</u> have decided not to buy property in that development;
    however, our friends have already bought <u>themselves</u> some land.

    A) We, ourself,
    B) their selves
    C) their self
    D) No change is necessary.

ANSWER KEY : PRACTICE EXERCISE FOR PRONOUN CASE

1) C   The possessive pronoun *theirs* doesn't need an apostrophe. Option A is incorrect because the subjective pronoun *he* is needed in this sentence. Option B is incorrect because the subjective pronoun *they*, not the objective pronouns *him* and *her*, is needed.

2) B   The subject/nominative case *whoever*--not the objective case *whomever*--is the subject of the relative clause *whoever will guarantee to drive it safely*. Option A is incorrect because *whom* is an objective pronoun. Option C is incorrect because *car* is singular and takes the pronoun *it*.

3) A   The subjective pronoun *he* is needed because it is the subject of the verb *laid*. Option B is incorrect because *them* is vague; the noun *body* is needed to clarify *it*. Option C is incorrect because *it* is vague, and the noun *sign* is necessary for clarification.

4) C   The subjective pronoun *I* is needed because the comparison is understood. Option A incorrectly uses the possessive *whose*. Option B is incorrect because the subjective pronoun *who*, and not the objective *whom*, is needed.

5) B   The reflexive pronoun *themselves* refers to the plural *friends*. Option A is incorrect because the plural *we* requires the reflexive *ourselves*. Option C is incorrect because the possessive pronoun *their* is never joined with either *self* or *selves*.

Adjectives are words that modify or describe nouns or pronouns. Adjectives usually precede the words they modify, but not always; for example, an adjective can occur after a linking verb.

Adverbs are words that modify verbs, adjectives, or other adverbs. They cannot modify nouns. Adverbs answer such questions as how, why, when, where, how much, or how often something is done. Many adverbs are formed by adding ly.

Error: The birthday cake tasted sweetly.

Problem: *Tasted* is a linking verb; the modifier that follows should be an adjective, not an adverb.

Correction: *The birthday cake tasted <u>sweet.</u>*

Error: You have done good with this project.

Problem: *Good* is an adjective and cannot be used to modify a verb phrase such as have done.

Correction: *You have done <u>well</u> with this project.*

Error: The coach was positive happy about the team's chance of winning.

Problem: The adjective *positive* cannot be used to modify another adjective, *happy*. An adverb is needed instead.

Correction: *The coach was <u>positively</u> happy about the team's chance of winning.*

Error: The fireman acted quick and brave to save the child from the burning building.

Problem: *Quick and brave* are adjectives and cannot be used to describe a verb. Adverbs are needed instead.

Correction: *The fireman acted <u>quickly and bravely</u> to save the child from the burning building.*

PRACTICE EXERCISE
ADJECTIVES AND ADVERBS

Choose the option that corrects an error in the underlined portion(s).
If no error exists, choose "No change is necessary."

1) Moving <u>quick</u> throughout the house, the burglar <u>removed</u> several priceless antiques before <u>carelessly</u> dropping his wallet.

   A) quickly
   B) remove
   C) careless
   D) No change is necessary.

2) The car <u>crashed loudly</u> into the retaining wall before spinning <u>wildly</u> on the sidewalk.

   A) crashes
   B) loudly
   C) wild
   D) No change is necessary.

3) The airplane <u>landed</u> <u>safe</u> on the runway after <u>nearly</u> colliding with a helicopter.

   A) land
   B) safely
   C) near
   D) No change is necessary.

4) The <u>horribly</u> <u>bad</u> special effects in the movie disappointed us <u>great</u>.

   A) horrible
   B) badly
   C) greatly
   D) No change is necessary.

5) The man promised to <u>faithfully</u> obey the rules of the social club.

   A) faithful
   B) faithfulness
   C) faith
   D) No change is necessary.

ANSWER KEY: PRACTICE EXERCISE FOR ADJECTIVES AND ADVERBS

1) A   The adverb *quickly* is needed to modify *moving*. Option B is incorrect because it uses the wrong form of the verb. Option C is incorrect because the adverb *carelessly* is needed before the verb *dropping,* not the adjective *careless.*

2) D   The sentence is correct as it is written. Adverbs *loudly* and *wildly* are needed to modify *crashed* and *spinning.* Option A incorrectly uses the verb *crashes* instead of the participle *crashing,* which acts as an adjective.

3) B   The adverb *safely* is needed to modify the verb *landed.* Option A is incorrect because *land* is a noun. Option C is incorrect because *near* is an adjective, not an adverb.

4) C   The adverb *greatly* is needed to modify the verb *disappointed.* Option A is incorrect because *horrible* is an adjective, not an adverb. Option B is incorrect because *bad* needs to modify the adverb *horribly.*

5) D   The adverb *faithfully* is the correct modifier of the verb *promised.* Option A is an adjective used to modify nouns. Neither Option B nor Option C, which are both nouns, is a modifier.

When comparisons are made, the correct form of the adjective or adverb must be used. The comparative form is used for two items. The superlative form is used for more than two.

	Comparative	Superlative
slow	slower	slowest
young	younger	youngest
tall	taller	tallest

With some words, *more* and *most* are used to make comparisons instead of *er* and *est.*

quiet	more quiet	most quiet
energetic	more energetic	most energetic
quick	more quickly	most quickly

Comparisons must be made between similar structures or items. In the sentence, "My house is similar in color to Steve's," one house is being compared to another house as understood by the use of the possessive Steve's.

On the other hand, if the sentence reads "My house is similar in color to Steve," the comparison would be faulty because it would be comparing the house to Steve, not to Steve's house.

Error: Last year's rides at the carnival were bigger than this year.

Problem: In the sentence as it is worded above, the rides at the carnival are being compared to this year, not to this year's rides.

Correction: *Last year's rides at the carnival were bigger than this _year's_.*

PRACTICE EXERCISE
LOGICAL COMPARISONS

Choose the sentence that logically and correctly expresses the comparison.

1)
   A. This year's standards are higher than last year.
   B. This year's standards are more high than last year.
   C. This year's standards are higher than last year's.

2)
   A. Tom's attitudes are very different from his father's.
   B. Toms attitudes are very different from his father.
   C. Tom's attitudes are very different from his father.

3)
   A. John is the stronger member of the gymnastics team.
   B. John is the strongest member of the gymnastics team.
   C. John is the most strong member of the gymnastics team.

4)
   A. Tracy's book report was longer than Tony's.
   B. Tracy's book report was more long than Tony's.
   C. Tracy's book report was longer than Tony.

5)
   A. Becoming a lawyer is as difficult as, if not more difficult than, becoming a doctor.

   B. Becoming a lawyer is as difficult, if not more difficult than, becoming a doctor.

   C. Becoming a lawyer is difficult, if not more difficult than, becoming a doctor.

6)
   A. Better than any movie of the modern era, Schindler's List portrays the destructiveness of hate.

   B. More better than any movie of the modern era, Schindler's List portrays the destructiveness of hate.

   C. Better than any other movie of the modern era, Schindler's List portrays the destructiveness of hate.

ANSWER KEY: PRACTICE EXERCISE FOR LOGICAL COMPARISONS

1) C   Option C is correct because the comparison is between this year's standards and last year's [standards is understood]. Option A compares the standards to last year. In Option B, the faulty comparative *more high* should be higher.

2) A   Option A is incorrect because Tom's attitudes are compared to his father's [attitudes is understood]. Option B deletes the necessary apostrophe to show possession (Tom's), and the comparison is faulty with *attitudes* compared to father. While Option C uses the correct possessive, it retains the faulty comparison shown in Option B.

3) B   In Option B, John is correctly the strongest member of a team that consists of more than two people. Option A uses the comparative *stronger* (comparison of two items) rather than the superlative *strongest* (comparison of more than two). Option C uses a faulty superlative most strong.

4) A   Option A is correct because the comparison is between Tracy's book report and Tony's (book report). Option B uses the faulty comparative *more long* instead of longer. Option C wrongly compares Tracy's book report to Tony.

5) A   In Option A, the dual comparison is correctly stated: *as difficult as, if not more difficult than*. Remember to test the dual comparison by taking out the intervening comparison. Option B deletes the necessary *as* after the first *difficult*. Option C deletes the *as* before and after the first *difficult*.

6) C   Option C includes the necessary word *other* in the comparison *better than any other movie*. The comparison in Option A is not complete, and Option B uses a faulty comparative *more better*.

Skill 20.2   Revise text to correct problems relating to sentence construction (e.g., those involving parallel structure, misplaced modifiers, run-on sentences)

Sentence structure

Recognize simple, compound, complex, and compound-complex sentences. Use dependent (subordinate) and independent clauses correctly to create these sentence structures.

Simple – Consists of one independent clause
> Joyce wrote a letter.

Compound – Consists of two or more independent clauses. The two clauses are usually connected by a coordinating conjunction preceded by a comma (and, but, or, nor, for, so, yet). Compound sentences are sometimes connected by semicolons.
> Joyce wrote a letter, and Dot drew a picture.

Complex- Consists of an independent clause plus one or more dependent clauses. The dependent clause may precede the independent clause or follow it.
> While Joyce wrote a letter, Dot drew a picture.

Compound/Complex – Consists of one or more dependent clauses plus two or more independent clauses .
> When Mother asked the girls to demonstrate their new-found skills, Joyce wrote a letter, and Dot drew a picture.

Note: Do **not** confuse compound sentence elements with compound sentences.

> Simple sentence with compound subject
> > <u>Joyce</u> and <u>Dot</u> wrote letters.
> > The <u>girl</u> in row three and the <u>boy</u> next to her were passing notes across the aisle.

> Simple sentence with compound predicate
> > Joyce <u>wrote letters</u> and <u>drew pictures</u>.
> > The captain of the high school debate team <u>graduated with honors</u> and <u>studied broadcast journalism in college</u>.

> Simple sentence with compound object of preposition
> > Coleen graded the students' essays for <u>style</u> and <u>mechanical accuracy</u>.

Types of Clauses

Clauses are connected word groups that are composed of *at least* one subject and one verb. (A subject is the doer of an action or the element that is being joined. A verb conveys either the action or the link.)

Students are waiting for the start of the assembly.
Subject   Verb

At the end of the play, students wait for the curtain to come down.
                        Subject   Verb

Clauses can be independent or dependent.

Independent clauses can stand alone or can be joined to other clauses.

Independent clause	for and nor	
Independent clause,	but or yet so	Independent clause
Independent clause	;	Independent clause
Dependent clause	,	Independent clause
Independent clause		Dependent clause

Dependent clauses, by definition, contain at least one subject and one verb. However, they cannot stand alone as a complete sentence. They are structurally dependent on the main clause.

There are two types of dependent clauses: (1) those with a subordinating conjunction, and (2) those with a relative pronoun

Sample subordinating conjunctions:
Although
When
If
Unless
Because

Unless a cure is discovered, many more people will die of the disease.
Dependent clause   +   Independent clause

Sample relative pronouns:
Who
Whom
Which
That

The White House has an official website which contains press releases, news updates, and biographies of the President and Vice-President.
(Independent clause + (relative pronoun + relative clause predicate=dependent clause)

Recognize correct placement of modifiers

Participial phrases that are not placed near the word they modify often result in misplaced modifiers. Participial phrases that do not relate to the subject being modified result in dangling modifiers.

Error: Weighing the options carefully, a decision was made regarding the punishment of the convicted murderer.

Problem: Who is weighing the options? No one capable of weighing is named in the sentence; thus, the participle phrase *weighing the options carefully* dangles. This problem can be corrected by adding a subject capable of doing the action.

Correction: *Weighing the options carefully, <u>the judge</u> made a decision regarding the punishment of the convicted murderer.*

Error: Returning to my favorite watering hole, brought back many fond memories.

Problem: The person who returned is never indicated, and the participial phrase dangles. This problem can be corrected by creating a dependent clause from the modifying phrase.

Correction: *When I returned to my favorite watering hole, many fond memories came back to me.*

Error: One damaged house stood only to remind townspeople of the hurricane.

Problem: The placement of the modifier *only* suggests that the sole reason the house remained was to serve as a reminder. The faulty modifier creates ambiguity.

Correction: *Only one damaged house stood, reminding townspeople of the hurricane.*

Error: Recovered from the five-mile hike, the obstacle course was a piece of cake for the Boy Scout troop.

Problem: The obstacle course is not recovered from the five-mile hike, so the modifying phrase must be placed closer to the word, *troop*, that it modifies.

Correction: *The obstacle course was a piece of cake for the Boy Scout troop, which had just recovered from a five-mile hike.*

PRACTICE EXERCISE
MISPLACED AND DANGLING MODIFIERS

Choose the sentence that expresses the thought most clearly and effectively and that has no error in structure.

1)   A. Attempting to remove the dog from the well, the paramedic tripped and fell in, also.

       B. As the paramedic attempted to remove the dog from the well, he tripped and fell in, also.

       C. The paramedic tripped and fell in also attempting to remove the dog from the well.

2)   A. To save the wounded child, a powerful explosion ripped through the operating room as the doctors worked.

       B. In the operating room, as the wounded child was being saved, a powerful explosion ripped through.

       C. To save the wounded child, the doctors worked as an explosion ripped through the operating room.

3)   A. One hot July morning, a herd of giraffes screamed wildly in the jungle next to the wildlife habitat.

       B. One hot July morning, a herd of giraffes screamed in the jungle wildly next to the wildlife habitat.

       C. One hot July morning, a herd of giraffes screamed in the jungle next to the wildlife habitat, wildly.

4)   A. Looking through the file cabinets in the office, the photographs of the crime scene revealed a new suspect in the investigation.

       B. Looking through the file cabinets in the office, the detective discovered photographs of the crime scene which revealed a new suspect in the investigation.

       C. A new suspect in the investigation was revealed in photographs of the crime scene that were discovered while looking through the file cabinets in the office.

LIBERAL ARTS & SCIENCE TEST   259

ANSWER KEY: PRACTICE EXERCISE FOR MISPLACED AND DANGLING MODIFIERS

1) B   Option B corrects the dangling participle *attempting to remove the dog from the well* by creating a dependent clause introducing the main clause. In Option A, the introductory participle phrase *Attempting...well* does not refer to a paramedic, the subject of the main clause. The word also in Option C incorrectly implies that the paramedic was doing something besides trying to remove the dog.

2) C   Option C corrects the dangling modifier *to save the wounded child* by adding the concrete subject <u>doctors</u> . Option A infers that an explosion was working to save the wounded child. Option B never tells who was trying to save the wounded child.

3) A   Option A places the adverb *wildly* closest to the verb screamed, which it modifies. Both Options B and C incorrectly place the modifier away from the verb.

4) B   Option B corrects the modifier *looking through the file cabinets in the office* by placing it next to the detective who is doing the looking. Option A sounds as though the photographs were looking; Option C has no one doing the looking.

Faulty parallelism

Two or more elements stated in a single clause should be expressed with the same (or parallel) structure (e.g., all adjectives, all verb forms or all nouns).

Error: She needed to be beautiful, successful, and have fame.

Problem: The phrase *to be* is followed by two different structures: *beautiful* and *successful* are adjectives, and *have fame* is a verb phrase.

Correction: *She needed to be <u>beautiful</u>, <u>successful</u>, and <u>famous</u>.*
          (adjective) (adjective)   (adjective)
                      OR
She needed <u>beauty</u>, <u>success</u>, and <u>fame</u>.
       (noun)   (noun)   (noun)

Error: I plan either to sell my car during the spring or during the summer.

Problem: Paired conjunctions (also called correlative conjunctions - such as either-or, both-and , neither-nor, not only-but also) need to be followed with similar structures. In the sentence above, *either* is followed by *to sell my car during the spring*, while *or* is followed only by the phrase *during the summer*.

Correction: *I plan to sell my car during either the spring or the summer.*

Error: The President pledged to lower taxes and that he would cut spending to lower the national debt.

Problem: Since the phrase *to lower taxes* follows the verb *pledged*, a similar structure of to is needed with the phrase *cut spending*.

Correction: *The President pledged to lower taxes and to cut spending to lower the national debt.*
                      OR
The President pledged that he would lower taxes and cut spending to lower the national debt.

PRACTICE EXERCISE
PARALLELISM

Choose the sentence that expresses the thought most clearly and effectively and that has no error in structure.

1. A. Andy found the family tree, researches the Irish descendents, and he was compiling a book for everyone to read.

   B. Andy found the family tree, researched the Irish descendents, and compiled a book for everyone to read.

   C. Andy finds the family tree, researched the Irish descendents, and compiled a book for everyone to read.

2. A. In the last ten years, computer technology has advanced so quickly that workers have had difficulty keeping up with the new equipment and the increased number of functions.

   B. Computer technology has advanced so quickly in the last ten years that workers have had difficulty to keep up with the new equipment and by increasing number of functions.

   C. In the last ten years, computer technology has advanced so quickly that workers have had difficulty keeping up with the new equipment and the number of functions are increasing.

3. A. The Florida State History Museum contains exhibits honoring famous residents, a video presentation about the state's history, an art gallery featuring paintings and sculptures, and they even display a replica of the Florida Statehouse.

   B. The Florida State History Museum contains exhibits honoring famous residents, a video presentation about the state's history, an art gallery featuring paintings and sculptures, and even a replica of the Florida Statehouse.

   C. The Florida State History Museum contains exhibits honoring famous residents, a video presentation about the state's history, an art gallery featuring paintings and sculptures, and there is even a replica of the Florida Statehouse.

TEACHER CERTIFICATION STUDY GUIDE

4.   A.   Either the criminal justice students had too much practical experience and limited academic preparation or too much academic preparation and little practical experience.

         B.   The criminal justice students either had too much practical experience and limited academic preparation or too much academic preparation and little practical experience.

         C.   The criminal justice students either had too much practical experience and limited academic preparation or had too much academic preparation and little practical experience.

5.   A.   Filmmaking is an arduous process in which the producer hires the cast and crew, chooses locations for filming, supervises the actual production, and guides the editing.

         B.   Because it is an arduous process, filmmaking requires the producer to hire a cast and crew and choose locations, supervise the actual production, and guides the editing.

         C.   Filmmaking is an arduous process in which the producer hires the cast and crew, chooses locations for filming, supervises the actual production, and guided the editing.

ANSWER KEY: PRACTICE EXERCISE FOR PARALLELISM

1. B   Option B uses parallelism by presenting a series of past tense verbs *found, researched*, and *compiled*. Option A interrupts the parallel structure of past tense verbs: *found, researches*, and *he was compiling*. Option C uses present tense verbs and then shifts to past tense: *finds, researched*, and *compiled*.

2. A   Option A uses parallel structure at the end of the sentence: *the new equipment and the increased amount of functions*. Option B creates a faulty structure with *to keep up with the new equipment and by increasing amount of functions*. Option C creates faulty parallelism with *the amount of functions are increasing*.

3. B   Option B uses parallelism by presenting a series of noun phrases acting as objects of the verb *contains*. Option A interrupts that parallelism by inserting *they even display*, and Option C interrupts the parallelism with the addition of *there is*.

4. C   In the either-or parallel construction, look for a balance on both sides. Option C creates that balanced parallel structure: *either had...or had*. Options A and B do not create the balance. In Option A, the structure is *Either the students...or too much*. In Option B, the structure is *either had...or too much*.

5. A   Option A uses parallelism by presenting a series of verbs with objects: *hires the cast and crew, chooses locations for filming, supervises the actual production, and guides the editing*. The structure of Option B incorrectly suggests that filmmaking chooses locations, supervises the actual production, and guides the editing. Option C interrupts the series of present tense verbs by inserting the participle *guided*, instead of the present tense guides.

Fragments

Fragments occur (1) if word groups standing alone are missing either a subject or a verb, and (2) if word groups containing a subject and verb and standing alone are actually made dependent because of the use of subordinating conjunctions or relative pronouns.

Error: The teacher waiting for the class to complete the assignment.

Problem: This sentence is not complete because an ing word alone does not function as a verb. When a helping verb is added (for example, was waiting), it will become a sentence.

Correction: *The teacher was waiting for the class to complete the assignment.*

Error: Until the last toy was removed from the floor.

Problem: Words such as *until*, *because*, *although*, *when*, and *if* make a clause dependent and, thus, incapable of standing alone. An independent clause must be added to make the sentence complete.

Correction: *Until the last toy was removed from the floor, the kids could not go outside to play.*

Error: The city will close the public library. Because of a shortage of funds.

Problem: The problem is the same as above. The dependent clause must be joined to the independent clause.

Correction: *The city will close the public library because of a shortage of funds.*

Error: Anyone planning to go on the trip should bring the necessary items. Such as a backpack, boots, a canteen, and bug spray.

Problem: The second word group is a phrase and cannot stand alone because there is neither a subject nor a verb. The fragment can be corrected by adding the phrase to the sentence.

Correction: *Anyone planning to go on the trip should bring the necessary items, such as a backpack, boots, a canteen, and bug spray.*

PRACTICE EXERCISE
FRAGMENTS

Choose the option that corrects the underlined portion(s) of the sentence.
If no error exists, choose "No change is necessary."

1)   Despite the lack of funds in the <u>budget it</u> was necessary to rebuild the
     roads that were damaged from the recent floods.

     A) budget: it
     B) budget, it
     C) budget; it
     D) No change is necessary

2)   After determining that the fire was caused by faulty <u>wiring, the</u>
     building inspector said the construction company should be fined.

     A) wiring. The
     B) wiring the
     C) wiring; the
     D) No change is necessary

3)   Many years after buying a grand <u>piano Henry</u> decided he'd rather play
     the violin instead.

     A) piano: Henry
     B) piano, Henry
     C) piano; Henry
     D) No change is necessary

4)   Computers are being used more and more <u>frequently. because</u> of
     their capacity to store information.

     A) frequently because
     B) frequently, because
     C) frequently; because
     D) No change is necessary

5)   Doug washed the floors <u>every day. to</u> keep them clean for the
     guests.

     A) every day to
     B) every day,
     C) every day;
     D) No change is necessary.

ANSWER KEY: PRACTICE EXERCISE FOR FRAGMENTS

1. B   The clause that begins with *despite* is dependent and must be separated from the clause that follows it by a comma. Option A is incorrect because a colon is used to set off a list or to emphasize what follows. In Option c, a semicolon, incorrectly suggests that the two clauses are independent.

2. D   In the test item, a comma correctly separates the dependent clause *After...wiring* at the beginning of the sentence from the independent clause that follows. Option A incorrectly breaks the two clauses into separate sentences, Option B omits the comma, and Option C incorrectly suggests that the phrase is an independent clause.

3. B   The *phrase Henry decided...instead* must be joined to the independent clause. Option A incorrectly puts a colon before *Henry decided*, and Option C incorrectly separates the phrase as if it were an independent clause.

4. A   The second clause *because...information* is dependent and must be joined to the independent clause. Option B is incorrect Because, as the dependent clause comes at the end of the sentence rather than at the beginning, a comma is not necessary. In Option C, a semi-colon incorrectly suggests that the two clauses are independent.

5. A   The second clause *to keep...guests* is dependent and must be joined to the first independent clause. Option B is incorrect because, as the dependent clause comes at the end of the sentence rather than at the beginning, a comma is not necessary. In Option C, a semi-colon incorrectly suggests that the two clauses are independent.

Run-on sentences and comma splices

Comma splices appear when two sentences are joined by only a comma, omitting the coordinating conjunction. Fused sentences appear when two sentences are run together with no punctuation at all.

Error: Dr. Sanders is a brilliant scientist, his research on genetic disorders won him a Nobel Prize.

Problem: A comma alone cannot join two independent clauses (complete sentences). The two clauses can be joined by a semi-colon, or they can be separated by a period.

Correction: *Dr. Sanders is a brilliant scientist; his research on genetic disorders won him a Nobel Prize.*
OR
Dr. Sanders is a brilliant scientist. His research on genetic disorders won him a Nobel Prize.
Or
Dr. Sanders is a brilliant scientist, and his research on genetic disorders won him a Nobel Prize.

Error: Florida is noted for its beaches they are long, sandy, and beautiful.

Problem: The first sentence ends with the word beaches, and the second sentence cannot be joined with the first. The fused sentence error can be corrected in several ways: (1) one clause may be made dependent on another with a subordinating conjunction or a relative pronoun; (2) a semi-colon may be used to combine two equally important ideas; (3) the two independent clauses may be separated by a period.

Correction: *Florida is noted for its beaches, which are long, sandy, and beautiful.*
OR
Florida is noted for its beaches; they are long, sandy, and beautiful.
OR
Florida is noted for its beaches. They are long, sandy, and beautiful.

Error: The number of hotels has increased, however, the number of visitors has grown also.

Problem: The first sentence ends with the word increased, and a comma is not strong enough to connect it to the second sentence. The adverbial transition however does not function the same way as a coordinating conjunction and cannot be used with commas to link two sentences. Several different corrections are available.

Correction: *The number of hotels has increased; however, the number of visitors has grown also.*
[Two separate but closely related sentences are created with the use of the semicolon.]
OR
The number of hotels has increased. However, the number of visitors has grown also.
[Two separate sentences are created.]
OR
Although the number of hotels have increased, the number of visitors has grown also.
[One idea is made subordinate to the other and separated with a comma.]
OR
The number of hotels has increased, but the number of visitors has grown also.
[The comma before the coordinating conjunction *but* is appropriate. The adverbial transition however does not function the same way as the coordinating conjunction *but* does.]

PRACTICE EXERCISE
FUSED SENTENCES AND COMMA SPLICES

Choose the option that corrects an error in the underlined portion(s). If no error exists, choose "No change is necessary".

1) Scientists are excited at the ability to clone a <u>sheep; however,</u> it is not yet known if the same can be done to humans.

    A) sheep, however,
    B) sheep. However,
    C) sheep, however;
    D) No change is necessary

2) Because of the rising cost of college <u>tuition the</u> federal government now offers special financial assistance, <u>such as loans,</u> to students.

    A) tuition, the
    B) tuition; the
    C) such as loans
    D) No change is necessary

3) As the number of homeless people continues to <u>rise, major cities</u> like <u>New York and Chicago,</u> are now investing millions of dollars in low-income housing.

    A) rise. The major cities
    B) rise; the major cities
    C) New York and Chicago
    D) No change is necessary

4) Unlike in <u>the 1950's, most</u> households find the husband and wife working full-time to make <u>ends meet.</u>

    A) the 1950's; most
    B) the 1950's most
    C) ends meet, in many
    D) No change is necessary

ANSWER KEY : PRACTICE EXERCISE FOR COMMA SPLICES AND FUSED SENTENCES

1) B   Option B correctly separates two independent clauses. The comma in Option A after the word sheep creates a run-on sentence. The semi-colon in Option C does not separate the two clauses but occurs at an inappropriate point.

2) A   The comma in Option A correctly separates the independent clause and the dependent clause. The semi-colon in Option B is incorrect because one of the clauses is independent. Option C requires a comma to prevent a run-on sentence.

3) C   Option C is correct because a comma creates a run-on. Option A is incorrect because the first clause is dependent. The semi-colon in Option B incorrectly divides the dependent clause from the independent clause.

4) D   Option D, no change, correctly separates the introductory adverbial phrase from the main clause using a comma.
Option A incorrectly uses a semi-colon to divide the elements.
The lack of a comma in Option B creates an improperly punctuated sentence. Option C puts a comma in an inappropriate place.

Skill 20.3 **Revise text to improve unity and coherence (e.g., eliminating unnecessary sentences or paragraphs, adding a topic sentence or introductory paragraph, clarifying transitions between, and relationships among, ideas presented)**

See Competency 17.0.

Skill 20.4 **Analyze problems related to the organization of a given text (e.g., logical flow of ideas, grouping of related ideas, development of main points)**

See Competency 17.0.

COMPETENCY 21.0   DEMONSTRATE THE ABILITY TO LOCATE, RETRIEVE, ORGANIZE, AND INTERPRET INFORMATION FROM A VARIETY OF TRADITIONAL AND ELECTRONIC SOURCES.

Skill 21.1   Demonstrate familiarity with basic reference tools (e.g., encyclopedias, almanacs, bibliographies, databases, atlases, periodical guides)

In our increasingly knowledge-based world, educators have found that it is not good enough to simply teach students factual information. The information teachers pass on to students is inherently going to be limited and soon out-dated. It is said that the body of knowledge in most academic fields doubles within a matter of years. That being said, we can assume that the factual information students do get in the classroom will not necessarily represent the most current, accurate information available.

Because of the rapidly accelerating amount of information available, educators cannot shirk the responsibility of teaching students how to access sources of information. References sources can be of great value, and, by teaching students how to access these first, students will later have skills that will help them access more in-depth databases and sources of information.

Encyclopedias are reference materials that appear in book or electronic form. Encyclopedias can be considered general or specific. General encyclopedias peripherally cover most fields of knowledge; specific encyclopedias include a smaller number of entries treated in greater depth. Encyclopedias are good first sources of information for students. While their total scope is limited, they can provide a quick introduction to topics so that students can get familiar with the topics before exploring topics in greater depth.

Almanacs provide statistical information on various topics. Typically, these references are rather specific. They often cover a specific period of time. One famous example is the *Farmer's Almanac*. This annual publication summarizes, among many other things, weather conditions for the previous year.

Bibliographies contain references for further research. Bibliographies are usually organized topically. They help point people to the in-depth resources they will need for a complete view of a topic.

Databases, typically all electronic now, are collections of material on specific topics. For example, teachers can go online and find many databases for science articles for students in a variety of topics.

Atlases are visual representations of geographic areas. Often, they cover specific attributes. Some atlases demonstrate geologic attributes, while others emphasize populations of various areas.

Finally, periodical guides categorize articles and special editions of journals and magazines to help archive and organize the vast amount of material that is put in periodicals each year.

In all, reference tools are highly valuable for students. Surprisingly, it takes a very long time for students to become competent with most reference tools, but the effort and time is definitely worth it.

Skill 21.2   Recognize the difference between primary and secondary sources

The resources used in the study of history can be divided into two major groups: primary sources and secondary sources.

Primary sources are works and records that were created during the period being studied or immediately after it. Secondary sources are works written significantly after the period being studied and are based upon primary sources. "Primary sources are the basic materials that provide the raw data and information for the historian. Secondary sources are the works that contain the explications of, and judgments on, this primary material." [Source: Norman F Cantor & Richard I. Schneider. HOW TO STUDY HISTORY, Harlan Davidson, Inc., 1967, pp. 23-24.]

Primary sources include the following kinds of materials:

- Documents that reflect the immediate, everyday concerns of people: memoranda, bills, deeds, charters, newspaper reports, pamphlets, graffiti, popular writings, journals or diaries, records of decision-making bodies, letters, receipts, snapshots, etc.
- Theoretical writings which reflect care and consideration in composition and an attempt to convince or persuade. The topic will generally be deeper and more pervasive values than is the case with "immediate" documents. These may include newspaper or magazine editorials, sermons, political speeches, philosophical writings, etc.
- Narrative accounts of events, ideas, trends, etc. written with intentionality by someone contemporary with the events described.
- Statistical data, although statistics may be misleading.
- Literature and nonverbal materials, novels, stories, poetry and essays from the period, as well as coins, archaeological artifacts, and art produced during the period.

Guidelines for the use of primary resources:

1. Be certain that you understand how language was used at the time of writing and that you understand the context in which it was produced.
2. Do not read history blindly; ascertain that you understand both explicit and implicit referenced in the material.
3. Read the entire text you are reviewing; do not simply extract a few sentences to read.
4. Although anthologies of materials may help you identify primary source materials, the full original text should be consulted.

Secondary sources include the following kinds of materials:

- Books written on the basis of primary materials about the period of time.
- Books written on the basis of primary materials about persons who played a major role in the events under consideration.
- Books and articles written on the basis of primary materials about the culture, the social norms, the language, and the values of the period.
- Quotations from primary sources.
- Statistical data on the period.
- The conclusions and inferences of other historians.
- Multiple interpretations of the ethos of the time.

Guidelines for the use of secondary sources:

1. Do not rely upon only a single secondary source.
2. Check facts and interpretations against primary sources whenever possible.
3. Do not accept the conclusions of other historians uncritically.
4. Place greatest reliance on secondary sources created by the best and most respected scholars.
5. Do not use the inferences of other scholars as if they were facts.
6. Ensure that you recognize any bias writers bring to their interpretation of history.
7. Understand the primary point of the book as a basis for evaluating the value of the material presented in it to your questions.

Skill 21.3 Formulate research questions and hypotheses

There are many different ways to find ideas for **research problems**. One of the most common ways is through experiencing and assessing relevant problems in a specific field. Researchers are often involved in the fields in which they choose to study, and thus encounter practical problems related to their areas of expertise on a daily basis. The can use their knowledge, expertise, and research ability to examine their selected research problem. This technique is not limited to qualified researchers engaged in specific fields; it can also be used by students. For students, all that this entails is being curious about the world around them. Research ideas can come from one's background, culture, education, experiences etc.

Another way to get research ideas is by exploring literature in a specific field and coming up with a question that extends or refines previous research.

Once a **topic** is decided, a research question must be formulated. A research question is a relevant, researchable, feasible statement that identifies the information to be studied. Once this initial question is formulated, it is a good idea to think of specific issues related to the topic. This will help to create a hypothesis. A research **hypothesis** is a statement of the researcher's expectations for the outcome of the research problem. It is a summary statement of the problem to be addressed in any research document. A good hypothesis states, clearly and concisely, the researchers' expected outcomes regarding the variables under investigation.

Once a hypothesis is decided, the rest of the research paper should focus on analyzing a set of information or arguing a specific point. Thus, there are two types of research papers: analytical and argumentative.

Analytical papers focus on examining and understanding the various parts of a research topic and reformulating them in a new way to support an initial statement. In this type of research paper, the research question is used as both a basis for investigation and as a topic for the paper. Once a variety of information is collected on the given topic, it is coalesced into a clear discussion

Argumentative papers focus on supporting a claim with evidence or reasoning. Instead of presenting research to provide information, an argumentative paper presents research in order to prove a debatable statement and interpretation.

Skill 21.4   Interpret data presented in visual, graphic, tabular, and quantitative forms (e.g., recognizing level of statistical significance)

Tables

To interpret data in tables, we read across rows and down columns. Each item of interest has different data points listed under different column headings.

Table 1. Sample Purchase Order

Item	Unit	$/Unit	Qty.	Tot. $
Coffee	lb.	2.79	45	125.55
Milk	gal.	1.05	72	75.60
Sugar	lb.	0.23	150	34.50

In Table 1 (above), the first column on the left contains the items in a purchase order. The other columns contain data about each item, labeled with column headings. The second column from the left gives the unit of measurement for each item, the third column gives the price per unit, the fourth column gives the quantity of each item ordered, and the fifth column gives the total cost of each item.

Examples: Use Table 1 to answer the following questions.

1. What does the 1.05 value in the table represent?

    Answer: Price in dollars per gallon of milk.

2. What is the total cost of the purchase order?

    Answer: $235.65

3. How many combined pounds of coffee and sugar does this purchase order include?

    Answer: 195 lbs.

Quantitative data is often easily presented in graphs and charts in many content areas. However, if students are unable to decipher the graph, its use becomes limited to students. Since information can clearly be displayed in a graph or chart form, accurate interpretation of the information is an important skill for students.

For graphs, students should be taught to evaluate all the features of the graph, including main title, what the horizontal axis represents, and what the vertical axis represents. Also, students should locate and evaluate the graph's key (if there is one) in the event that there is more than one variable on the graph. For example, line graphs are often used to plot data from a scientific experiment. If more than one variable was used, a key or legend would indicate what each line on the line graph represented. Then, once students have evaluated the axes and titles, they can begin to assess the results of the experiment.

For charts (such as a pie chart), the process is similar to interpreting bar or line graphs. The key, which depicts what each section of the pie chart represents, is very important in interpreting the pie chart. Be sure to provide students with lots of assistance and practice with reading and interpreting graphs and charts.

Many educational disciplines require the ability to recognize representations of written information in graphic or tabular form. Tables help condense and organize written data, and graphs help reveal and emphasize comparisons and trends.

Example: A survey asked five elementary school students to list the number and type of pets that they had at home. The first student had three dogs and three fish. The second student had two cats and one dog. The third student had three fish and two dogs. The fourth student had one rabbit, two cats, and one dog. The fifth student had no pets.

Construct a data table and line graph that represents the survey information.

Solution: The following is a table that appropriately represents the data.

Student #	# of Dogs	# of Cats	# of Fish	# of Rabbits	Total # of Pets
1	3	0	3	0	6
2	1	2	0	0	3
3	2	0	3	0	5
4	1	2	0	1	4
5	0	0	0	0	0

The following is a line graph that appropriately represents the total number of pets each student has.

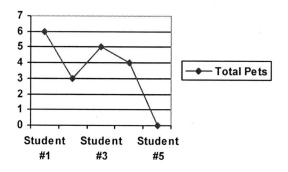

Skill 21.5   Organize information into logical and coherent outlines

A good thesis gives structure to an essay and helps show focus of thoughts. When forming a thesis, look at your prewriting material from clustering, questioning, or brainstorming. Then decide quickly which two or three major areas to discuss. Remember to limit *the scope* of the paper because of the time factor.

The **outline** lists main areas and topics for each paragraph.
Looking at the prewriting cluster on computers might result in choosing several areas in which computers help us, for example in science and medicine, business, and education. Considerations of people's reliance on this "wonder" might also be included. A formal outline for this essay might look like the one below:

I.   Introduction and thesis
II. Computers used in science and medicine
II. Computers used in business
IV. Computers used in education
V. People's reliance on computers
VI. Conclusion

Under time pressure, however a shorter organizational plan, such as abbreviated key words in a list, might be advisable. For example

1. intro: wonders of the computer OR
2. science
3. med
4. schools
5. business
6. conclusion

a. intro: wonders of computers - science
b. in the space industry
c. in medical technology
d. conclusion

Developing an essay

With a working thesis and outline, you can begin writing the essay. The essay should be in three main sections:

1) The **introduction** sets up the essay and leads to the thesis statement.
2) The **body paragraphs** are developed with concrete information supporting the **topic sentences**.
3) The **conclusion** ties the essay together.

Introduction

Put the thesis statement into a clear, coherent opening paragraph. One effective device is to use a funnel approach in which a brief description of the broader issue leads to a clearly focused and specific thesis statement.

Consider the following introductions to the essay on computers. The length of each is an obvious difference. Read each, and consider other differences.

> Does each introduce the subject generally?
> Does each lead to a stated thesis?
> Does each relate to the topic prompt?

Introduction 1: *Computers are used every day. They have many uses. Some people who use them are workers, teachers and doctors.*

Analysis: This introduction does give the general topic, computers used every day, but it does not explain what those uses are. This introduction does not offer a point of view in a clearly stated thesis, nor does it convey the idea that computers are a modem wonder.

Introduction 2: *Computers are used just about everywhere these days. I don't think there's an office around that doesn't use computers, and we use them a lot in all kinds of jobs. Computers are great for making life easier and work better. I don't think we'd get along without the computer.*

Analysis: This introduction gives the general topic about computers and mentions one area that uses computers. The thesis states that people couldn't get along without computers, but it does not state the specific areas the essay discusses. Note, too, the meaning is not helped by vague diction such as *a lot* or *great*.

Introduction 3: *Each day, we either use computers or see them being used around us. We wake to the sound of a digital alarm operated by a micro-chip. Our cars run by computerized machinery. We use computers to help us learn. We receive phone calls and letters transferred from computers across continents. Our astronauts walked on the moon and returned safely because of computer technology. The computer a wonderful electronic brain that we have come to rely on and has changed our world through advances in science, business, and education.*

Analysis: This introduction is the most thorough and fluent because it provides interest in the general topic and offers specific information about computers as a modern wonder. It also leads to a thesis that directs the reader to the scope of the discussion--advances in science, business, and education.

Topic Sentences
Just as the essay must have an overall focus reflected in the thesis statement, each paragraph must have a central idea reflected in the topic sentence. A good topic sentence also provides transition from the previous paragraph and relates to the essay's thesis. Good topic sentences, therefore, provide unity throughout the essay.

Consider the following potential topic sentences. Be sure that each provides transition and clearly states the subject of the paragraph.

Topic Sentence 1: *Computers are used in science.*

Analysis: This sentence simply states the topic--computers used in science. It does not relate to the thesis or provide transition from the introduction. The reader still does not know how computers are used.

Topic Sentence 2: *Now I will talk about computers used in science.*

Analysis: Like the faulty "announcer" thesis statement, this "announcer" topic sentence is vague and merely names the topic.

Topic Sentence 3: *First, computers used in science have improved our lives.*

Analysis: The transition word *First* helps link the introduction and this paragraph. It adds unity to the essay. It does not, however, give specifics about the improvements computers have made in our lives.

Topic Sentence 4: *First used in scientific research and spaceflights, computers are now used extensively in the diagnosis and treatment of disease.*

Analysis: This sentence is the most thorough and fluent. It provides specific areas that will be discussed in the paragraph and offers more than an announcement of the topic. The writer gives concrete information about the content of the paragraph that will follow.

Summary Guidelines for Writing Topic Sentences
1. Specifically relate the topic to the thesis statement.
2. State clearly and concretely the subject of the paragraph
3. Provide some transition from the previous paragraph
4. Avoid topic sentences that are facts, questions, or announcers.

Skill 21.6   Evaluate the reliability of different sources of information

The sky is blue", "the sky looks like rain", one is a fact, and the other is an opinion. This is because one is **readily provable by objective empirical data**; while the other is a **subjective evaluation based upon personal bias**. This means that facts are things that can be proved by the usual means of study and experimentation. We can look and see the color of the sky. Since the shade we are observing is expressed as the color blue and is an accepted norm, the observation that the sky is blue is a fact. (Of course, this depends on other external factors such as time and weather conditions).

This brings us to our next idea: that it looks like rain. This is a subjective observation in that an individual's perception will differ from someone else's. What looks like rain to one person will not necessarily look like that to another person. The question thus remains as to how to differentiate fact from opinion. The best and only way is to ask oneself if what is being stated can be proved from other sources, by other methods, or by the simple process of **reasoning**.

See also Skill 21.2.

COMPETENCY 22.0   PREPARE AN ORGANIZED, DEVELOPED
COMPOSITION IN EDITED AMERICAN ENGLISH IN
RESPONSE TO INSTRUCTIONS REGARDING
AUDIENCE, PURPOSE, AND CONTENT

This section of the test consists of a written assignment. You are to prepare a written response of about 300–600 words on the assigned topic. Your response to the written assignment will be evaluated on the basis of the following criteria:

• **FOCUS AND UNITY:** Comprehend and focus on a unified, controlling topic.

• **APPROPRIATENESS:** Select and use a strategy of expression that is appropriate for the intended audience and purpose.

• **REASON AND ORGANIZATION:** Present a reasoned, organized argument or exposition.

• **SUPPORT AND DEVELOPMENT:** Use support and evidence to develop and bolster ideas, and account for the views of others.

• **STRUCTURE AND CONVENTIONS:** Ensure that sentence and paragraph structure, choice and use of words, and mechanics (i.e., spelling, punctuation, capitalization) reflect careful revision and editing.

Your response will be evaluated based on your demonstrated ability to express and support opinions, not on the nature or content of the opinions expressed. The final version of your response should conform to the conventions of edited American English. This should be your original work, written in your own words, and not copied or paraphrased from some other work.

Topics will vary, and you will be asked to respond in a specific manner. For example, you may:

• Take a position on an issue of contemporary concern, and defend that position with reasoned arguments and supporting examples

• Analyze and respond to an opinion presented in an excerpt

• Compare and contrast conflicting viewpoints on a social, political, or educational topic explored in one or more excerpts

• Evaluate information, and propose a solution to a stated problem

• Synthesize information presented in two or more excerpts

WRITING ASSIGNMENT:

In the field of education, the concept of homework has been hotly debated. Presented below are brief summaries of arguments for and against homework:

For Homework – Homework is an important part of the cognitive, social, and personal development of students. It encourages students to develop discipline and responsibility, and it furthers students' learning beyond the short school day.

Against Homework – Homework often consists of busy-work. It rarely encourages deeper or better learning, and it often deprives students of time to pursue personal interests. It is a tradition that adds little to students' learning or development.

Write an essay in which you offer your opinion about this topic. Provide a well-reasoned argument with supporting evidence to back up your claims.

SAMPLE STRONG ESSAY:

Homework has been a mainstay in American education for decades. It has served as a time for practicing academic skills and as an opportunity to instill, personal responsibility and time-management skills. Expertise takes great time to develop, and homework time simply extends the limited time students get in the classroom to learn complex subjects. However, homework also has been seen by many as a vehicle for useless, repetitive practice that contributes little to students' learning. Considering that more and more of the school day is taken up by academics (and less time is reserved for social time, play, or electives), homework simply adds more of the basic subjects to students' daily lives and reduces their chances of doing things to develop personal interests. It also reduces chances that students will engage in physical activities, and, therefore, contributes more to sedentary behaviors. Overall, both sides have strong arguments; the problem is not inherently with homework. The problem is with the ways in which homework is used. Homework would be a positive element in students' academic lives if it fostered true intellectual growth and if it was limited only to truly prioritized topics.

First, homework should increase intellectual stimulation. Students should be able to truly learn things from their work. For example, teachers can ask students to conduct mini-experiments at home. In units on argumentative writing, for example, teachers can ask students to go home and conduct a short survey with neighbors and family members. Additionally, long-term, extensive projects that require a great deal of initiative, time-management, and conceptualization— all done at home—can provide students with a good experience in working on a project of interest to them while still honing necessary academic skills.

Second, there are many learning experiences students should have that cannot reasonably be completed in the classroom or during the school day. For example, as mentioned above, assignments that ask students to do surveys or mini-research activities should be done in natural places, rather than in schools. Conducting such activities as experiments or surveys gives students the opportunity to practice real-world academic activities that they cannot get in the classroom. Additionally, extensive reading assignments, which are necessary for good reading development, should be done on students' own time so that valuable class time can be reserved for discussion and analysis.

In general, homework is a valuable tool when it is used right. When homework is used as a vehicle for mindless, repetitive activity, it fails to provide students with valuable opportunities to grow intellectually and socially. Homework really can be used as a stimulant to productive growth, and, therefore, if homework is assigned, the value of the work should be extensive and highly apparent.

Sample Test – Written Analysis and Expression

DIRECTIONS: *The passage below contains several errors. Read the passage. Then answer each test item by choosing the option that corrects an error in the underlined portion(s). No more than one underlined error will appear in each item. If no error exists, choose "No change is necessary."*

Every job places different kinds of demands on their employees. For example, whereas such jobs as accounting and bookkeeping require mathematical ability; graphic design requires creative/artistic ability.

Doing good at one job does not usually guarantee success at another. However, one of the elements crucial to all jobs are especially notable: the chance to accomplish a goal.

The accomplishment of the employees varies according to the job. In many jobs the employees become accustom to the accomplishment provided by the work they do every day.

In medicine, for example, every doctor tests him self by treating badly injured or critically ill people. In the operating room, a team of Surgeons, is responsible for operating on many of these patients. In addition to the feeling of accomplishment that the workers achieve, some jobs also give a sense of identity to the employees'. Profesions like law, education, and sales offer huge financial and emotional rewards. Politicians are public servants: who work for the federal and state governments.

President bush is basically employed by the American people to make laws and run the country.

Finally; the contributions that employees make to their companies and to the world cannot be taken for granted. Through their work, employees are performing a service for their employers and are contributing something to the world.

1. **Every job <u>places</u> different kinds of demands on <u>their</u> <u>employees</u>.**

    A. place
    B. its
    C. employes
    D. No change is necessary

2. **<u>For example,</u> <u>whereas</u> such jobs as accounting and bookkeeping require mathematical <u>ability;</u> graphic design requires creative/artistic ability.**

    A. For example
    B. whereas,
    C. ability,
    D. No change is necessary

3. **Doing <u>good</u> at one job does not <u>usually</u> guarantee <u>success</u> at another.**

    A. well
    B. usualy
    C. succeeding
    D. No change is necessary

4. <u>However,</u> one of the elements crucial to all jobs <u>are</u> especially <u>notable:</u> the accomplishment of a goal.

    A. However
    B. is
    C. notable;
    D. No change is necessary

5. The <u>accomplishment</u> of the <u>employees</u> <u>varies</u> according to the job.

    A. accomplishment,
    B. employee's
    C. vary
    D. No change is necessary

6. In many jobs the employees <u>become</u> <u>accustom</u> to the accomplishment <u>provided</u> by the work they do every day.

    A. became
    B. accustomed
    C. provides
    D. No change is necessary

7. In addition to the feeling of accomplishment that the workers <u>achieve</u>, some jobs also <u>give</u> a sense of self-identity to the <u>employees'.</u>

    A. acheive
    B. gave
    C. employees
    D. No change is necessary

8. Politicians <u>are</u> public <u>servants: who</u> <u>work</u> for the federal and state governments.

    A. were
    B. servants who
    C. worked
    D. No change is necessary

Read the following passage and answer the questions that follow.

One of the most difficult problems plaguing American education is the assessment of teachers. No one denies that teachers ought to be answerable for what they do, but what exactly does that mean? The Oxford American Dictionary defines accountability as: the obligation to give a reckoning or explanation for one's actions.

Does a student have to learn for teaching to have taken place? Historically, teaching has not been defined in this restrictive manner; the teacher was thought to be responsible for the quantity and quality of material covered and the way in which it was presented. However, some definitions of teaching now imply that students must learn in order for teaching to have taken place.

As a teacher who tries my best to keep current on all the latest teaching strategies, I believe that those teachers who do not bother even to pick up an educational journal every once in a while should be kept under close watch. There are many teachers out there who have been teaching for decades and refuse to change their ways even if research has proven that their methods are outdated and ineffective. There is no place in the profession of teaching for these types of individuals. It is time that the American educational system clean house, for the sake of our children.

9. **What is the organizational pattern of the second paragraph?**

   A. Cause and effect
   B. Classification
   C. Addition
   D. Explanation

10. **What is the main idea of the passage?**

    A. Teachers should not be answerable for what they do.
    B. Teachers who do not do their job should be fired.
    C. The author is a good teacher.
    D. Assessment of teachers is a serious problem in society today.

11. **From the passage, one can infer that**

    A. The author considers herself a good teacher.
    B. Poor teachers will be fired.
    C. Students have to learn for teaching to take place.
    D. The author will be fired.

12. **Teachers who do not keep current on educational trends should be fired. Is this a fact or an opinion?**

    A. Fact
    B. Opinion

13. **What is the author's purpose in writing this?**

    A. To entertain
    B. To narrate
    C. To describe
    D. To persuade

14. **Is there evidence of bias in this passage?**

    A. Yes
    B. No

15. **The author's tone is one of**

    A. Disbelief
    B. Excitement
    C. Support
    D. Concern

16. **What is meant by the word "plaguing" in the first sentence?**

    A. Causing problems
    B. Causing illness
    C. Causing anger
    D. Causing failure

17. **Where does the author get her definition of "accountability?"**

    A. Webster's Dictionary
    B. Encyclopedia Brittanica
    C. Oxford Dictionary
    D. World Book Encyclopedia

18. A figure of speech in which someone absent or something inhuman is addressed as though present and able to respond describes

A. personification.
B. synechdoche.
C. metonymy
D. apostrophe.

19. A sixth-grade science teacher has given her class a paper to read on the relationship between food and weight gain. The writing contains signal words such as "because," "consequently," "this is how," and "due to." This paper has which text structure?

A. cause & effect
B. compare & contrast
C. description
D. sequencing

20. Which of the following is *not* a figure of speech (figurative language)?

A. Simile
B. Euphemism
C. Onomatopoeia
D. Allusion

Answer Key: Written Analysis and Expression

1. B.
2. C.
3. A
4. B
5. C
6. B
7. C
8. B
9. D.
10. D.
11. A.
12. B.
13. D.
14. A.
15. D.
16. A.
17. C.
18. A.
19. A.
20. D.

Rationales for Sample Questions: Written Analysis and Expression

1. **B.** The singular possessive pronoun *its* must agree with its antecedent *job*, which is singular also. Option A is incorrect because *place* is a plural form and the subject, *job*, is singular. Option C is incorrect because the correct spelling of employees is given in the sentence.

2. **C.** An introductory dependent clause is set off with a comma, not a semicolon. Option A is incorrect because the transitional phrase *for example* should be set off with a comma. Option B is incorrect because the adverb *whereas* functions like *while* and does not take a comma after it.

3. **A** The adverb *well* modifies the word *doing*. Option B is incorrect because *usually* is spelled correctly in the sentence. Option C is incorrect because *succeeding* is in the wrong tense.

4. **B** The singular verb *is* is needed to agree with the singular subject *one*. Option A is incorrect because a comma is needed to set off the transitional word *however*. Option C is incorrect because a colon, not a semicolon, is needed to set off an item.

5. **C** The singular verb *vary* is needed to agree with the singular subject *accomplishment*. Option A is incorrect because a comma after *accomplishment* would suggest that the modifying phrase *of the employees* is additional instead of essential. Option B is incorrect because *employees* is not possessive.

6. **B** The past participle *accustomed* is needed with the verb *become*. Option A is incorrect because the verb tense does not need to change to the past *became*. Option C is incorrect because *provides* is the wrong tense.

7. **C** Option C is correct because *employees* is not possessive. Option A is incorrect because *achieve* is spelled correctly in the sentence. Option B is incorrect because *gave* is the wrong tense.

8. **B** A colon is not needed to set off the introduction of the sentence. In Option A, *were*, is the incorrect tense of the verb. In Option C, *worked*, is in the wrong tense.

9. **D.** The meaning of this word is directly stated in the same sentence.

10. **D.** Most of the passage is dedicated to elaborating on why teacher assessment is such a problem.

11. **A.** The first sentence of the third paragraph alludes to this.

12. **B.** There may be those who feel they can be good teachers by using old methods.

13. **D.** The author does some describing, but the majority of her statements seemed geared towards convincing the reader that teachers who are lazy or who do not keep current should be fired.

14. **A.** The entire third paragraph is the author's opinion on the matter.

15. **D.** The author appears concerned with the future of education.

16. **A.** The first paragraph makes this definition clear.

17. **C.** This is directly stated in the third sentence of the first paragraph.

18. **A.** Personification gives human reactions and thoughts to animals, things, and abstract ideas alike. This figure of speech is often present in allegory: for instance, the Giant Despair in John Bunyon's *Pilgrim's Progress.* Also, fables use personification to make animals able to speak.

19. **A.** Cause and effect is the relationship between two things when one thing makes something else happen. Writers use this text structure to show order, inform, speculate, and change behavior. This text structure uses the process of identifying potential causes of a problem or issue in an orderly way. It is often used to teach social studies and science concepts. It is characterized by signal words such as because, so, so that, if... then, consequently, thus, since, for, for this reason, as a result of, therefore, due to, this is how, nevertheless, and accordingly.

20. **D.** Allusion is an implied reference to a person, event, thing, or a part of another text. A simile is an indirect comparison between two things. Euphemism is the substitution of an agreeable or inoffensive term for one that might offend. Onomatopoeia is a word that vocally imitates the meaning it denotes, some sound.

XAMonline, INC. 21 Orient Ave. Melrose, MA 02176

Toll Free number 800-509-4128

TO ORDER Fax 781-662-9268 OR www.XAMonline.com

NEW YORK STATE TEACHER CERTIFICATION EXAMINATION   - NYSTCE - 2008

PO#   Store/School:

Address 1:

Address 2 (Ship to other):

City, State Zip

Credit card number_____-_____-_____-_____   expiration_____

EMAIL _____

PHONE_____   FAX

ISBN	TITLE	Qty	Retail	Total
978-1-58197-660-1	NYSTCE ATS-W ASSESSMENT OF TEACHING SKILLS- WRITTEN 91			
978-1-58197-260-3	NYSTCE ATAS ASSESSMENT OF TEACHING ASSISTANT SKILLS 095			
978-1-58197-289-4	CST BIOLOGY 006			
978-1-58197-855-1	CST CHEMISTRY 007			
978-1-58197-865-0	CQST COMMUNICATION AND QUANTITATIVE SKILLS TEST 080			
978-1-58197-632-8	CST EARTH SCIENCE 008			
978-1-58197-267-2	CST ENGLISH 003			
978-1-58197-858-2	CST FRENCH SAMPLE TEST 012			
978-1-58197-344-0	LAST LIBERAL ARTS AND SCIENCE TEST 001			
978-1-58197-863-6	CST LIBRARY MEDIA SPECIALIST 074			
978-1-58197-623-6	CST LITERACY 065			
978-1-58197-296-2	CST MATH 004			
978-1-58197-290-0	CST MUTIPLE SUBJECTS 002			
978-1-58197-579-6	CST PHYSICAL EDUCATION 076			
978-1-58197-042-0	CST PHYSICS 009			
978-1-58197-265-8	CST SOCIAL STUDIES 005			
978-1-58197-396-9	CST SPANISH 020			
978-1-58197-258-0	CST STUDENTS WITH DISABILITIES 060			
			SUBTOTAL	
	FOR PRODUCT PRICES VISIT WWW.XAMONLINE.COM		Ship	$8.25
			TOTAL	

9 781581 973440